VICE IN CHICAGO

PATTERSON SMITH REPRINT SERIES IN
CRIMINOLOGY, LAW ENFORCEMENT, AND SOCIAL PROBLEMS

A listing of publications in the SERIES *will be found at rear of volume*

PUBLICATION NO. 84: PATTERSON SMITH REPRINT SERIES IN
CRIMINOLOGY, LAW ENFORCEMENT, AND SOCIAL PROBLEMS

VICE
IN CHICAGO

WALTER C. RECKLESS

Associate Professor of Sociology
Vanderbilt University

Montclair, New Jersey

PATTERSON SMITH

1969

Copyright 1933 by The University of Chicago
Reprinted 1969, with permission, by
Patterson Smith Publishing Corporation
Montclair, New Jersey

SBN 87585-084-7

Library of Congress Catalog Card Number: 69-16243

PREFACE

Many changes in the problem of commercialized vice in Chicago have occurred since Chicago's Vice Commission reported on its findings in 1911 and since the segregated district was closed in 1912. The present study attempts to rehearse and measure, wherever possible, these changes.

The available data show that there are not as many open houses of prostitution today as in the 1910 era; that vice emporia today run more sporadically and under cover; that they have fewer prostitutes per resort; that they have sought out more decentralized neighborhoods of the city in contrast to the almost complete concentration of resorts in the near central (downtown) areas of 1910; that Negro prostitution has grown enormously, due to the social unadjustment following the wholesale immigration of Negroes into Chicago's undesirable and disorganized neighborhoods; that the caste of the prostitute has broken down; that many prostitutes are now able to lead an existence independent of syndicated brothels and to escape "identification with the prostitute class"; that organized, protected or syndicated vice has continued to a diminishing extent from the days of the segregated district in spite of suppressive measures, due to affiliations with the police, political machines, and gang rule; that since 1910 or the pre-suppression era there has been a notable growth of cabarets and roadhouses which have had a direct or indirect relation to the shift in the business of vice, to developments in commercialized recreation, and to changes in the life and habits of city dwellers; that within the city vice resorts tend to locate themselves in neighborhoods or areas which show the highest incidence of related social problems and the most marked indexes of population disturbance, that is, in areas of greatest social disorganization—areas where vice can thrive, although sporadically, in spite of the hammer blows of public suppression.

My impression is that the changes in the problem of commercialized vice in Chicago in large part have been due to modern urban trends and to underlying causes of modern city growth, and only in small part to law-enforcement drives. At no time in the twenty years of attempted vice suppression in Chicago have the forces of public suppression been constant, uniform, or at a maximum. There are certain indications that in the future the combined and concerted action of the public and private law-enforcement agencies may reach a much higher level in efficiency. When and if this happens, it should further the decline of organized vice resorts and brothel prostitution and it should force prostitution to be practiced more subtly and hiddenly by semi-professionals or amateurs who will no longer be identified as out-and-out prostitutes. Assuming the forces for suppression at their maximum, can commercialized vice be annihilated as the Chicago Vice Commission believed? Would such be possible even in an unchanging urban environment? Is it only possible, as many now believe who view conditions in a more objective light than the early vice crusaders viewed them, to keep commercialized vice at a minimum in an unsyndicated, subdued form?

The present study had its inception ten years ago as a part of several correlated studies of urban community life in Chicago. At this time the underlying notion was that if we could explain the distribution of social problems which varied according to different areas in the urban community, we could go far in understanding the underlying forces and background causes of urban problems such as crime, delinquency, boys' gangs, homeless men, suicide, divorce, poverty, and so forth.

The emphasis on the distributive aspects of these problems, their concentration, or varying incidence in certain areas of the city was conceived as a new ecological approach in sociology.

The draft of my early researches into the problem of commercialized vice in Chicago was submitted as a Doctor's dissertation to the University of Chicago under the title of the *Natural History of Vice Areas in Chicago* (1925). In this early study the stress was laid on the growth of vice localities as a result of the underlying forces which determined the growth of urban community life.

At that time the doors of several agencies, both private and public, which possessed important records and data for research of this character, were closed. By 1928 these agencies had become more co-operative in allowing their records to be used for research purposes.

It was then felt that the vice study could be continued and extended in avenues heretofore obstructed. The American Institute of Criminal Law and Criminology made a grant which enabled the data to be collected and organized. The Committee on Grants-in-Aid, of the Social Science Research Council, made a grant taking care of certain exigencies which developed as the study neared completion. The Local Community Research Committee and the Department of Sociology of the University of Chicago were of valuable assistance in affording use of certain data already on file and in sponsoring the publication of the study in the series on Urban Sociology.

I am greatly indebted to Dr. Robert E. Park for many stimulating suggestions and for his editing of the manuscript; to Dr. E. W. Burgess for his help and advice in the organization of the resources for the continuation of the study; to Mr. A. A. Bruce, president of the American Institute of Criminal Law and Criminology; to Mr. Walter R. Sharpe, of the Social Science Research Council; to Mr. Charles E. Miner, general director of the Committee of Fifteen of Chicago, for his most hearty co-operation; to Mr. Clifford R. Shaw, research sociologist of the Institute of Juvenile Research of Chicago, for use of already collected data on file; to Miss Jessie F. Binford, of the Juvenile Protective Association of Chicago, for use of certain case records and the data from special investigations; to Mr. John Landesco, for use of newspaper files on vice and crime conditions in Chicago; to the directors of four important venereal disease clinics in Chicago for use of their case records; to authorities of the Municipal Court and Morals Court of Chicago and especially for the help of Mrs. Julia L. McGuire, head of the social service department of the Morals Court; to my father, Mr. Walter B. Reckless, for clipping the important vice and crime news stories in the Chicago papers during the last four years.

WALTER C. RECKLESS

December, 1932

TABLE OF CONTENTS

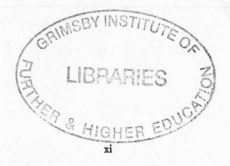

LIST OF MAPS

LIST OF TABLES

CHAPTER I

TWENTY YEARS OF VICE SUPPRESSION

The crusade which wiped out most of the so-called red light districts in American cities was more dramatic in some ways than that which closed the saloon. Chicago led, closing its red light district in 1912. Other American cities followed. A few years later a checkup of the so-called segregated districts in American cities revealed the facts given in Table 1. Vice continued in America after the breaking up of segregated vice areas, but due to the change in law enforcement policy, the character of the commerce in women changed. The problem has assumed a new form; it has not ceased to exist.

THE SCOPE OF PRESENT STUDY

What has happened to commercialized vice since the closing of the red light districts? In what areas of the city are resorts now located? Who are now the prostitutes? Has prostitution really declined? These questions are more easily asked than answered. The ramifications of the problem are many. Data on all aspects of the problem are not available in many places. Under the circumstances it seems wise to narrow the scope of our enquiry and concentrate on the study of vice in one city, Chicago. If Chicago's trends in vice are unique, further studies of conditions in other American cities will show the local variability.

THE ANTI-VICE CRUSADE

Prostitution was never quite a legalized or even a tolerated institution in Chicago or in other American cities. It

1

TABLE 1

AMERICAN CITIES REPORTED AS CLOSING THEIR RED LIGHT
DISTRICTS, 1912–17*

Place	Population	Year of Investigation	Year of Closing of District
Atlanta............	154,839	1912	1912
Baltimore..........	558,485	1913	1915
Bay City..........	451,166	1913	1913
Bridgeport.........	102,054	1915	1915
Chicago...........	2,185,283	1910	1912
Cleveland.........	560,663	1911	1915
Denver............	213,381	1913	1913
Elmira............	37,176	1913	1913
Grand Rapids.......	112,571	1912	1912
Hartford..........	98,915	1912	1912
Honolulu..........	52,183	1913	1917
Kansas City, Mo....	250,000	1911	1913
Lancaster.........	47,227	1913	1914
Lexington.........	40,000	1915	1915
Little Rock........	45,941	1912	1913
Louisville.........	223,928	1915	1917
Minneapolis........	301,408	1911	1913
Newark............	347,469	1914	1917
New York..........	4,766,883	1912	1916
Philadelphia........	1,549,008	1912	1913
Pittsburgh.........	533,905	1912	1914
Portland, Me......	58,571	1913	1915
Portland, Ore......	207,214	1912	1913
Richmond.........	127,628	1914	1914
St. Louis..........	687,029	1914	1914
Shreveport.........	28,015	1913	1917
Springfield.........	51,678	1914	1915
Syracuse..........	137,249	1912	1913
Toronto...........	376,538	1913	1913

* Joseph Mayer, "Passing of the Red Light District," *Social Hygiene*, IV (1918), 199.

merely had been permitted to exist (in spite of statutory law) during a period when public discussion of it was tabu.

Once this tabu was lifted there followed a period in which public discussion of the social evil was carried on with extraordinary freedom and candor. In newspapers, magazines, periodicals, and books, conditions were exposed and described with unusual freedom. The movement reached a climax just prior to the closing of the red light district in Chicago.

On October 12, 1909, Gipsy Smith, evangelist and reformer,[1] led a band of 12,000 Christian men and women through the Twenty-second Street red light district of Chicago, in an attempt, like the crusaders of old, to reclaim the region to Christianity.[2]

On September 29, 1912—only three days before the closing of Chicago's red light area—10,000 civic welfare paraders made a public demonstration and appealed for a "clean Chicago." "Rain which fell with dismal persistence yesterday dampened the clothing but failed to wilt the ardor of several thousand of Chicago's Anti-Vice forces, who changed Michigan Avenue's wonted refrain of tooting automobiles to reverberating gospel hymns."[3]

The most telling blows against the underworld in Chicago did not come from the dramatic method of attack, but rather from the federation of the moral forces, which sought to arouse public opinion and put pressure on city authorities.

On January 31, 1910, at a meeting of the Church Federation, composed of clergy representing six hundred congregations in Chicago, a discussion of the problem of the

---

[1] Rodney Smith, born of gipsy parents, near Epping Forest, England, in 1860, represented "a voice from the wilderness." His mother died when he was very young; and as a result his father became intensely religious, later being converted in a mission, and converting many of his tribe and family. "Rodney Smith was thus, in boyhood, converted with a simple model of primitive piety and evangelism." See *The Missionary Review*, XXX (March, 1907), 176–80.

[2] *Chicago Record-Herald*, October 19, 1909.

[3] See account in *Inter-Ocean*, September 29, 1912. The parade marched through the downtown districts.

social evil was led by Dean Walter T. Sumner, of the Episcopal Cathedral of SS. Peter and Paul, in the heart of the West Side levee district. A resolution, asking for the appointment of a civic-minded Vice Commission, was unanimously adopted at the conclusion of this meeting. The Commission was appointed by the mayor and its investigation of the Chicago vice situation was reported on fifteen months later.[4]

THE CLOSING OF THE "RED LIGHTS" IN CHICAGO

In connection with the September (1912) grand jury investigation into vice conditions, attempts were made by the reform leaders to place the responsibility for the existing situation on those officials whose duty it was, under the laws of the state of Illinois and the ordinances of the city, to suppress commercialized vice.[5] The investigation focused itself upon the State's Attorney, who was charged not only with allowing vice to exist in West Hammond, on the outskirts of the city, but also with blocking the progress of the investigation. State's Attorney Wayman took up the challenge for law enforcement, filed complaints against the keepers of houses of ill-fame, particularly those in the Twenty-second Street "red light" district, and obtained warrants for their arrest.[6]

[4] The Chicago Vice Commission report, *The Social Evil in Chicago* (1911), p. 1.

[5] Houses of ill-fame were prohibited under the statutes of Illinois and the Municipal Code very early in the history of both state and city. (See *The Social Evil in Chicago,* Appendices on Laws and Ordinances, pp. 309 ff.) However, in spite of these prohibitions, it had become customary for public and officials, in the absence of public pressure, to tolerate the existence of these places.

[6] The charge was later made that State's Attorney Wayman was the

The wholesale closing of the houses of ill-fame, in view of the previous history of the city, was a radical step. The public officials and the police were practically unanimous for "segregation" or "toleration." The Mayor was inclined to believe that segregation was the best way of handling the problem, although he suggested a popular referendum on the question of the closing of the "red light" district.[7] The city council took up for consideration the policy which ought to be accepted in regard to commercialized vice. A committee of nine aldermen was appointed by the Mayor, in response to a resolution by the city council, which declared: "Elimination and segregation are to be carefully considered together with the social evil in all its phases, and a report is to be made to the City Council for its action."[8] The members of the community at large kept their eyes on the sessions of this committee. The leaders of the reform movement considered their cause lost, believing that the committee would favor segregation, and that pressure would be brought to reopen the red light district.

The reform movement in Chicago rallied its forces in a stupendous effort to hold the ground already won, to keep the red light district closed, and to prevent the return to police segregation. The Rev. Charles Bayard Mitchell attacked the Mayor in a sermon for his "middle-course" stand. He is reported to have said: "Think of the moral obliquity of a Mayor who knows that the social evil legally cannot be tolerated and yet talks of letting the people of

tool for the Santa Fe railroad interests, who wanted the property in the Twenty-second Street red light district for terminal purposes.

[7] *Chicago Tribune,* October 5, 1912.

[8] *Chicago Examiner,* October 15, 1912.

Chicago decide whether they will keep or break the state laws on the question!"[9]

The Church Federation of Chicago, representing over 600 Protestant churches, vigorously protested the reestablishment of the segregated district.[10]

The Young People's Civic League took measures to arouse sentiment against the reopening of the red light district.[11]

Resolutions, directed against the indorsement of the segregation policy by the City Council, were passed by the Men's League of the Sunday Evening Club.[12]

The forces of suppression finally won in Chicago, as in other American cities. Toleration of vice in the form of segregation or police regulation was abandoned. The initial police raids started by State's Attorney Wayman, inaugurating the policy of law enforcement, were continued, not only in the Twenty-second Street district, but also in other parts of the city, where open vice could be apprehended. A more or less continuous drive against commercialized vice by law-enforcement agencies, augmented from time to time by raiding demonstrations on the part of the police, was maintained during the whole period of suppression.

THE FIRST REACTIONS OF VICE TO SUPPRESSION

But commercialized vice was not as easily eliminated by a program of law enforcement as had been generally expected. The ancient evil was stubborn, yielded here and

[9] *Chicago Tribune,* November 4, 1912.

[10] *Chicago Record-Herald,* October 11, 1912.

[11] *Chicago Tribune,* November 11, 1912.

[12] *Chicago Record-Herald,* November 14, 1912.

there but did not disappear. As soon as there was any re-
laxation in law-enforcing activities, vice tended to return
to its old haunts and did not always abandon its new ones.
The many "lid tiltings" in Chicago show to what extent
vice has persisted.

Within a week's time after Wayman's initial assault in
the underworld raids had become less frequent and less
effective.[13] About a month later it was found that the "red
light" district itself showed signs of activity, in spite of
direct orders from the Mayor that the district was to be
kept closed.[14] Two days after this exposure, the red light
district was closed again by police activity.[15]

LID TILTINGS AND OFFICE POLICY

The underworld forces showed signs of activity when
State's Attorney Wayman retired from office and was succeeded by Maclay Hoyne, who made it understood that he
intended to take no part in the anti-vice crusade.[16]

Changes in the city administration as well as in the
State's Attorney's office have invariably affected the enforcement of the policy of vice suppression. The two
notable examples of this are the Thompson rule (1915–23,
1927–31) which stood for the "open town" and the Dever

[13] See *Chicago Daily Examiner*, October 11, 1912.

[14] *Chicago Record-Herald*, November 20, 1912.

[15] *Chicago Record-Herald*, November 22, 1912. The suggestion is made
in this newspaper account of a possible "tip-off," a factor with which the
raiding squads of the police have had to deal in enforcing repression. In
many cases the activity in a house of prostitution or a gambling place
has been suspended before the police arrived. Who gets the tip-off is one
of those baffling, intangible questions common to politics of American
cities.

[16] See the *Chicago Tribune* and *Record-Herald*, December 3, 1912.

régime (1923–27) which held out for the "closed town."

In general, however, the history of commercialized vice in Chicago since the initial closing of the red light district is a repetition of "openings and closings."

These monotonous fluctuations in vice activity and public suppression have continued from the Wayman raids (1912) until the present (1932). Even at present writing the Mayor has announced a city-wide ban on vice resorts.[17] The moral forces are still organizing drives, the mayor's and chief of police's offices are still issuing orders, the newspapers are still running front-page stories on vice conditions—today as twenty years previously. One wonders that the recurrence of the vice situation cycle—exposure of conditions by a newspaper, agency or investigation; reaction from the "law and order" organizations; public announcement from mayor's office, police headquarters or State's Attorney's office after pressure has been felt— has not caused the reflective public to question the results of as well as the tactics used in vice suppression.

While commercialized vice in Chicago has persisted in spite of "lids," closings and moral crusades, it has never returned in the flagrant form in which it existed in 1912 and it has not concentrated in an open, accessible mart like that of the old Twenty-second Street district. Chicago's vice resorts, dispersed through a wide area of the city, are subdued and unobtrusive.

POLICE ACTIVITY

The external effects of this pulsating pressure of public opinion for suppression may be gauged by rates of police activity. These rates show enormous increases and de-

[17] *Chicago Tribune*, September 18, 1931.

creases for a twenty-year period although the trend is
toward a huge increase. Using the data on police arrests
for the principal types of offenses involving commercialized
vice, it is possible to get an index of the department's per
capita activity (corrected for yearly population increase)
for years 1908 to 1928. (See Table 2, p. 10.) The year
1908 was chosen as the basal year because it is indicative
of police activity on the vice situation prior to the beginning of the era of public suppression and law enforcement
(October, 1912).[18]

Table 2 indicates a spurt in vice activity in 1912 (the
year of the inauguration of suppression of open brothels)
and in 1913 and 1914 when a high point is reached. From
that period on there is a general slipping back to lower
levels of activity until the advent of the Dever administration (starting in 1923) when another spurt reaches a peak
in 1926, the high point for the whole period. With the return of the Thompson administration in 1927, a decline is
registered although a considerable recovery is made toward
the high level in 1928.

The pulse of repression is thus seen in an irregular trend
toward higher levels of police drive against commercialized
vice. The dips and the rises should be considered in terms
of the "lids off and lids on," the changes in administrative
attitude and policy, and the waxing and waning of public sentiment. During this twenty-year period the increase
in vice arrests outstripped the increase in total arrests several fold. A reading of the index numbers for vice arrests
and total arrests indicates this conclusion, which is con-

[18] While the anti-vice and anti-white slave forces were organizing at
this time, no great pressure had been brought on the police department
to change its policy of toleration.

VICE IN CHICAGO

TABLE 2

INDEXES OF CHICAGO POLICE ACTIVITY AGAINST VICE AS GAUGED BY ARRESTS, 1908–28

Year	Index Vice Arrests	Index Total Arrests	Per Cent Vice Arrests of Total Arrests
1908	100*	100*	3.8†
1909	132	101	4.9
1910	121	114	3.9
1911	118	112	3.9
1912	175	112	5.8
1913	239	138	6.4
1914	304	145	8.6
1915	279	122	8.4
1916	157	111	5.3
1917	261	136	7.1
1918	157	117	4.9
1919	96	93	3.9
1920	111	88	4.5
1921	164	116	5.2
1922	132	108	4.6
1923	257	147	6.5
1924	404	191	7.8
1925	461	212	8.0
1926	511	200	9.4
1927	368	157	8.7
1928	454	143	11.6

* Based on Table 58. Arrests per policeman per capita population were taken as the figure from which the index numbers were computed. Expressed algebraically, this figure for any given year was $\frac{a}{bc}$, where a=number of arrests (either vice arrests or total arrests), b=number of police, and c=the population.

† Based on Table 58. The actual number of total arrests was divided into the actual number of combined vice arrests.

firmed by the treble increase in the percentage of vice arrests in the total arrests for the entire period. In 1908 the vice arrests comprised 3.8 per cent of the total police arrests in Chicago, while in 1928 they constituted 11.6 per cent.

FROM CONCENTRATION TO DISPERSION

If we compare the concentration of houses of prostitution in the Twenty-second, the West Madison, and the

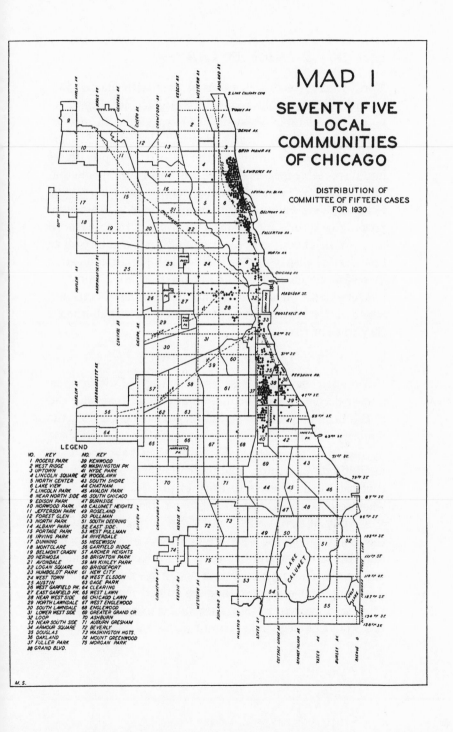

MAP I

SEVENTY FIVE LOCAL COMMUNITIES OF CHICAGO

DISTRIBUTION OF
COMMITTEE OF FIFTEEN CASES
FOR 1930

LEGEND

NO.	KEY	NO.	KEY
1	ROGERS PARK	39	KENWOOD
2	WEST RIDGE	40	WASHINGTON PK
3	UPTOWN	41	HYDE PARK
4	LINCOLN SQUARE	42	WOODLAWN
5	NORTH CENTER	43	SOUTH SHORE
6	LAKE VIEW	44	CHATHAM
7	LINCOLN PARK	45	AVALON PARK
8	NEAR NORTH SIDE	46	SOUTH CHICAGO
9	EDISON PARK	47	BURNSIDE
10	NORWOOD PARK	48	CALUMET HEIGHTS
11	JEFFERSON PARK	49	ROSELAND
12	FOREST GLEN	50	PULLMAN
13	NORTH PARK	51	SOUTH DEERING
14	ALBANY PARK	52	EAST SIDE
15	PORTAGE PARK	53	WEST PULLMAN
16	IRVING PARK	54	RIVERDALE
17	DUNNING	55	HEGEWISCH
18	MONTCLARE	56	GARFIELD RIDGE
19	BELMONT CRAGIN	57	ARCHER HEIGHTS
20	HERMOSA	58	BRIGHTON PARK
21	AVONDALE	59	McKINLEY PARK
22	LOGAN SQUARE	60	BRIDGEPORT
23	HUMBOLDT PARK	61	NEW CITY
24	WEST TOWN	62	WEST ELSDON
25	AUSTIN	63	GAGE PARK
26	WEST GARFIELD PK.	64	CLEARING
27	EAST GARFIELD PK.	65	WEST LAWN
28	NEAR WEST SIDE	66	CHICAGO LAWN
29	NORTH LAWNDALE	67	WEST ENGLEWOOD
30	SOUTH LAWNDALE	68	ENGLEWOOD
31	LOWER WEST SIDE	69	GREATER GRAND CR
32	LOOP	70	ASHBURN
33	NEAR SOUTH SIDE	71	AUBURN GRESHAM
34	ARMOUR SQUARE	72	BEVERLY
35	DOUGLAS	73	WASHINGTON HGTS.
36	OAKLAND	74	MOUNT GREENWOOD
37	FULLER PARK	75	MORGAN PARK
38	GRAND BLVD.		

M.S.

North Clark streets districts as of 1912 with the distribution of vice resorts in 1930 which is given in Map 1, we notice considerable dispersion and scattering. In view of the warning of the "segregationists" that the reformers and law enforcers would scatter resorts and prostitutes into respectable neighborhoods, it is important to note that in the twenty years of public suppression there were relatively few underworld invasions of good residential areas. Vice resorts for the most part in spreading outward invaded neighborhoods of declining respectability. The bold fact of dispersion, as indicated in the 1930 location of resorts as compared with the 1912 location, must be tempered with the additional fact that neighborhoods into which vice is scattered in 1930 are not the neighborhoods they were in 1912.

LOW RATE OF PERSISTENCE

Although commercialized resorts of vice in Chicago show a more decentralized distribution at present than they did at the beginning of the period of public suppression, the majority of them are not permanently located. Bobbing up here and there for a short run, they have lost their institutional character. The present situation is in direct contrast to the relative security of pre-suppression days, when resorts maintained an unbroken operation for years.

A study of the Morals Court cases during 1928 reveals the fact that, of the separate addresses at which police raids occurred during that year, 67 per cent were raided one time, while 92 per cent were raided less than five times. Assuming that a separate address raided more than five times in a year is an indication of persistence (although this would be negligible form of persistence as compared with the flagrantly operated resorts in red light days), less than 8 per cent of the vice resorts in Chicago show any semblance of persistence.[19]

TABLE 3

AN ANALYSIS OF POLICE RAIDS AT SEPARATE ADDRESSES
TAKEN FROM MORALS COURT CASES, CHICAGO, 1928

No. of Times Raided	No. of Separate Addresses	Per Cent
1	1,225	67.7
2	262	14.4
3	136	7.5
4	50	2.8
5	34	1.9
6	31	1.7
7	16	0.9
8	16	0.9
9	13	0.7
10	5	0.3
11	1	*
12	5	0.3
13	1	*
14	2	0.1
15	2	0.1
16	3	0.2
17	3	0.2
19	1	*
20	1	*
22	1	*
24	1	*
39	1	*
Totals	1,810	100.0

* Less than one-tenth of 1 per cent.

The Committee of Fifteen of Chicago, whose full-time job it is to investigate and suppress vice resorts, finds that

[19] The overwhelming majority of the Morals Court cases consists in dealing with commercialized vice in some form. The number of other cases coming into court, like adultery and fornication, are so small in proportion that the foregoing conclusion would not be seriously modified if those non-commercialized vice cases were thrown out.

only a small number of resorts once closed reopen at the same addresses. "A check was made in December 1928 on 1,166 resorts closed prior to 1927. Only twelve of this number were found to be operating. Out of 211 resorts closed in 1927, 13 had reopened. Of the 303 closed in 1928, the reinvestigation disclosed 10 to be operating again."[20] Taking the Committee's 1929 cases, we find that of the 459 places at which evidence of commercialized vice was found (in 1929) 68 (14.8 per cent) showed up just once and failed to reappear on further investigations. Of the 459, 342 (74.5 per cent) were closed by the action of the committee, while 49 (10.7 per cent) resorts continued on the books as still doing business when the new year began. About one-half of the 49 resorts continuing on the books "unclosed" consisted of places which had been reported so late in the year that the Committee's action was not completed before the new year set in. The remaining number of unclosed resorts (about 5 per cent of the total 459) may be considered as showing signs of stubbornness and persistence.

A more specific idea of the average span of life (in days) of vice resorts may be obtained from a study which was made by Mr. Charles E. Miner, general director of the Committee of Fifteen of Chicago. He took the cases of vice resorts on the Committee's records for 1929 and in each instance calculated the total number of days which each resort had lived (that is, from the date of first appearance to the last appearance on the books). The average persistence for all 1929 resorts in Chicago was found to be 174 days, which is less than half a year.

[20] *Chicago Daily News*, March 6, 1929.

THE NUMBER OF VICE RESORTS: 1910–31

If commercialized vice resorts have become dispersed and sporadic, does this mean too that they have decreased in actual numbers? The Vice Commission estimated the total houses of prostitution in Chicago as of 1910 to be 1,020.[21] The number of detected vice resorts in 1931 from the most reliable sources of field investigation was 731. This total is a combination of Committee of Fifteen and special police cases, corrected for duplication and is arrived at with the following data.

In 1931 the police under a plan adopted in 1929 sent information on 306 vice resorts, which had been raided by them at least twice, to the State's Attorney's office for prosecution under the Abatement and Injunction Law. During the same year the Committee acted against 470 resorts for prostitution, 45 of which were duplications of the police cases. The reason there was not a larger number of duplications is simply that the police prepared cases mainly against the obvious, cheap Negro resorts. A check of the police cases showed that 271 or 87 per cent of the 306 offending places contained colored inmates and were located in the poorest Negro neighborhoods. Since the police under the 1929 plan were found to be concentrating on the cheap Negro resorts, the Committee of Fifteen thereafter tried to avoid duplication of effort.

Combining the reported police cases with the Committee of Fifteen's cases for 1931, a total of 731 is obtained when the 45 duplications are subtracted. It is almost impossible to establish the number of vice resorts which evaded investigation. However, the 1,020 resorts reported by the

[21] *The Social Evil in Chicago*, p. 70.

Chicago Vice Commission (as of 1910) are in some measure comparable with the 731 (as of 1931), since both figures represent the results of field investigation and checking against police lists. In spite of the large population increase in Chicago over the last two decades, it appears that there was a smaller number of detected vice resorts in 1931 than in 1910.

But certain qualifications of this conclusion should be made. It may safely be assumed that practically all of the 1,020 (1910) resorts were white. The 1931 situation was considerably different. The Committee of Fifteen reported 371 white resorts out of a total of 470 against which it took action in 1931, while of the 306 referred police cases 35 were discovered to be white resorts. (I am using the Committee's field definitions here: a white resort is one which contains white inmates only; a colored resort, colored inmates only or partly.) A total of 400 white resorts is obtained from the 1931 data, when corrected for duplications (13 per cent or 6 of the 45 duplications may be considered as white resorts). Four hundred white vice emporia in 1931 as against 1,000 in 1910 would perhaps be a safer comparison than 731 vs. 1,020, since the former (i.e., 400) rule out the enormous growth of Negro prostitution in Chicago since the presuppression days of two decades ago.

OTHER COUNTS AND ESTIMATES

There have been from time to time other counts and estimates of the number of vice resorts in Chicago. Some of the important of these are inserted more for their historical than comparable value. Twelve years after the Chicago Vice Commission's investigation the Juvenile Protective Association of Chicago made a survey by paid investigators and presented its findings to a grand jury during January and February, 1923. In about four weeks' search in the field the investigators found 168 "open" houses of prostitution in Chicago. These represented the places which supposedly any man could find by inquiry. Of this number 48 had previous records with the Morals Court and other agencies extending back over a period at the most of two or three years. The Juvenile Protective Association suspected that these 48 houses were "protected" or "syndicate" resorts. At any rate they represented the more persistent houses of prostitution as compared with the 120 remaining places which might be said to be the temporary resorts. At this time Judge Daniel P. Trude of the Morals Court of Chicago testified that there were 500 houses of prostitution operating in Chicago.[22] The Committee of Fifteen found evidence of law violation at 387 separate addresses during the year 1922. About 300 of these were houses of prostitution, the remainder being cabarets, saloons, immoral shows and "dope" parlors. Chief of Police Fitzmorris stated that during March, 1923, there were 134 houses of prostitution picketed by the police, and that 117 were still being picketed in April, 1923.[23] He added: "I have never believed, and I do not believe now, that there are or have been at any given time during my administration as Chief of Police, in excess of 175 places of ill-fame—either prostitution or assignation—

[22] *Chicago Tribune,* February 22, 1923.

[23] The police picketing consisted of stationing one or two uniformed policemen outside the known houses of prostitution to prevent entrance except for a legitimate reason. This surveillance activity followed the pressure brought to bear by the grand jury investigation of the previous January and February.

in the 200 square miles within the city limits of Chicago."[24]

For 1922 and 1923 we have therefore the following figures from low to high: (a) 117 (picketed by police in April 1923), (b) 134 (picketed by police in March 1923), (c) 168 (found by the Juvenile Protective Association in four weeks December 1922), (d) not in excess of 175 (Fitzmorris's claim for his term of office as chief of police), (e) 300 (found by the Committee of Fifteen during all of 1922), (f) 500 (Judge Trude's estimate, February, 1922).

Figures (a), (b), and (c) are consistent with (e) because the latter figure represents the total number of different places found open for the entire year of 1922 and it is quite possible that during any given month, say at the end of 1922 or the beginning of 1923, 117, 134, or 168 places were running. Figures (d), (e) and (f) are not consistent, and logically it seems that figure (e) would recommend itself, it being between the two extremes (175 and 500). The 300 figure (e) has this additional fact to recommend it, namely it is based on field investigations intended to secure competent evidence against houses of prostitution.

Five or six years later, that is, 1928 and 1929, we find that the available figures on the number of open houses of prostitution vary from low to high as follows: (e) 480 (found by the Committee of Fifteen during 1928), (b) 893 (Moral Court convictions at separate addresses for 1928), (c) 2,000 (estimate of newspapers in exposures of gang, political, vice gambling, booze hook ups). Figure (a) or 480, again, represents the result of a year's continual field investigation. Figure (b) or 893 was obtained from

[24] Letter of Chief of Police to the Committee of Fifteen, dated April 2, 1923.

the Morals Court records. During that year a record was kept on the raids, which the police brought into court, by street addresses.

As already noted there were 1,810 separate addresses at which one or more raids were made during 1928. But not every raid finally results in a conviction in court and legally there is no violation unless a conviction is obtained. Consequently the raids were sorted out according as one or more persons at the address raided were given a fine, sentence or a term of probation. Dispositions, such as Good Behavior, Dismissal for Want of Prosecution, "Nolle Pros.," etc., were discarded. Finally, it was found that 893 separate addresses had been the scene of one or more police raids, leading to the conviction of one or more persons in the Morals Court of Chicago.

The discrepancy between 480 (the Committee of Fifteen figure for 1928) and 893 (the Morals Court figure for 1928) is due to the fact that police raids bring into court cases of law violation with which the Committee of Fifteen is not likely to deal, such as disorderly conduct on or in front of premises. Besides, the police take official cognizance of certain doubtful cases of "assembling," collecting or solicitation of women on the street or in front of an address noted at the time of raid. These latter instances of law violation may not have any direct connection with the address at which they are booked by the police. A large percentage of cases which come into the Morals Court and result in convictions, are of this character. The records are such that it is impossible to tell just how many of these cases there were in 1928 and still more impossible to tell how many there were by separate addresses. If the percentage was as high as 45, the Morals

Court figure (893) and the Committee of Fifteen figure (480) would be practically the same.

On the other hand, the Committee of Fifteen only deals with instances of commercialized vice where the actual practice of prostitution is in evidence on and within premises. Consequently, we should expect the Committee's figure to be lower and at the same time more indicative of the actual number of vice resorts in operation than the police raids and court convictions at separate addresses.[25] Recent newspaper exposures of "booze," vice, gambling, and gang hook-ups have placed the number of vice resorts in Chicago at 2,000. There is no reason to believe that this figure is anything but excessive.

THE TREND IN THE LAST FIFTEEN YEARS

The Committee of Fifteen's records are the only available data which yield consistent figures, especially since 1912. In Table 4 we notice the number of places of prostitution as found by the Committee during each year from 1914 to 1931.[26]

[25] The claim might be made that if the Committee had more investigators it would return a higher yearly figure. Taking into account its methods of investigation and territory assignments, I should say this is doubtful. It might be contended, further, that the Committee's investigators become known and are denied entrance to places. This would only apply to a minority number of "syndicate" houses of prostitution. I find, however, that the Committee's investigators have been barred in only a few places where the door men have suspected them. And in 1929 this applied mainly to a half dozen syndicate resorts on the Near West Side. On the other hand, investigators are more likely to find and gain access to quiet running resorts in flats and apartments which fail to draw the attention of the police.

[26] The number of resorts has been compiled by years as far back as 1910 but prior to 1914 much of the Committee's work was centered on the prosecution of white slave pandering cases. Beginning with 1914

TABLE 4

NUMBER OF SEPARATE VICE RESORTS AT WHICH EVIDENCE WAS
SECURED BY COMMITTEE OF FIFTEEN, CHICAGO, 1914–31

YEAR	NUMBER	YEAR	NUMBER
1914	272	1923	305
1915	259	1924	238
1916	288	1925	389
1917	380	1926	446
1918	332	1927	441
1919	303	1928	480
1920	291	1929	459
1921	374	1930	441
1922	387	1931	470

In this series the year 1924 is left out of the reckoning
because at that time the Committee's staff was not at its
full numerical strength.

With minor fluctuations there is a noticeable increase
from 1914 to 1925. If we take the lowest figure of the series
(excluding 1924) as the base (259 in 1915) and compare
it with the highest (480 in 1928), we obtain an 85 per cent
increase which is higher than the increase in Chicago's
population during the last twenty years (estimated at 50
per cent). If we simply compare 1914 with 1929, a 69 per
cent increase is noted, an increase which lies closer to the
percentage increase of the population in the last twenty
years.

This 85 per cent or 69 per cent increase in vice resorts
according to the Committee of Fifteen's data is an un-
qualified accounting. In 1914 or 1915—in fact in any of
those pre-war or early war-time years—there were very
few houses of prostitution with colored inmates. The 272
(1914) or the 259 (1915) which are used here as a base are

practically all of the Committee's attention is given to the investigation
of open houses of prostitution.

composed almost entirely of strictly "white" resorts. Of the 459 separate resorts investigated by the Committee in 1929, 203 (or 44 per cent) were colored resorts (see Table 6); while 250 were found to be white resorts (according to the color of the inmates seen). If we compare the 272 resorts in 1914 or the 259 in 1915, which were practically all white, with the white count of 250 in 1929, we discover a slight increase in the face of an increasing population. Once again, if we take the number of known resorts in 1910 which was placed at 1,020 by the Chicago Vice Commission (practically all of them white), the comparison with the 250 white resorts in 1929 indicates a 400 per cent decline, which would be even greater if corrected for a 50 per cent increased population in 1929 as against 1910.

THE NUMBER OF PROSTITUTES PER RESORT

If the figures on the number of resorts for prostitution in Chicago may be interpreted to mean a failure on the part of commercialized vice even to approach its numerical strength (proportionally considered) as of 1910, what of the numbers of inmates per resort? Has this average increased or decreased? The Vice Commission estimated that there were about 5,000 women who devoted their full time to the business of prostitution (including maids, madams as well as prostitutes) in Chicago in 1910.[27] If we divide this figure by the estimated number of resorts for prostitution found at the time (1,020 or 1,000 to make the average come out even), we derive an average of five women per resort. In 1923 when Judge Trude claimed there were 500 resorts in the city, he also estimated 2,500 prostitutes

[27] *The Social Evil in Chicago*, p. 70.

or 5 per resort.[28] According to statements made by Mr. Samuel P. Thrasher, superintendent of the Committee of Fifteen, at this time, there were 900 girls for 300 places of prostitution or an average of 3 per resort. Tabulating the number of women taken by police in raids in 1928 where one or more persons were convicted, we find an average of 1.89 per place raided. If the single cases, which represent for most part the doubtful cases of solicitation not associated with definite resorts, could be isolated, this average would probably go above 2.0 per place. The distribution of the number of girls according to the Morals Court data is given in Table 5 below.

TABLE 5

AVERAGE NUMBER OF GIRLS CAUGHT IN POLICE RAIDS WHERE ONE OR MORE PERSONS WERE CONVICTED IN THE MORALS COURT, CHICAGO, 1928

No. of Girls Reported in Raid	No. of Instances	Product Col. 1 by Col. 2	Weighted Average
0	6	0	
1	608	608	
2	423	846	
3	172	516	
4	46	184	
5	23	115	
6	10	60	
7	1	7	
8	1	8	
Total	1,290	2,344	1.89

If we were to assume that 50 per cent of the 608 singleton women caught in police raids were not identified with the place in front of which they were arrested for suspected solicitation or disorderly conduct, the weighted average of 1.89 would be corrected to stand at 2.1 (2040/

[28] *Chicago Tribune,* February 22, 1923.

986). The average number of girls seen in places at which the Committee of Fifteen found evidence of prostitution during 1929 was 1.98 (910 inmates in 459 resorts). This is a maximum figure, because the highest number of inmates seen on the premises was taken where more than one investigation had been made at a given address. For sake of ready comparison if we place the corrected Morals Court figure and the Committee of Fifteen average at 2 girls per resort (1928–29), we find that there has been a very marked decline in the number of inmates per resort since 1910, when the Chicago Vice Commission's data yielded an average of 5.

Both the decrease in the number of resorts of prostitution and the average number of girls per resort in Chicago from 1910 to 1930, must be taken into consideration with the additional fact that street walking and solicitation in public amusement places have dwindled in Chicago so as to be practically a negligible factor in the total commercialized vice (see chap. vi). If the number of inmates per resort had declined and the amount of street walking and public solicitation had increased measurably, the latter increase might then be considered as a counter balance. But street walking and public solicitation by prostitutes has declined just as have the number of resorts and the average number of women per resort. (See Table 17 and pp. 157–59.) Consequently, there has been no diversion of the stream of commercialized vice in the next most obvious channel of professional prostitution after the house of prostitution itself. Just where the outlets and substitutions are will be indicated in later chapters.

THE GROWTH OF NEGRO PROSTITUTION

One of the most noticeable developments in Chicago's era of suppression is that of Negro prostitution which, from certain meager numerical soundings, appears to be greater in proportion to the colored population than white prostitution is to the white population. For the most part, the policy of suppression itself has had very little to do with this development; since it has come about as an incident of the recent immigration of Negroes to Chicago.

While no figures are available, Negro prostitution was not large enough to command attention as a problem in the old red light era. That a few Negro girls were inmates in houses of prostitution in the old levee districts is confirmed by observers at the time. That many Negroes found work as maids and porters in the red light resorts was also true. That there was any well-developed Negro prostitution, for colored, white or both races, is not consistent with the reports of the pre-suppression times.

Of the 459 places at which the Committee of Fifteen found evidence of prostitution in 1929, 44.2 per cent consisted of resorts in which inmates were exclusively colored; 1.3 per cent in which both white and colored women were engaged in prostitution and 54.5 per cent, at which prostitutes were white exclusively. A 44 per cent return colored for the total resorts found by the Committee of Fifteen in 1929, is quite out of the proportion with the percentage the colored population occupies in the total for Chicago. For in the 1930 census Negroes constituted only 6.9 per cent of the total population of Chicago.

The combined police and Committee of Fifteen data for 1931 already mentioned, when corrected for duplication, reveal that 45 per cent of the investigated vice resorts in Chicago for that year were colored houses of prostitution (731 total, 400 white, 331 colored), which percentage is approximately the same as that obtained from the 1929 data.

The overwhelming majority of Negro places of prostitution in 1929 were found in the Douglas, Grand Boulevard, and Washington Park section.[29] This area encompasses the greatest part of Chicago's South Side Black Belt. The remaining colored places are distributed mostly in the Negro sections of the Near West and the Lower North Sides of Chicago. Table 6 gives the distribution by local areas of Chicago, of white and colored places at which evidence of prostitution was found by the Committee of Fifteen in 1929.

The available statistics from the Morals Court of Chicago indicate that Negro women in 1929 represented the decided majority of incoming cases, whereas nine and fifteen years earlier they were far in the minority. We find that Negro women constituted about 16 per cent of the total number tabulated as to race in the Morals Court in 1914, while Negroes only represented 2 per cent in the total population of Chicago for 1910. But in 1929 Negro women comprised 70 per cent of the Morals Court load, while the

[29] For statistical purposes in population studies of various local areas in Chicago, the Department of Sociology of the University of Chicago has defined the boundaries as follows: Douglas—26th street (north); 39th street (south); and lake, west on 35th street, south on Vincennes Avenue (east); the New York Central RR's tracks (west). Grand Boulevard—39th street (north); 51st street (south); Cottage Grove Ave. (east); N. Y. C. RR's tracks (west). Washington Park—51st street (north); N. Y. C. RR's tracks (south); Cottage Grove Ave., west on East 60th street, south on South Park Ave. (east); N. Y. C. RR's tracks (west).

TABLE 6

CLASSIFICATION BY COLOR OF WOMEN IN 459 DIFFERENT VICE
RESORTS INVESTIGATED BY THE COMMITTEE OF FIFTEEN
OF CHICAGO DURING 1929

	W.	Per Cent	C.	Per Cent	W. C.	Per Cent	Total
Uptown	96	100.0	0	0.0	0	0.0	96
Near West	21	67.7	9	29.0	1	3.2	31
Douglas	8	16.0	39	78.0	3	6.0	50
Grand Boulevard	3	2.3	122	97.6	0	0.0	125
Loop	5	100.0	0	0.0	0	0.0	5
Washington Park	2	7.7	23	88.5	1	3.8	26
Kenwood	10	90.9	1	9.0	0	0.0	11
Near South	7	77.7	1	11.1	1	11.1	9
Oakland	5	83.3	1	16.6	0	0.0	6
Hyde Park	2	100.0	0	0.0	0	0.0	2
Rogers Park	1	100.0	0	0.0	0	0.0	1
Lower North	26	78.8	7	21.2	0	0.0	33
Lakeview	58	100.0	0	0.0	0	0.0	58
Lincoln	6	100.0	0	0.0	0	0.0	6
Total	250	54.5	203	44.2	6	1.3	459

TABLE 7

NUMBER AND PER CENT OF WOMEN IN THE MORALS COURT OF
CHICAGO, REPORTED ON AS TO COLOR, 1914–1929*

YEAR	WHITE		COLORED		TOTAL
	No.	Per Cent	No.	Per Cent	
1914†	2,254	83.5	444	16.5	2,698
1920	1,527	79.2	400	20.8	1,927
1921	2,257	69.3	1,002	30.7	3,259
1922	2,217	59.2	1,530	40.8	3,747
1923	1,683	50.7	1,638	49.3	3,321
1924	2,233	43.8	2,870	56.2	5,103
1925	1,790	47.7	1,963	52.3	3,753
1929	2,467	30.5	5,633	69.5	8,100

* The figures in Table 7 can only be taken as the legend indicates: women reported on as to color. They cannot be taken to indicate the total case load of the Morals Court.

† Figures for 1914 are given only for the last six months. No figures are available for years 1915–19 and 1926–28. Figures for 1920–29 are given for separate individuals; for 1914, by unseparated cases.

Negro population was less than 7 per cent of the total 1930 population in Chicago.[30] It seems that the big increase in the Negro percentage came after 1920; for by 1920 the number of colored prostitutes had only increased from 16 per cent to 21 per cent (1920), at which time Negroes made up just 4 per cent of the general population of Chicago. The fast-rising increase after 1920 might be expected in view of the fact that large numbers of Negro women were completing the cycle of immigration from the South already begun by the men in great numbers before 1920, especially during the war period. If the percentage of colored women in the total load of the Morals Court continues to increase, the court will in a few years become practically an agency dealing with Negro female sex delinquents.

WHY THE DISPROPORTION?

This high figure for Negro women in the Morals Court demands some explanation. It is a generally accepted fact that Negroes are more liable to arrest by police than whites. On this point official statements of ten years ago were summarized by the Chicago Commission of Race Relations in this wise: "The testimony is practically unanimous that Negroes are much more liable to arrest than whites, since police officers share in the general public opinion that Negroes 'are more criminal than whites,' and also feel that there is little risk of trouble in arresting Negroes, while greater care must be exercised in arresting

[30] Using the total population instead of numerical strength of colored versus white women in Chicago would make very little difference, because for Chicago in 1910 the ratio of white males to white females was 106.1; of colored males to colored females, 105.9. In 1920 the respective ratios were 102.6 (white) and 104.5 (negro).

whites."[31] This applies to Negro women in the Morals Court. Furthermore, the recent migrations of Negroes from the rural south to metropolitan Chicago has tended to the demoralization of Negro communities. The fact that Negro migrants have had to occupy the least desirable neighborhoods in Chicago must also be considered. Negro communities in Chicago have frequently been located in the neighborhood of white vice districts and many of the early Negro immigrants found their only available occupation as maids and porters, if not prostitutes, in houses of prostitution. Ten years ago Judge Wells M. Cook was reported as saying that: "The colored people, living largely in one section of the city, and being naturally of a social, emotional temperament, are apt to congregate in places and resorts where the police could more easily raid them, and are much more easily apprehended. That is about the only reason I can see for the disproportionate number of colored defendants brought into the Morals Court. It is not that there is any greater percentage of immorality, but prostitution among whites was more clandestine."[32] The open Negro community life—undoubtedly a pattern transferred from the gregariousness of plantations and "black-bottoms" in the South to Chicago's "bad land" neighborhoods traditionally suspected by surveilling police—is likewise in part responsible for greater liability of arrest of Negro women.

The testimony of various students of crime in the Chicago Race Relations Commission's report was to the effect

[31] *The Negro in Chicago, A Study of Race Relations and a Race Riot* (Chicago, 1922), p. 347. The collection of data for this survey was made in the period December, 1919, to November, 1920.

[32] *The Negro in Chicago* (Chicago, 1922), p. 347.

that Negro crime and vice (ten years ago) was not "organized." The extent to which Negro commercialized vice is becoming organized will have to remain for further studies to determine, although the reported activities of Dan Jackson and Oscar De Priest in corralling the Negro vote and vice on the South Side for the Thompson machine might have lead one to suspect that Negro political-underworld situation was tending to become organized.

SUMMARY

While certain other trends in vice development in Chicago, such as are registered in the decline of white slavery, the persistence of organized vice, the growth of roadhouses and cabarets, will be pictured in later chapters, our survey of vice in Chicago during the period of suppression informs us that:

1. Commercialized vice was not eliminated by the closing of the red light district but has persisted under different marketing conditions.

2. The policy of public suppression has been characterized by short periodic efforts at law enforcement and control, "lid tiltings," and vacillations in administrative policy towards a "wide open" or a "closed" town.

3. The pulse of suppression is recorded by enormous increases and decreases in police drive against vice. The general trend in the amount of police activity is decidedly upward, since in 1928 the police were seven times more active in vice arrests than they were in 1908.

4. The centrifugal spread of vice resorts has resulted from the changes and declines in decentralized neighborhoods incidental to the city's growth just as much as from the reaction to suppressive efforts.

5. Resorts for prostitution today have, on the average, a low rate of persistence at separate addresses as contrasted to the secure, well-established status of brothels in the red light district.

6. The most reliable data, at present, indicate that the actual number of investigated vice resorts was smaller in 1931 than in 1910. A smaller number of resorts operated on a short-time, sporadic basis, is indeed a contrast to the full-time flagrant business of vice in red light districts.

7. Available data indicate that the average number of prostitutes per resort today is 2 as compared with 5 in 1910.

8. There has been a considerable growth of Negro prostitution since 1910 when it was almost negligible. From the available data it appears that Negroes have much more than their proportionate amount of prostitution considering their small number in the total population and that the causes for this are to be found in the heavy Negro immigration, the attending unadjustment, the restricted occupational outlets for Negro women, the disorganized neighborhood conditions in which most Negroes must live, and greater liability of police arrest—rather than to be sought in Negro sex psychology or in a supposed proneness to criminality.

CHAPTER II

FROM WHITE SLAVERY TO RECONSTRUCTION

The traffic in women and especially young girls has been much more shocking to the public than the existence of open brothels. White slaves were supposed to be the "fuel" for the "red lights." The conception grew in the minds of the public that brothel prostitution, on a large scale and in an institutional form, could not exist without systematic seduction of innocent girls. Consequently, the crusade against the segregated district in America involved a movement against white slavery.

White slavery is confessedly a misnomer, since Negro and Chinese girls may become "slave girls." As the term is used in popular discourse it applies to the exploitation of women of any sort for purposes of prostitution or to the trapping of women for profit. In the course of the vice crusades, white slavery assumed, in the mind of the public, almost legendary proportions, and the sentiments which the agitation has aroused have centered about the figure and the fate of the Missing Girl.

THE MISSING GIRL

There had long been great concern about the disappearance of young girls and in the years between 1909 and 1912, when the press was familiarizing the public with the conception of a widespread international traffic in girls, the public was more concerned about missing girls than ever before. As very little was actually known about the circumstances under which these disappearances took place, the detailed stories that got into circulation and were

32

repeated again and again, tended to conform more and more to a conventional pattern.

The innocent victims, enticed away from home and lured into prostitution, were represented as fatally condemned to a quick and certain end.

It is a significant fact that when the body of a young girl was recently taken to the morgue in Chicago, nearly five hundred persons—relatives of other missing girls—called or wrote during the time allowed for identification to see if it was their lost one. Where are those lost girls? On the outskirts of one of the western cities, there is a cemetery where 451 nameless girls are buried. The unhappy fact that the daughters of every State of the Union are menaced by the cowardly agents of this clandestine traffic should be made known.[1]

The downfall and tragic end of missing girls was regarded as an incident of a gigantic traffic in women. "This business has become established in America," so wrote Janney. "It is more or less clandestinely but extensively carried on in the United States, where some of the shrewdest and most unscrupulous traders have harvested large profits from a sort of brokerage system of trafficking in women. It is a business carried on for profit."[2]

CAUGHT AND HELD

Not all the women in brothels were supposed to be white slaves, but the supply of those who entered of their own free will was said to be far behind the demand—hence the need for procuring innocent victims.[3]

[1] Adapted from *The White Slave Traffic in America* by O. Edward Janney, New York, 1911, pp. 22–23.

[2] *Ibid*, pp. 13–14.

[3] Clifford Roe, *Panders and Their White Slaves*, New York and Chicago, 1910, p. 108.

The white slaves were said to be lured by promises of luxury and marriage, by flattering attention, appeals to vanity, the dazzle and whirl of bright lights in cities, and sometimes by forced abduction. Once the girl was trapped she was presumably held as a prisoner in a brothel, to be abused, beaten, and forced to turn over her earnings to a pimp. "The human chattels of these traffickers," according to Janney, "are practically slaves, for the girls and women who are lured, deceived through affection, or in some instances forced into prostitution, are held in bondage by subtle but compelling means. Whether the victim is confined behind closed doors, or is allowed to go out under close watch, or kept in submission by fear of personal violence, she is, under any of these conditions, *a slave*— one forced to do her master's bidding and obliged to give him the money she receives."[4]

A THRICE TOLD TALE

It was in purity lectures addressed to women that the story of the Missing Girl and the white slave traffic, shorn of all actual details, assumed finally an almost epic character.

Briefly—for no one cares to linger long in a charnel house—the situation is this: We have in our nation between 300,000 and 500,000 girls and women whose only income is their wage of shame. Most of these creatures belong actually or potentially to another class of people who have commercialized vice, who make these girls their capital, and who reap immense profits from their pitiful sales.

These women do not live long, so their owners must be constantly on the outlook for others to take their places; there must be no lack of a face at the window or profits will fall off. Today no one ques-

[4] O. Edward Janney, *The White Slave Traffic in America*, New York, 1911, p. 15.

tions the fact that girls are bought and sold in America even as cattle and sheep and hogs are bought and sold; that men go in and out our great stores, factories, laundries, everywhere looking the girls over and deciding which ones they want just as keen-eyed stock buyers go through a herd of cattle or flock of sheep. Having decided whom they want, they go about getting them. They learn the vulnerable point in the girl's armour; it may be love of dress, love of fun, love of ease, love of admiration, love of love itself, no matter, they will undertake to supply it. The trip on the boat, the park, the dance, the theatre with supper afterward—but why enumerate? These human sharks pick up the helpless immigrant, the unsuspecting traveler, the homesick working girl, the love-hungry country girl, it is all the same to them.[5]

Stories oft repeated and reinterpreted tend to assume the character of myth and conform to the sentiments of those who tell them and those who hear them told. And yet the public can be stirred into action by rumor more easily than by dull and undramatic fact. Under the influence of rumor, estimates as to the number of white slave victims in the United States were given currency with almost the imputed validity of an actual enumeration.

20,000 GIRLS ARE SNARED ANNUALLY

From 15,000 to 20,000 girls between the ages of 13 and 25 years, a majority of whom are native born Americans, are the victims each year of the white slave traffic in the U. S.

About 50,000 men and women make an "easy" living every year selling, buying and living on the earnings of these girls.

So easy is the living to be made out of the white slave traffic, says Mr. Finch, that conscienceless crooks of all kinds in the country have turned to trafficking in young girls and there are today, conservatively estimated, no less than 250,000 women living a life of shame in semipublic or officially tolerated places of disrepute.[6]

[5] Adapted from *The White Slave Traffic versus the American Home* by M. Madeline Southard, Louisville, 1914, pp. 9–11.

[6] *Chicago Interocean*, September 8, 1912.

A STORY TOLD FIRST HAND

The following story of a white slave was published at a time when public interest in the white slave traffic was still undiminished by more complete knowledge of the facts. It is selected from among others published at the time, first, because it is cited by Clifford Roe who prosecuted white slave cases in Chicago, and second, because it is not the usual story of the young immigrant girl, fifteen or sixteen years of age, who falls into the clutches of ruthless foreign procurers. The story is no doubt true, but the actual facts are obscured by the addition of literary details by the writer or his informants.

A thin, frail young woman, aided by a physician, walked slowly into the court room and took her place on the witness stand. She said that she lived with her parents on the North Side of Chicago; that she was twenty years old and was a high school graduate.

"Do you remember meeting a certain young man about a month ago?" I asked her.

"Yes," she answered. "I was then employed in an office down-town and one of the girls working in the same building with me suggested that we attend a dance on Saturday night. This dance was held at a dance hall, I believe, near the corner of Thirty-first Street and Indiana Avenue. It was there I met this young man, whose first name was John."

John invited her to have a drink of lemonade.

"When I began to drink the lemonade I noticed a peculiar taste about it. After drinking it I felt dizzy. It seemed as though my head was whirling round and round. I was sick, and in a few minutes I entirely forgot where I was."

When she regained consciousness she found herself in bed in an entirely strange room.

"My head was sore and I put up my arm to feel for something and my hand clutched bedclothing. In a moment a door opened and a bright light shone into the room and a person passed through the door towards me. She came over and put her hand upon my head and soothingly said, 'Dearie, how are you?' I tried to answer, but my voice failed me. I lay still for a while, and finally I gasped out, 'Where am I?'

" 'You are all right,' said the Negress, 'and you will like it here.'

"She then went out and came back in a short time with a glass of wine, which she put to my lips, and I drank it and fell into a sleep.

"A day or so later I became stronger and it was then that I first learned where I was.

"I asked her for my clothes that I might go home and she told me that the madam had them locked up.

" 'Please, may I see the madam?' I cried out, for I was becoming terribly frightened. The Negress disappeared and came back with a stout blond woman, wearing a kimono and a great many diamonds and other jewels.

"The woman came up to me and took me by the hand and said, 'Why, you know where you are; you can't go home now. You owe me a debt and until that debt is paid you cannot leave this house.'

" 'I owe you a debt,' I cried, 'and for what?'

" 'Why, don't you think you owe me anything for taking care of you here and for the clothes I have bought for you and for the money I have paid the young man who brought you here for his trouble and expense? Of course you do.'

"For days and days I pleaded with the madam to let me go home. I was sick. I could not endure the drinking and the awful life any longer.

"They knocked me about and even whipped me. They watched me as a cat does a mouse for fear that I would say something or tell something which I had been forbidden to tell.

"At first they sent a man to me, whom I thought from his manner I could trust, and I told him of my trouble, and he sympathized with me in my terrible plight and said he would help me escape and tell my family where I was. It was for this that I was whipped, for I found that he was what they called 'a ringer,' and had been sent to me purposely to see whether or not I would tell that I was being kept in this place against my will.

"The girls are cowed into submission in this way and are afraid and suspicious of every man they meet, and they have been whipped and have seen others whipped until their spirits are broken. They are forced into a life from which they cannot escape."[7]

In contrast with literary artifice employed in the foregoing story the actual statement of the complaining witness and the court record in one of the most sensational of 77 extant records of white slave cases in Chicago during 1910–13 is startling in its realism. The original data in these cases are still available in record. The unvarnished statement of the girl herself as taken down by Officer Bell after her apprehension is given here, *in toto,* supplemented by a summary of the process of the case.

THE GIRL'S OWN STATEMENT

November 13, 1911—I am twenty years old. I came to this country one month ago from H—[small town], Sweden, and went to live with my uncle at XXX C— street [Chicago]. The first night that I was here I met a young man who took me out on the grass plot and tried to have [relations] with me but I fought him off; but in the squabble I lost my cousin's watch. Then I became frightened about losing the watch and left my uncle's home, and walked the streets all night. I had about $1.50. About four A. M. the next morning I rented a room at 24th and State Sts. from a colored man. He registered my name in a book and I paid him fifty cents. At eleven A. M. that morning I went out and walked the streets all day until evening, when I met a colored man in the same neighborhood, and I asked him if he knew where I could get a room and he took me to a room and I stayed all night with him and he gave me $5.00. He had [relations] with me. The next day I met a colored woman named Mrs. D. at 24th and Dearborn. I asked her if she knew where I could get a room, and she asked me to come to her house XXXX Dearborn St. in the basement. She then asked me if

---

[7] Adapted from *Panders and Their White Slaves* by Clifford G. Roe, Fleming H. Revell & Company, New York and Chicago, 1910, pp. 11–17.

I liked to make money and I said yes; so Mrs. D. took me into a room and powdered me up and then we went to saloons hustling for prostitution and took our men to XXXX Dearborn St. [the same basement] and Mrs. D. charged them fifty cents for a room and one dollar for the girl. I hustled at this place for two weeks when Mrs. D. saw in the newspapers that I was missing from home; she asked me about it and I told her it was true. Then she asked me if I wanted to go home and I told her I did, but I wanted her to go with me to explain matters. She got an automobile and took me to the corner near my uncle's place and left me there. I was afraid to go home; then I got on a car and went back to 24th and State Sts. and met another colored man and I asked him if he knew where I could get a room. He took me to his room at 12th and State Sts. This is where the officers arrested me, and got a card with the colored man's name on it. Mrs. D. is from 30 to 35 years of age; 5 ft. 4 inches tall; weighs 135 lbs. and has pock-marked yellow skin.

THE PROCESS OF THE CASE

Girl disappeared October 14, 1911. A friend of girl's uncle appealed to Clifford Roe [October 25, 1911] for help after police had case for 11 days and had been unable to find the girl, although they advanced the theory that she must be held against her will in a resort. An investigator found her in rear room of saloon at 30th and State Streets. He reported that he was attracted by the fact that a colored woman was accompanied by a very pretty girl. The white girl, he reports, did not speak English. He obtained cards of both Mrs. D. and the girl at the time. This was at 1 A. M. [Nov. 8, 1911]. The next evening [same day November 8, 1911] arrest was made. The Swedish Council [November 9, 1911] took up girl's case with United States Immigration Bureau and "they planned" to deport her. No data given of any final action on this point. Mrs. D., the colored woman, was fined $300 and sentenced to one year in House of Correction (Nov. 23, 1911). A charge of abduction was made against one of the Negro men in the case [not clear which one], but girl was reported to have refused to prosecute him.[8]

[8] See Case 17—Chicago Vice Study File.

BANDS AND CONTRABANDS

Not to be forgotten in the stereotyped picture of white slavery are the bands of white slavers themselves. In America they were said to operate from coast to coast, in town and country, with tentacles in foreign lands, east and west, and across the American borders. The most sensational of these were said to be the French, Italian, and Jewish rings who preyed on innocent girls of their respective nationalities at ports of entry into the United States or ensnared them at the ports of embarkment in Europe and even in their home towns. The public was so incensed as a result of such rumors that a special immigration commission was appointed to investigate exploitation of immigrant girls by white slavers (1907). The commission found nothing so startling as conditions were rumored to be. Very doubtful instances of organized rings of traffickers were discovered. Later (1910) a Special Grand Jury, with John D. Rockefeller, Jr., as foreman, charged with the investigation of organized traffic in women in New York City, also found practically no evidence to support the rumors. "They reported that while they had not been able to find any evidence of organizations engaged in the traffic, they had discovered that a trafficking in the bodies of women does exist and is carried on by individuals acting for their own individual benefit, and that these persons are known to each other and are more or less informally associated."[9]

The Chicago Vice Commission's statement on an organized traffic in women is perhaps the most moderate and conservative part of the whole survey.

[9] Edwin R. A. Seligman, *The Social Evil in New York,* second edition of the Committee of Fifteen report, 1912, p. 27.

This investigation has shown that panders often work in groups and are in communication with gangs in other cities. Individuals, working independently are also willing and eager to procure prostitutes for houses not only in this city, but for houses in other cities and countries.

These individuals and members of these gangs are very often waiters in saloons, bartenders and proprietors of saloons and houses of prostitution. They are scattered all over the city, and the individuals are known to each other, and confer together when their services are demanded.

It has been demonstrated that men and women engaged in the so-called "white slave" traffic are not organized. Their operations, however, are so similar and they use the same methods to such an extent that it is safe to infer that they are in some way working together.

This fact is illustrated by the following incidents brought to light through the court records as cited in conference with the Commission by the prosecuting attorney of the offenders.

The first is the case of Mollie Hart. In the trial of this case, it was shown that Albert Hoffer, Michael Hart, David Garfinkle, Maurice Van Bever, Julia Van Bever, Dick Tyler and Frenchy Tolman all belonged to the same crowd, and operated together. The headquarters of this gang in Chicago was operated by Maurice Van Bever. This man was found guilty of pandering and sentenced for one year and to pay a fine of $1,000. His wife, Julia, was also found guilty.

The Van Bevers had two houses of prostitution in Chicago. These two houses back up against each other. This gang operated in a clever manner, which still further proved that the combination existed. This gang had a combination with other gangs in other cities.[10]

SELF-APPOINTED ATTACHES AS THE PROCURERS

The statement that pandering and procuring were largely in the hands of individual men—self-appointed attachés to vice resorts—is borne out by the examination of

[10] *The Social Evil in Chicago* (Chicago, 1911), pp. 176–77.

the 77 Chicago white slave cases. I could find no evidence in any of the cases of the existence of gangs of white slavers organized for the purpose of waylaying girls and enslaving them. There was very little evidence to support the charge that men were purposely and consciously sent out to trap girls by the managers of a resort or syndicate of resorts. If present-day Chicago gangs with their efficient feudal organization had been engaged in white slavery twenty years ago, the actual facts in regard to bands of "traffickers" might have equalled the unwarranted sensational rumors in both kind and degree.

That individual men placed girls whom they married, seduced, intimidated, or coaxed in houses of prostitution is quite in accord with the actual data. That they got so much per head for delivering the girls is not apparent from the evidence. What is apparent is that the procurer took so much from the girl's earning account in advance and that this was charged to the girl. The girls themselves ultimately paid for their being brought to a resort; the keepers did not pay as far as the evidence goes. The men who brought girls to resorts and obtained an initial payment (charged to the new inmate), were almost invariably the same ones who came to collect more money from their women. These same men sometimes lived with them, and no doubt occasionally abused them. In other words, the male procurers were the pimps, panders, lovers, and beaters.

MAN'S INHUMANITY TO WOMAN: A PATRIARCHAL PATTERN

An impression one receives in reading the data in the 77 white slave records in Chicago (1910–13) is that procuring —pimping—pandering was an accepted pattern of male activity. It seemed to be the customary thing in the under-

world.   Every one "had him a woman."   Some even had
more than one.   The procuring—pimping—pandering com-
plex seemed to be a survival of this lingering patriarchal
pattern of family life and male human nature transferred
in perverted expression to a modern urban situation where
it took the form of exploitation.

WHAT THE CASES SHOW

(a) *Young girls but no children*.—The study of 77 white
slave cases of 1910–13, whose records were available, reveals certain interesting conclusions, which may help to
put Chicago's former white slave market in its proper per-
spective.   These cases were investigated for the most part
by officers Bell, Kinder, and Bowler and prosecuted by
Roe, Waldron, and Thrasher for the anti-white-slavery
forces.   Out of the 77 cases studied, 63 showed actual
evidence of pandering; 12 of the 63 came up in 1910; 25,
in 1911; 21, in 1912 and 5, 1913.   The age distribution of
the girls in the cases runs as follows: 15, 2; 16, 7; 17, 12;
18, 3; 19, 5; 20, 5; 21, 3; 22, 2; 23, 2; 24, 3; over 24, 2;
age not given, 17.   This age distribution should not be
taken as indicative of the ages of prostitutes in Chicago at
the time but merely as indicative of the cases which anti-
white-slave forces gave greatest attention to—namely
young girls.   We notice, however, that even with this extreme selection of cases there are none under 15 years in
spite of what the public believed about girls scarcely in
their "teens" being lured into prostitution.   In the 77 cases
I found only one girl that was under 15.   She ran away to
Chicago on an adventure with her cousin but investigation
did not show any evidence of exploitation and was not
included in the 63 tabulated.

(*b*) *Six immigrant girls.*—Only 6 of the 63 girls were reported as immigrant (1 Irish, 1 Danish, 2 Swedish, 1 Hungarian, and 1 Serbian). None of these was a "just-arrived" immigrant. Most of the 6 had been in this country over 5 years. The Serbian girl had been here 11 years. Twenty of the girls were reported as American and in 37 remaining cases the data did not reveal nativity.

(*c*) *The men: 9 Italian, 7 Polish, 3 Greek.*—In absence of any definite and reliable data on nativity of the men exploiters in these cases, I give what nationality and racial names appeared for the men in the records. Nine of the men were reported as being Italian; 7, as Polish; 3, as Greek; 2, as Negro; 5, as American (white, I assume). If it is permissible to assume that the foreign nationalities reported signified foreign-born, then 19 out of 63 were reported as foreign-born while 7 would be American-born, 37 not being reported on this condition. But it is interesting to note that Italians, Poles, and Greeks were representative of the most recent (in about that order of sequence) immigrant groups in America at the time (1910).

(*d*) *Chicago's own girls outnumber the small town victims.*—Seventeen of the 63 white slaves had come from small towns; 15, from large towns; 27, from Chicago itself; and 4 cases were not reported on as to location of home. It would seem from this that, contrary to the belief then, the largest single number (43 per cent) came from Chicago itself, while only 17 (27 per cent) came from small towns and 15 (24 per cent)—an almost equal number—came from large towns. And yet the popular impression at the time was that small town (as well as immigrant) girls fell victims in the largest proportions.

(*e*) *Wayward rather then virtuous victims.*—In the 63

cases (with the girls telling their own stories with lawyers and officers helping them), only 4 instances are reported where the procurer—pimp—pander was actually the violator of the girl's chastity. On the other hand, in 16 instances the data seems to indicate that the girl had been wayward before meeting the defendant in the case. One is unable to say whether this 1 to 4 ratio would hold in the 43 cases where the data did not indicate this aspect of the girls' histories. It would be logical to assume so, since criminologists agree that most girls who enter prostitution have been delinquent and have had previous experience prior to entering the life.

(*f*) *Three held prisoner and 15 abused.*—In regard to girls' being held prisoner against will and their being brutally treated by their pimps, the data in the 63 cases only yield 3 instances of the former and 15 of the latter. The 3 cases of being held prisoner are given in the following summaries.

1911, M. B. 18, Mg. B. [her sister] 16, C. H. [a cousin] 18—3 girls—came to Chicago from a small Wisconsin town, April 1911. M. B. claimed she came to stay with her aunt, held a position in general housework and sewing for two months, met F. at a saloon, took her to J.'s place (a resort), F. promised to marry her, stayed with him there that night, next morning J. (the woman keeper) told the girl she could make $65 per week and she could have half of what she made, girl refused, F. then took her to another resort, girl told the police booker she was 18 (contrary to F.'s orders which were 19) and the bookers would not let her stay, social worker takes girl back to her aunt's, 3 days later met F. again and took girl back to J.'s place where she practiced prostitution for 5 months, girl was whipped with rawhide by J.'s husband, J. took all money girl earned, an opium joint in the place, left the place October 1911.[11]

C. H. [cousin of the other two girls] came to Chicago with them,

[11] Case 5a—Chicago Vice Study File.

worked about also as a domestic, went home to Wisconsin town, later returned to Chicago, called on M. B. [Sept. 1911] at J.'s place, stayed there over night, went for a visit to a friend of her [C. H.'s] mother in Chicago, stayed there for 3 days, this woman returned to Wisconsin town [same as home town of girl], C. H. then went to J.'s resort. "After being there a number of days I found out that there was not much money in it and did not like the life, because I had to drink wine and beer [with men who were] introduced to me and was told to stay with them and only had one day off a week." "We would never go out to mail a letter or go to [the] store without asking J. otherwise we could never go out only when she allowed us to." [After] "I was there about ten days M. got in a quarrel with J. about some money so we both left the place." F. and J. were each sentenced to a year in the house of correction and fined $100 each for pandering. The girls were sent home.[12]

1911 born in Hungary, came to the United States in 1908, married in New York City 5 months after arrival, lived with him 6 months, left him because he turned out to be a drunkard and because he beat her, came to Chicago, worked as waitress in northside restaurant, met G. [Bohemian evidently] at her rooming house in the Bohemian area, he was 50 years of age and a cripple, he sent a woman to see her, H. got on friendly terms with girl, taken by H. to South Chicago vice district on promise of better work, this was a ruse evidently and the better work was at a resort, forced to stay with men, prevented from leaving, owner of house in the Strand [South Chicago] caught in another case and brought to trial [August 1911].[13]

A RUMOR INVESTIGATED AND FOUND UNWARRANTED

In one case investigated on a complaint by a deaconess that a Swedish immigrant girl was being held against her will in a Japanese-Chinese resort in the Twenty-second Street district of Chicago, officers Bell and Bowler turned in the following written report (given *in toto*).

[12] Case 5c—Chicago Vice Study File.
[13] Case 39—Chicago Vice Study File.

6-23-11

CARL WALDRON

SIR

In regard to the complaint filed by Deaconess Detrick about one, Lillian, a Swede, being held against her will at the Japanese and Chinese House of Ill Fame located at XXX—W. 21st Street, top flat, and run by Madame Daisy Davies, we find that she was an inmate of this place only the evenings for the last 6 months, and that she lived out on the Southside with a colored man and that he paid her way about 2 weeks ago to her sisters in Michigan and she is still there. And the Madame thought she was in this country about 5 or 6 years and that she hustled at XXY—W. 21st Street before she came to her house.   Respectfully

Bell—Bowler [14]

THE WORST CASE OF BRUTALITY

The most dramatic of the 15 cases where "beating" was reported is given in summary.

1913, 21 divorced, met L. at a house of ill-fame over a year ago, went to various hotels to live with him and to hustle, turned over her earnings to him, then he made arrangements for her to enter one of the most notorious places in the 22nd Street district, 30 to 40 girls there, 40 per cent commission for drinks, all earnings here were turned over to L., L. bought her clothes and paid the rent, stayed here about 10 months, then he sent her to Bloomington and she returned 2 days later and would not go back, L. beat her one evening in a hotel at which they were living so that her screams attracted the officers in the neighborhood and the arrest was made. She was found nude, crying and bleeding at the mouth. He had beaten her several times previously but not as violently as on the night of the arrest. The reason he gave for beating her was that she had made no money to turn over to him that day and had, instead, gone out with a friend. L. was sentenced to H. of C. for one year and fined $1,000. No data in the file on what became of the girl.[15]

[14] Case 57—Chicago Vice Study File.
[15] Case 29—Chicago Vice Study File.

We cannot tell from the available data in this case, or any of the cases for that matter, whether the beating developed out of just pure financial troubles and crossing of ire or whether there was something more sadistic involved. The more obvious conjecture in absence of definite proof would be to ascribe the abusiveness to the patriarchal pattern according to which wife beating was a male prerogative. In none of the 15 cases reported as to beating did any of the girls claim that the beating was an every day or even a frequent occurrence.

ENTERING LIFE OF OWN FREE WILL

Curiously enough in the 77 records of supposed white slave cases it was found that 14 of them showed no evidence of pandering whatsoever. Out of these 14, 3 of the girls went into prostitution of their "own free wills." In other words no men were involved in their cases at all. The remaining 11 girls were taken advantage of and exposed morally but did not go into prostitution. The available data from the cases of the three girls who entered the life apparently of their own free wills are given below.

1912, 17, born and living with parents in Chicago, in spring of 1911 was employed as a domestic in Chicago suburbs, became pregnant by local man, went to her own home (westside of Chicago) for 5 months, then to a refuge until child was born (Jan. 1912), returned to home, left home in June 1912, 3 weeks later went to a resort by herself in 22nd Street district, asked to be allowed to become an inmate, told police she was 20 years old and had hustled on streets for 2 years previously, girl had venereal disease at time (syphilis), stayed there for 6 weeks when case came up (against manager of resort for having a juvenile in house of prostitution), girl averaged $25 to $30 per week at the resort, girl was boarding her child with some friends. No pander or pimp in the case.[16]

[16] See Case 26—Chicago Vice Study File.

1910, 19 years, born in small town in Indiana, came to Chicago
five months ago to visit sister who was a prostitute, hustled in the
same saloon (on the Near Northside) sister worked in, officers told
her to leave as she was too young, went to her home in Indiana, but
returned to Chicago a week later, went to the same saloon again,
about two weeks later Mother sent for both sister and the girl on
account of sickness, the sister returned in about two weeks to Chicago and the girl returned in about five weeks, she says "of my own
free will," the girls left this saloon about six weeks later and went to
work at another resort (still on the Near Northside), they lived elsewhere in the neighborhood while practicing prostitution, the girl said
she was a prostitute in her home town before coming to Chicago and
that her Mother knew that she and her sister were prostitutes and
that they used to send her money. The statement of the sister indicates the same sequence of events. It adds that the girl was not her
real sister but had lived at her home for three years and called her
sister. The sister also claimed that the girl had mentioned that the
owner of the saloon was in her home town during the last visit and
that she (the girl) had returned to Chicago with him. The girl does
not mention this man but the sister does.[17]

1912, 17, living in Chicago with parents, left home 3 weeks previously and went to room with girl friend at a cheap hotel, had been a
ward of Juvenile court for 1 year, met J. J. Sunday night [2 weeks
previously] on street corner in neighborhood, went downtown together, girl said she went of own accord to a resort that she had
learned about through a girl acquaintance [now in the Bridewell],
while at resort called another man friend who brought along J. S.
[defendant in case whom girl said she had known for over a year],
he made 3 visits to her, she gave him small sums of money [$2 and
$1] on two occasions, when attorney asked how it was she gave him
money she said "I don't know how I happened to give it. I had it
and he didn't have any money and so I just gave him the money."
She claimed that J. S. told her to go back home and she said "If I
got married I would go home." Girl had gone to City Hall to get a
license when she was arrested, J. S. had promised to marry her.
The girl's story is full of conflicts and seems to be shielding J. S. Dis-

<hr />

[17] See Case 32—Chicago Vice Study File.

position of case not given. Once during the 3 weeks adventure she made a visit home and told her Mother she was working in a private family. Investigation showed girl was living at this resort (which was a hotel, resort and cafe all together) with a man—not clear whether it was J. S. or some other man.[18]

It might be urged that the girl in Case 32 was brought back to Chicago by the saloon keeper the last time and the fact that she did not mention him, saying she came of her "own free will," is an instance of shielding. To make this claim is transcending the data. My own impression is that if there had been enough evidence in the case of coercion the officers and authorities would have uncovered it. But the girl in Case 4P tells such a round-about story that one suspects that the whole truth has not been told. A suspicion, however, is no justification for placing this case under those in which procuring and pandering are verifiable.

USED BUT NOT PANDERED

Cases which follow are instances of girls who, although exploited, were not led into prostitution. The first one is the case of a "poor working girl"—a type much advertised in the discussion of the causes of prostitution. This working girl was exposed and exploited, as far as the record goes, but did not become a prostitute. In the second case, a homeless man, a Greek, gives a girl presents in return for her favors, incidentally he exposes her to exploitation of Jewish shop keepers. And in the third case Chinese laundrymen, likewise homeless and sexually isolated men, are using neighborhood girls. In the last case cited (Case 20), a girl of 17 is lured from home by an "experienced" girl of 20 who might in time have led her into prostitution.

[18] See Case 4P—Chicago Vice Study File.

The motives for the girl's going off with the "vampire" and the vampire's disposition to "take up" with the girl are not indicated. They are probably adventure and romance on the part of the girl and companionship in the case of the vampire.

THE POOR WORKING GIRL LED ASTRAY BUT NOT EXPLOITED

7–13–1911 (Investigator's Report)

Teresa Jahn came to Chicago about 3 months ago—worked as a nurse girl on the North Side. On July 1st she met H. H. at Wilson Ave. beach, bathing. He got her to leave that night at 10 P. M. and took her to the Pierce Hotel where they took a room as man and wife. He stayed with her that night and a part of Sunday. During the next four days he called to see her several times and said he had a lot of business outside. He did not stay with her again till Friday night. Saturday night he paid the hotel bill and they both left. He took her to the boat landing at the foot of Clark Street and told her they would take the night boat for Michigan. He left a few minutes to go and see his doctor and never came back. She thinks he is a travelling man but doesn't know his business or the company he works for.

9–12–12 (Investigator's Report)

Teresa Jahn [alias John] called in this office and said that she was working in Ice Cream Parlor at XXXX So. Halsted St., and lived with her cousin at XXXX C ——, near North Ave. [on North Side].

10–9–12 (Investigator's Report)

I investigated the complaint of Teresa Jahn who was working for J. M., Proprietor of Greek Restaurant, at XXXX W. Chicago Ave. Her complaint was that the Greek cook put his hand on her breast and said she was stuffed with newspapers and he would have 5 boys meet her tonight. I told Teresa to get her things and go home to her cousin's and go and see the Community Woman's League and try to get a job with some private family.

10–11–12 (From further interviews with girl)

Threatened with death by four men because she would not accept their attentions, Miss Teresa Jahn, cashier in a restaurant at XXX West Chicago Avenue, telephoned to the office of State's Attorney Wayman, asking for protection. She declared that a brother-in-law of the manager, whose name she did not know, was the ringleader in the gang and the first to force his attentions on her when she went to work at the place last Thursday.

"Sunday he forced me to go to several moving theatres with him, threatening to have me discharged if I refused," said Miss John. "He insisted on having some pictures taken and later showed them to the cook and a boy who works here. They then tried to force me to go with them. This morning they brought two friends into the shop and all made threats to kill me on the way home some night if I continued to refuse to go out with them. It is not safe for any girl to work here and I shall get myself another position as soon as possible." An officer from State's Attorney's office escorted Miss John to her home XXXX Clearmont Avenue, and will investigate the case.

10–14–12 (Investigator's Report)

Went to the Community Woman's League with Teresa John and talked with Mrs. X. about a position for her and she called up Mrs. Y. and she said she would like Teresa to come out there but Teresa must mind her and not run out nights and to have her come out tomorrow afternoon. No further data in file.[19]

1911, 18 Polish girl, born and living in Chicago, met G. (a Greek) 3 weeks ago through a Polish man friend (X), G. and X. took this girl and another one to the rear of a store belonging to two Jews, got girls drunk on wine and stayed with them, G. took girl home and gave her $1.50 and told her to call around at the restaurant where he worked, next time he took her to his room and then gave her $1, the next time to the Jew's store again, one of these stayed with her also, the two Jews tried to get her to hustle in the back of their store, girl met him at his restaurant, took her to his room, then to the restaurant of his cousin (another Greek), tried to get her a job as a waitress there, then back to his room, they were arrested there, the land-

[19] See Case 45—Chicago Vice Study File.

lady had found out that G. was bringing girl to his room, G. had bought her a $14 coat and gave her $2 on other occasions and bought her a $5 ring (he said) and gave her a key to his room.[20]

1912, 21, living in Chicago, a girl friend [G. K.] introduced her to G. W. a Chinese laundryman, G. K. had given the Chinese her picture, he gave the girl $1 and gave G. K. $10 for bringing her and other girls around, four or five days later returned to laundry with G. K., G. W. gave the girl $2 and G. K. got some money from C. C. another Chinese at the laundry, two or three days later the girls went to the laundry again and got $5 a piece from the Chinese who told them to meet them down at the M. Hotel [cheap hotel] on Sunday afternoon, stayed with the Chinese and received more money [the girl got $3 this time], went with G. K. to the laundry once the next week and J. F. another Chinese there asked for a girl for himself and promised G. K. a nice present, that same afternoon G. K. went home and got her own sister [M. K.] and J. F. gave G. K. and M. K. $5 to be split between them, M. K. told her Mother so G. K. had to get J. F. another girl and got him K. B., J. F. gave both of them money, on the following Sunday all three girls [the girl in the case, G. K. and K. B.] went to the hotel and stayed with the three Chinamen, the girl got $3 this time from G. W., the rest got money too, all three girls went to same hotel the next Sunday, this time the girl got $7 from G. W. and this was last time she went there, J. F. gave G. K. $20 to buy K. B. a new suit; she paid $12.98 for it plus $1.98 for a collar and K. gave G. the rest.[21]

1911, 17, living in Chicago with parents, girl met S. [a girl of about 20] at a dance hall garden on Southside, Nov. 1911, S. asked her to go to her home with her to live and in that event she [S.] would not take her servant when she fitted out the new apartment, 3 days later the girl after being written to and called on phone by S. went to her house, took her to rooms on Northside, S. got dates for both that evening, S. and girl went to hotel with J. and M. respectively, later in week made some pick up acquaintances at dance halls, the rooming house keeper censured S. and girl for staying away all night, S. took girl to other lodgings, S. and girl met two new men on

[20] See Case 13—Chicago Vice Study File.
[21] See Case 38—Chicago Vice Study File.

streets, all returned to rooms, S. stayed with one, girl refused the other man, S. tried to date up the girl with men for next evening, girl refused, S. stayed out all night and told girl she had made $2, both went for an auto ride on second evening following, two evenings from this S. and girl went to a dance hall, met some new fellows, officers there recognized girl as one who was "missing," when her picture appeared in paper as "missing" the girl wanted to return home but S. would not let her, S. had asked her to go to Boston with her, told girl she had been arrested 4 times, once with a man who took her [S.] to Milwaukee and was arrested on "white slave charge," the little money the girl and S. made was spent together by both. Girl's parents prosecuted the case. No disposition recorded in the file.[22]

AN OUTCAST GROUP

All these traits and conditions of white slaves, some actual, some doubtful and some even fictitious, were of such a spectacular nature that the public lost sight of the most fundamental fact about prostitutes of the 1910 era and before. This was that they had formed an outcast group segregated and cut off from respectable society by place of residence, mode of living, manners and dress, and the stigma attaching to the profession. In classical antiquity this separateness from respectable society was translated into law, according to which prostitutes were confined to the slave classes, already an outcast group.[23]

In the "half world" or underworld to which prostitutes were banished there was the tendency on the part of these

[22] See Case 2—Chicago Vice Study File.

[23] Solon, instituting the classical system of state regulation of prostitution, confined the prostitutes to the slave classes and only those slaves brought from foreign lands. The prostitutes were really state slaves, and like other slaves were subject to a state tax, the payment of which stigmatized them as non-citizens (see Bloch, *Die Prostitution*, I, 215, 440–41). This system was also adopted, with certain more stringent regulations, by the Romans.

"fallen" women to acquire certain habits and manners, which further marked them off from the rest of the community. The prostitute was free to do what was tabu for the respectable woman. She could be grossly unconventional; for that was the secret of her profession. In matters of dress and ornament, she again was decidedly different, perhaps individual—in some cases leading fashion.[24] In classical times, particularly in Rome, the prostitutes were prohibited by law from wearing the clothing and ornaments of respectable women—the *institia, stola, vitae* —and were required to wear a toga-like garb, the so-called "toga meretricia." In medieval London the women of bad repute were restricted to a certain garb, and were prohibited by royal proclamation of Edward I from wearing miniver (spotted ermine) or cendale (a particular kind of thin silk) on their hoods and dresses.[25] The conflict in the Middle Ages over the dress of the prostitute, which in certain places led to prohibitions, was felt mainly by the ladies of the noble classes, who were themselves exhibiting certain signs of individuality. The great masses of women were untouched by this struggle for supremacy in fashion; for they had not emerged out of the stage symbolized by the *tracht*.

THE PAINTED LADY

Until recently the prostitute has had an uncontested monopoly on the use of rouge, the bleaching of the hair, and strong perfumes, all of which have been means of sexual attraction, very old in the history of prostitution.[26]

[24] Havelock Ellis, *Sex in Relation to Society*, p. 299.

[25] H. B. Wheatley, *The Story of London*, pp. 44–45.

[26] Iwan Block, *op. cit.*, pp. 45–46, 167–71. Rouging the face or bleaching the hair is considered by Bloch as a survival from primitive sex life.

These were recognized attributes of a professional and pariah class as late as 1910. While such decoration has had a professional value, it has also, like differences in dress, set off the prostitutes from the respectable women of society. The fact that she has been referred to as the "painted lady," was a recognition of the fact that the prostitute formed a caste. This is illustrated in the case of two prostitutes, who tried to prepare their unsophisticated protegée for her new role but curiously failed in the attempt.

I am fifteen years old and live with my Mother at [Near West Side Chicago]. I first met Mrs. D —— and became acquainted with her in F. —'s store [right across street] where she was working several months ago. About a month ago she took me to her home one day and talked to me and asked me if I did not want to go to Bill C——'s saloon and be a sport. I told her I did not want to go. On June 27th she took me to the X. [cheap] hotel at 11 A.M. and I sang up in the Flossy's room for Flossy and Mrs. D—— and two men named "Red" and "Tom" and drank a glass of beer and they drank and smoked cigarettes.

About 1 P.M. Mrs. D—— took me down to Bill C——'s saloon and C— came out side to see us and Mrs. D—— said to come inside but I said I did not want to go; C—— said "Oh yes come inside and have a drink." We went inside and she ordered whiskey for both of us and C—— brought it himself, brought in two glasses.

Before I went to C——'s saloon and while I was up at Flossy's room at the X. [cheap hotel], Mrs. D—— and Flossy dressed me up and powdered and painted me and dressed my hair to make me look like a sport. I have the clothes at home which they put on me. They made me go home and get my silk petticoat and bring my Mother's silk skirt for Mrs. D——. They put a big shawl in my waist for a bust. Flossy told me to stay with men at C——'s saloon and get the money first and put it in my stocking and took out a roll of bills out of her pocket and showed it to me. She told me that if I would be a sport the doctor would always take care of me when I was sick and that it was an easy life.

On Wednesday Mrs. D—— came to my house and took me for a walk and took me down to XX C — street and tried to get me to go in there and become an inmate for prostitution and said she used to work in there. From there to M——'s saloon [corner Washington and Carpenter St.]. Mrs. O—— told M—— to give me a drink of whiskey and M—— said "No she is too young." She had five whiskeys and I had two glasses of pop. M—— told her she had better take me home before she got pinched.

Then Mrs. L—— took me down on the street and I went and stayed two days with Mrs. N—— at XXXX W. Madison Street and did house work and got $1.50. On July 8th Mrs. D—— took me to a saloon and met two fellows Red and Earl and all four of us went to a rooming house. Both the fellows took rooms and both had [relations] with Mrs. D——, but not with me.[27]

After a girl entered the life of prostitution, her departure was difficult, although not impossible. Since the history of the girl in Case 31 is incomplete, we do not know what finally became of her. Obviously the re-entry into society might take place via matrimony, a job or the return home. Any return to respectibility was precarious at best at a time when even divorces were frowned upon. What then became of prostitutes? Reformers claimed that fallen women died in two to seven years but there seems to be little evidence to support this claim.[28] What happens to girls who have once practiced prostitution, today? No investigations so far made offer information upon which to base a positive statement.

THE BREAKDOWN OF THE CASTE

It does seem, however, that the escape from prostitution has become less difficult. The prostitute today is not necessarily doomed to live a marginal existence, cut off from any

[27] See Case 31—Chicago Vice Study File.

[28] Abraham Flexner, *Prostitution in Europe*, pp. 21–22.

hope of a respectable future. This is because women of
ill-fame no longer form a distinct caste readily distin-
guished from other women by dress, manners, and place
of residence. The activities of modern women—slumming, night life, exaggerations in dress, an unchaperoned
life outside the home, entrance into business and sports—
have erased the outward distinction between the painted
sport and the paler protected lady. The breakdown of
the barriers of caste has made the escape easier from the
life of commercialized vice. It has made the life itself less
of a hardship—less of a form of slavery. The inhumanity
of the earlier form of exploitation of women consisted in
the fact that once she had crossed the threshold of a house
of prostitution there was no escape. Prostitution in these
modern times has thus tended to become a transitory status
for unadjusted girls and women. While following their
temporary careers as prostitutes, girls are now able to
maintain their family connections and to return, when they
desire, to temporary or permanent respectability. The less
clever, with the caste of the prostitute disappearing, still
fall into the hands of pimps and constitute the load which
is carried into the Morals Court by police raids and arrests.
However, the extent to which girls are, by avoiding arrest
by police, detection by investigators, and exploitation by
pimps, able to escape identification with the prostitute
class is still a matter for speculation.

RECONSTRUCTION VIA RESCUE WORK

The majority of prostitutes have had to assist themselves in getting out of their profession. They have had to
make their own adjustments to a new world. Only a few
have ever been reached and saved by welfare agencies.

In the era of the segregated district in Chicago rescue missions visited the vice areas to save souls. Mission workers, offering to help them in every way possible, tried to get girls to quit the life. Their success was not great because the outlook offered them was dark. Tender-minded girls who could not endure the wear and tear of brothel existence and desired to run away were assisted by rescue mission workers. Women's civic clubs, always interested in fallen girls, aided a few individuals offering clothing, carfare, job. Still more infrequently the police interested themselves in returning young girls who were found in resorts. But most girls, if young and unsophisticated, were instructed what to tell the police when they called—usually they were "21 years of age" and "had hustled in another town." Organizations interested in combating white slavery were able to send a few young girls, who had been victimized, to their homes. All in all, the welfare work with fallen women reached but a short distance and in no sense did it involve expert guidance and supervision. Prostitutes who unassisted found for themselves a way out did so because they discovered some niche in society into which they could fit, probably not in their home town.

THE WORK AT PRESENT

Until 1931, little improvement was made in the welfare work done for delinquent women in the Morals Court. There were two social service workers in the court who, after identifying recidivists and keeping court statistics, had little time for constructive case work. At best material relief in the form of shelter, clothing, food, railroad fare, employment, etc., were provided for a small number of cases by referring them to other agencies. But no thoroughgoing case work was done at court. After the administrative changes in 1931, two trained workers were assigned to the Morals Court. Although now relieved of identification and statistical work, they are allowed merely to handle cases of girls who voluntarily ask for aid. Besides the trained workers assigned to the court, there is a volunteer worker who does the type of rescue work mission workers did years ago. Prior to 1931, the Juvenile Protective Association was called upon from time to time to take over the cases of young girls who have appeared in the Morals Court. Although not equipped to handle large numbers, the Juvenile Protective Association attempted to deal with the girls referred to them according to the best canons of present day case work. The experience of the agency with Morals Court girls has been that they are not merely the most difficult but also the most unsatisfactory cases to work with.

SAMPLE DIFFICULTIES IN CASE WORK WITH YOUNG PROSTITUTES

In order to learn something of the difficulties and limitations experienced in attempting case work with Morals Court girls, I cleared the extant list of names of girls who had been referred from the Court to the Juvenile Protective Association in 1925. These cases—most of them under 21 and all of them venereally infected—were referred only indirectly from the Court since they were called to the attention of the agency by a trained public-health nurse who was assigned to court for the purpose of looking after the girls who had to be sent to Lawndale Hospital (the contagious disease hospital) for treatment for venereal disease. Out of an extant list of 20 names, I was able to locate 16 records in the Juvenile Protective Association's file. But in examining these 16 cases more closely, I found that three of the number were delinquent women, but women who were not sent to Lawndale from the Morals Court. As one reads these records he is impressed with the unsatisfactory way the cases turn out. And one begins to see the inherent difficulties in the way of successful outcomes. In two of the 16 cases, the girls dropped out of sight after preliminary investigations had been made. It is safe to say that if case work were attempted on a large number of Morals Court women one chief difficulty would be to keep them under supervision. Nineteen-year-old Carolyn in the case cited below moves and leaves no address.

Carolyn, 19 years old, picked up by police in Wilson Avenue district, referred as needing supervision, had a court record 3 months previous, had then only taken treatment twice for syphilis at clinic to which she was sent, now [12-16-25] at Lawndale Hospital, had a grandmother living in neighborhood not far from where girl was arrested, had a father in Minneapolis and a brother in Denver [both living at hotels]; 12-26-25 contact with grandmother who lives in a rooming house and looks after children in evening, because of her absence she claimed C. went out a great deal at night, said she would look after C. if given the opportunity, said C. has not been able to work steadily during last 2 years, because of sickness; 12-30-25 public health nurse on case feels that grandmother knows more about C's delinquencies than she told the worker. Letter from agency in Minneapolis stating that C's father had just left for Chicago and could be found at such and such address in the Wilson Avenue district and that contact should be made promptly since he may go to some other state; 1-5-26 C's case in Court. Placed on probation after released from Lawndale Hospital; 1-21-26 agency sent letter to grandmother stating that C., since her release from Lawndale, has written a colored girl there whom the nurses thought unfavorably

of, that C. gave her address to a prostitute there whom she had previously known in the House of Good Shepherd, that "I understand
Carolyn is working and I hope she will make good but I wanted to
have you know this in order that you can check up on the company
she is keeping"; 2–9–26 called at the grandmother's residence and
found that C. and her grandmother had moved about 3 weeks ago;
their address is unknown; 2–14–16 spoke to the public health nurse
on the case who felt that C. will get into bad company wherever
she is.[29]

Two of the 16 cases, due to the presence of counteract-
ing forces, got completely beyond the control of the agency,
rendering effective social case work practically impossible.
One of the two is cited.

Nancy, 18 years, venereally infected, 5 months pregnant, arrested
in North Clark Street resort, husband a pimp, mother in X. Iowa;
4–13–25 in Lawndale; referred to agency 4–14–25; 4–15–25 letter
from Associated Charities of X. stating that contact with N's family
dates back to 1917 when her parents applied for help, parents had
domestic difficulties, father lazy and shiftless, N. had convulsions in
1917, teacher at subnormal school said N. was a menace to girls in
her grade, N's mother said N's condition due to fact that the girl's
[paternal] grandfather had committed rape with her when N. was
five years old, N's mother reported as having gonorrhea in 1917, had
9 miscarriages as result of several infections, N's paternal grand-
parents had also been dependents; 4–16–25 letter from Associated
Charities of X. stating N. had married Roy [her pimp husband] June
1924 in Y. Iowa, that N's mother said when she went to see them
he was staying nights with women next door, N. tired of this left X.
February, 1925, home for short time then left leaving no word, wrote
April 7 from Chicago, address General Delivery, asked mother to
keep her whereabouts a secret, said she was well and happy and
some day would have "plenty," N's teacher in the subnormal school

[29] Summarized from Record No. 50119.40, Juvenile Protective Association, Chicago. The other uncited lost-track-of case is No. 49909.40.
Names and places (where necessary) have been changed in the following
cases.

said that she was afraid the mother would use N. as a prostitute, that N. was promoted to 7B in 1923 but did not return after vacation; 5–13–25 case in court. Girl released from Lawndale. Roy, husband, failed to appear, forfeiting bond. He had disappeared taking N's wardrobe including her marriage certificate. N. said that no matter what he did she still loved him. She would not tell of his whereabouts although she had received letters from him while in Lawndale. N. admitted that she had left X. with Roy in men's clothing [a corduroy knicker suit] and came to Chicago with him. N. was put on 6 months probation. Was put on her train for X. 5–14–25 letter from Travelers Aid stating N. arrived at X. and was met by her mother; 5–22–25 letter to Associated Charities of X. stating that N. was a high grade moron according to examination of city alienist, that she will need care of physician for venereal infection, that N's husband is pimp and is likely to turn up in X; 6–5–25 letter to Associated Charities of X. stating that place at which N. arrested on North Clark Street, Chicago, was the kind that changes hands and girls at each conviction, that N. did not admit in court that she was pandered by her husband, that N. would be a good farm colony case as she will probably always be at the mercy of unscrupulous men, that while at Lawndale physicians said she was physically and mentally indolent, that her stay there was characterized by "a disinclination to leave her bed except to go to the table and when she was supplied with candy and peanuts she seemed perfectly happy" [so a Lawndale nurse reported]; 6–4–25 letter from Associated Charities of X. stating that because of heat and expected confinement in two months she is unable to go downtown for treatments and a physician is coming to her home [from a local hospital], that agency arranged for her to go to a health center but it is probable she will not go for treatments unless forced; 8–18–25. The Judge of the Morals Court received a letter from N. saying that she was at home with her mother and that she had a fine baby girl born in July; 10–3–25 telegram from Associated Charities of X. stating that N. broke parole, that mother and Rescue Home are unable to manage her, that she attempted escape from police and is now in jail with baby, that matron [of jail] awaits agency's advice [no record of any advice if sent]; 11–14–25 letter from Associated Charities in X, reporting that N's husband is back in X.[30]

We have in Nancy a case of a girl who presents the greatest handicaps and the poorest material for social case work to deal with. Bad family background, poor mental equipment, instability, an indolent disposition, venereally infected, an attachment to a pimp husband, pregnancy and offspring, constitute the difficulties which must be surmounted in her case. It would not be too much to say that the chances are against any permanent reconstruction at present through case work no matter how adequate and intensive. For case work with Morals Court girls would certainly show the best results when the human material which must be refashioned is good and when the girl herself is willing to be reformed and sees the value of what social workers try to do for her.

One case in the group cleared showed an exaggerated difficulty which is somewhat prevalent among Morals Court girls and which certainly throws obstacles in the path of case work. When girls so far from giving the agencies their co-operation concoct information about their backgrounds, social work can hardly begin. As we shall see later, probation work with Morals Court girls is rendered practically impossible thereby. They can "get by" giving misinformation and thus escape supervision by probation officers.

A little girl of 17 told a social worker how she was raised by a half-Indian father whose shack was the headquarters for a gang of bootleggers near Quebec, Canada; how her father abused her and forced her at 15 to give in to a mem-

[30] Summarized from Record No. 48890.40, Juvenile Protective Association, Chicago. The other uncited case is No. 48338.40. This case is just as difficult, except for absence of a low mentality and an attachment to a pimp.

ber of the gang (a half-breed); how her father deserted
her and how she was rescued from the clutches of the
villainous half-breed and taken to Chicago. While at the
Lawndale Hospital she wrote two letters to her supposed
rescuer in Quebec. These, like her story, were pure flights
of imagination. When she finally admitted the truth about
herself, it was learned that she was covering up so she
would not be sent home. But the city alienist had already
called her a pathological liar.

This case was referred to the Juvenile Protective Association June 20, 1925. Requested investigations by
agencies in Quebec and Ottawa (Ontario) failed to verify
any of the clues in her story and letters. By August 12,
1925, almost two months later, the workers on the case
were able to discover that she was a runaway from a small
farming community in southern Illinois. After persistence
on the part of the social workers, the girl finally admitted
the truth. Arrangements were made to send her home,
in spite of fact that girl said she would rather be committed
to an institution than return home and have her mother
"bawl her out."[31]

The outlook for reformation is certainly not bright when
a girl is sent home against her will. The girl in the foregoing case would rather be sent to the girls' reformatory
than go home. Another girl of 18 after being sent home,
wrote back to an old offender in the Lawndale Hospital
that she would rather stay two years in Lawndale (and
that would be an ordeal) than to come back to Canada.[32]
In the former instance the trouble seemed to be an un-
sympathetic parent; in the latter, the dullness of living at

[31] Excerpts and summary from Record No. 49253.40, Juvenile Protective Association, Chicago.

home and working in a restaurant. But in social work practice, if a girl has a decent home to return to there is no alternative but to send her there.

The social agency is sometimes put in a dilemma when parents refuse to take the erring daughter back. In the case of a little girl 16, who was arrested for living with a man although she claimed she had been working steadily as a waitress, and had only been immoral with one other man, the father (an Illinois farmer) was notified to come to Chicago for his daughter. When he went to Lawndale Hospital for his child, she refused to tell him where she had been and what she had been doing for the last seven months (her last letter home was sent seven months ago). Whereupon he refused to take her home and all this after the agency had already been side tracked by the girl's having given a wrong name, false address, and age. The girl was finally transferred to the Juvenile Court with a request for a mental and physical examination, the latter because of a report that she was pregnant.[33]

It sometimes happens that while the agency is making its investigations preliminary to taking action, the case is disposed of by the public authorities without consultation or making an investigation. One of the cases in group studied was of this nature. A girl of 24, although over the age limit for girls' cases usually taken by the Juvenile Protective Association, was referred to this agency by the public health nurse working with Lawndale Hospital cases. Investigation showed that she had been a wild, irresponsible girl; had worked infrequently; had run with men; had a child four years of age; had been known to the Juvenile

[32] See Record No. 47945.40, Juvenile Protective Association, Chicago.
[33] See Record No. 48791.40, Juvenile Protective Association, Chicago.

Court in a nearby city; had an aged, incompetent father who could not look after her and a mother in a State Hospital for the insane. The girl herself was said to be a mental farm colony case. She had been arrested also with a man who was thought to be a panderer. While the agency was collecting information on her background and connections, she was turned over by the court and hospital authorities to an aunt unknown and uninvestigated, who came for her.[34]

Other times the situation is such that very little can be done for Morals Court girls. A girl of 22, thought to be an old offender in the Morals Court although not identified as such, claimed that she had left her foster home in a small town near Chicago about seven years ago, after her foster mother had died. A letter from a nephew of the supposed foster father in this farming community stated that he knew of no one by the name given but knew of a girl by another name who had run away five years ago. This was evidently taken to mean that the possible connection was not worth following up; for no further entry occurs in the record after this letter was received. Just prior to receiving this letter showing dubious foster connections, the agency received a memorandum from the public health nurse on the case saying that the girl "does not seem to be ambitious to do anything besides earning a living and we cannot see that there is much that can be done for her."[35] If the referring social worker or agency gives up the ghost, there is no reason why the agency to whom the case has been referred should continue with it.

Not all the difficulties, actual or potential, in case work

[34] See Record No. 48677.40, Juvenile Protective Association, Chicago.
[35] See Record No. 38952.40, Juvenile Protective Association, Chicago.

with Morals Court girls in Chicago have been considered. We have examined enough of them perhaps to realize the force of the statement, coming from the Juvenile Protective Association, that these cases are extremely unsatisfactory to work with and yield hardly any results for a great deal of effort.

In summary we may conclude that while white slavery was never so extensive or coercive as rumor had it, the greatest aid to the women who are in or getting out of the life of commercialized vice has been the breakdown of the prostitute caste. Reconstruction of the lives of prostitutes has come about only when the girls themselves desired and co-operated in achieving it. This has probably taken place most often through marriage with men willing to overlook the past.

CHAPTER III

THE RESISTANCE OF ORGANIZED VICE

In the red light district vice flourished under police protection. With the initiation of the period of suppression commercialized vice went underground. Vice resorts located in the ancient vice areas on Chicago's Near North Side, Near West Side, and Near South Side, lingered on but were steadily declining in number under constant attacks carried out with the assistance of the new administrative weapons forged in the heat of the anti-vice crusade. The percentage of vice resorts found active and open in these central vice areas steadily declined from 1914 to 1930.[1] But those that survived were able to do so because, in the central areas of the city, it was possible to effect an alliance with the local political organizations or with influential personages connected with these organizations, and through them secure police protection. The rings or privileged vice syndicates, which came into prominence at this time, were, however, not a new phenomenon.

THE CONTINUITY OF ORGANIZED VICE

The *Illinois Crime Survey* (1929) reported that "organized crime is not, as many think, a recent phenomenon in Chicago. A study of vice, crime and gambling during the last twenty-five years shows the existence of crime and vice gangs during that period and how they have become more and more highly organized and powerful."[2] As early

---

[1] See Table 13, pp. 139–40.

[2] John Landesco, "Organized Crime in Chicago," *Illinois Crime Survey* (1929), p. 845.

as 1912 and even before that time the business of vice was getting into the hands of rings, which were able to protect themselves by directing the zeal of the reformers against their independent and unsyndicated rivals.

In July, 1911, "Mike de Pike" Heitler, described as "a long notorious keeper," was reported to have opened up a new district on Carpenter Street after having been driven out of Curtis Street by protests of the people in the neighborhood. It was reported that he paid the police $5,000 for the privilege of a monopoly and exacted an initial payment of $150 and a monthly tribute of $40 to $50 from each keeper. The police confined their attack to the resorts that were not protected.[3]

The notorious Everleigh Club in the Twenty-second Street district "was closed," so it was reported, "because it was a rival of Freiberg's of the trust."[4] After closing, Freiberg's quadrupled its business. Miss Kate Adams, in an article (October 29, 1912), based on a canvass, stated that 200 resorts in the old South Side levee were reputed at that time to be owned by a powerful vice trust.[5]

Almost two years after the closing of the red light district, the *Chicago Tribune* found three organized vice rings in the old (near) South Side vice area. The most powerful of these rings was the alliance of Colosimo, Torrio, and Van Bever. In this triumvirate Colosimo was the responsible leader. The second ring was headed by Julius and Charlie Maibaum and included Ed Weiss, Jakie Adler, and Harry Hopkins. The third was led by the Marshall Brothers who were associated with Eddie Woods. The in-

[3] *Chicago Daily Socialist,* July 11, 1911.

[4] *Illinois Crime Survey* (1929), pp. 847–48.

[5] *Ibid.,* p. 847.

dependents were Joe Grabiner, Harry Cusick, Judy Williams, John Jordan, and the Rothchilds.[6]

This was in 1914. In 1916 Ike Bloom and Ed Weiss, representing organized vice on the South Side managed to regain their licenses which had been revoked for operating saloon-cabarets in violation of the Sunday one o'clock closing ordinance. In October, 1917, State's Attorney Hoyne made public a list of 75 resorts on the South and West Sides. In October, 1919, Police Civil Service Commission discovered that Captain Cronnin of the Warren Avenue police district (Near West Side) had been in league with organized vice on Chicago's West Side.

Colosimo's death in 1920 was reported to have resulted from a clash of the so-called vice lords for control on the Near South Side. During Mayor Dever's administration (1923–27) Chicago was operating under the "closed town" policy. At this time much of the syndicated vice migrated to roadhouses on the outskirts of Chicago.

Exposures of August, 1927, revealed the fact that organized vice on the South Side was more favored by police than that on the West and North Sides, and that the Cusick-Capone combine, successors to the Colosimo-Torrio ring, was fighting for the South Side territory. Grand Jury investigations of September, 1928, disclosed the fact that Capone was securing control of organized vice on the South Side. Eleven vice resorts were reported to be included in the South Side territory dominated by this heavily advertised gangster.[7] "Monkey Face" Charley Genker, formerly allied with "Mike de Pike," was reported to be in control on the West Side in July, 1929. Genker was

[6] *Chicago Tribune,* July 21, 1914.

[7] *Chicago Daily Journal,* September 11, 1928.

said, at this time, to have been in the "disgraceful business" for thirty-six years. The story of his career became
public in the wake of an attempt on his life, the result of a
clash with the West Side organization of "Mike de Pike."[8]

The newspaper reports here reviewed afford some indication of the confused struggle which took place between
the vice interests and the law enforcement agencies during the period in which the people of Chicago were seeking to abolish professional prostitution (commercialized
vice) by the suppression of the segregated vice areas. It
was in the very nature of this struggle that the vice interests should seek to avoid the force of the attack by cor-
rupting the agents of law enforcement wherever and whenever possible. But it was just as inevitable that those
interested in law enforcement should attempt to fix responsibility for their failure, if not their success, upon
those personages whom the spotlight of publicity had
made conspicuous, particularly the mayor, the chief of
police and the State's Attorney. Public opinion cannot
operate as a renovating and reforming agency in public
affairs unless it is directed against an obvious abuse. It
operates with the greatest energy when the object against
which it is directed is an individual, who can be regarded
as responsible for the conditions it is seeking to reform.

The fixing of responsibility is not, however, so simple a
matter as the man is likely to assume who is unacquainted
with the conditions under which, in our American system
of government, political alliances are made and police
regulations are enforced.

In the first place, ward politics seems to be largely a
matter of personal friendships. One votes with the party

[8] *Chicago Daily Journal,* July 30, 1929.

and one votes with one's friends.   There is no place in the
city where voters are so in need of friends as in the slums,
where so large a number of persons are engaged in occupa-
tions which bring them under the surveillance of the police.
The casual laborers, who invariably herd together in the
areas of transition about the center of the city which has
been described as Hobohemia; the immigrant peoples who
in Chicago live in what are called the River Wards; the
rooming-house population, young, restless, and unsettled
individuals eager to know the life of the city but not concerned at the moment about the enforcement of laws to
make the city life safer and less exciting—these are the
voters upon whom local bosses rely.

It is the existence of these three classes of voters, living
in these deteriorated residential areas, that makes possible
the sort of political machine that exists in these wards.
But the ward organization, once established, is not always
as easily controlled, as the term "machine" implies.   Not
infrequently responsible leaders have found themselves
committed to more concessions to organized vice and to
a greater toleration of semi-criminal practices, than they
had expected or intended.

When political machines increase in size they multiply
the numbers of henchmen and intermediaries between the
leaders, the voters and the seekers of privileges. With the
advent of high-priced elections and of a gangland interested not only in the older outlawed business, such as
vice and gambling, but in the more lucrative vocations like
beer running and racketeering, the local political machine
has sometimes gotten quite out of control.

Meanwhile the gangsters, who have been characterized
as beer barons and vice lords in recognition of their rôle

in the regulation of prostitution and gambling, once they have achieved an alliance with politics and the police and feel themselves more or less tolerated by the public, are led finally to assume that they are performing a quasi-public function. They exist to exercise control and regulate conduct in fields where official and legally sanctioned control has failed. They come to believe, finally, that they have a kind of vested interest in the illegal activities which they control and regulate during the period which inevitably intervenes between writing of a law on the statute book and its acceptance not merely by the community as a public regulation but by the individual man and woman as an actual rule of conduct.

Insofar as the gangsters have been able to supersede the police in the control of vice, they have superseded the older, simpler and more democratic methods of campaign contribution and division of political spoils, for maintaining political organizations by the more direct method of laying tribute, and have sought to carry elections by the forced delivery of votes, by means of fraud, terror, and general chicanery.

If commercialized vice did not disappear with the passing of the segregated district, it is also true that the difficulties of dealing with vice, now that it was organized, intrenched, and protected, were greatly increased. The vice lords and their syndicated resorts and their alliances with local politics, have been able to organize a resistance which the forces of reforms have thus far not been able to successfully overcome. What form this resistance assumed and to what extent it has been successful is indicated by the fate of the so-called "Morals Squad" under Major Funkhouser. The Morals Squad was one of the instruments of law enforcement, which was devised to carry into effect the policy of suppression.

As a result of the recommendation in the Chicago Vice Commission report and of the initiation of the period of suppression by the Wayman raids, the office of Second Deputy Police Commissioner was established. Major Funkhouser was put in this office, beginning March, 1913. His duty was to pay particular attention to vice conditions in the city. He appointed W. C. Dannenberg as Morals Inspector and Chief of the Morals Squad. The work of Funkhouser's department and Dannenberg's men seems to have been largely nullified by their inability to secure the co-operation of the regular police. Organized vice developed a "tip-off" system by which the resorts were warned in advance of the coming of the Morals Squad. Gangsters tried to bribe Dannenberg offering him $2,200 per month to "lay off." In April, 1914, one of Dannenberg's men was stabbed in Roy Jones' saloon-resort which belonged to the South Side syndicate. At this time Dannenberg was trying to get the facts in regard to the murder of Henagow which had taken place there. The press made the comment that "the attack on Dannenberg's man was a warning to Funkhouser and the officers of the Morals Division."

A few months later (July, 1914) Sergeant Stanley Birns of the Morals Squad was shot and killed. This was interpreted by the press to mean that organized vice in the old South Side levee district had had enough of vice snooping. The district at the time was reported to be under the protection of Captain Ryan, supported by Alderman "Hinky

Dink" Kenna and his partner in first ward control, "Bath-house" John Coughlin.[9] State's Attorney Hoyne started a series of Grand Jury investigations which continued until the expiration of his term of office. Organized vice, in spite of these exposures, continued and survived them. State's Attorney Hoyne's Grand Jury investigation led no-where, for he could not finally get a conviction for the mur-der of Sergeant Birns.[10]

Under pressure from the reform forces Mayor Harrison revoked the licenses of Jim Colosimo and Ike Bloom. Bloom was at that time running Freiberg's dance hall. This step was taken August 24, 1914. Colosimo's license was restored January 28, 1915. A former head-waiter (Bergamini) at the Congress Hotel, acted as the "dummy." Ike Bloom's license was restored, December 25, 1915. The Hop Ling Co. acted as the "dummy." Ed Weiss' Bristol Café license, which had introduced organized vice into Englewood, was revoked December 30, 1915, and re-issued January 13, 1916.

Just after the advent of William Hale Thompson to the office of mayor in April, 1915, Corporation Counsel Ettel-son issued an opinion on the one o'clock closing ordinance to the effect that while no drinks could be sold after one o'clock the guests could remain thereafter. This was in-terpreted as a victory of organized vice over the reformers and an indication that the Thompson administration was friendly to the vested interests of vice.

Shortly after this the Thompson faction, supposedly as a favor to organized vice, made a drive to abolish the office of Second Deputy and disperse the Morals Squad.

[9] *Chicago Tribune,* July 18, 1914.

[10] *Illinois Crime Survey* (1929), p. 851.

In March, 1916, Francis D. Hanna, Morals Inspector for Funkhouser was discharged and the officers assigned to Funkhouser's office were withdrawn. The office of Second Deputy lingered on for two more years. Finally, in June, 1918, the city council finance committee failed to recommend the appropriation for the office and it came to an end. With Funkhouser eliminated nothing stood in the way of organized vice except the agitation of the reform group and the investigations of State's Attorney Hoyne.

In 1916, Mike de Pike Heitler of the West Side fell afoul of the Federal Government which has never been as easy as the local government for the criminal elements to circumvent. It seemed that Heitler was not content with his limited operations in Chicago but had developed an interstate business in vice. His traffic included Pittsburgh, Indianapolis, Milwaukee, St. Louis, Gary, Indiana, and Burnham, Illinois, on the state line. He was convicted of white slavery under the Mann Act, June 2, 1916. This was a victory for law and order, but it made very little impression on the other vice lords of Chicago who have rarely exposed themselves to the jurisdiction of the United States courts and the penalty of a sentence to Leavenworth.

In 1916 Hoyne was again active in his investigations. When Captain W. P. O'Brien was made "the goat" of Thompson's Police Civil Service Commission's investigation and suspended, he turned state's witness and told how vice ran wild in his Black Belt. He testified that he had been given orders by Chief of Police Healey not to disturb certain politically powerful dives, and that the Chief tried to put a stop to police captains' "going reform." In January, 1917, Hoyne exposed the police graft and collection

from organized vice on the West Side, producing Lieutenant White's (of Lake Street district) notebook with the
names of dives, their weekly graft rate, and the list of "can
be raided" and "can't be raided" places. In October,
1919, the Police Civil Service Commission inquiry under
Captain Coffin went into conditions in Captain Cronin's
Warren Avenue district (West Side). It was found that
Cronin and his officers collected regularly, although in
small amounts, from dives and that these places remained
open.[11] Cronin was held responsible and suspended November 20, 1919. This inquiry took the edge off of a city-
wide investigation which Hoyne had started in September,
1919, at which time he claimed that vice and gambling resorts flourished all over Chicago and were "operated under
the wing of certain city hall favorites."[12] Colosimo's murder in 1920 showed the apparent helplessness of law and
order to do more than stand by and let the underworld faction settle the issue as to the control of illegal business.
In April, 1920, Hoyne charged that the Lundin-Thompson
machine promised vice and gambling, an open town, in
return for support at the primary elections[13]; that the city
hall machine had perpetuated wholesale violations, un-
checked by the police.[14]

The *Chicago Daily News* exposure of October, 1921,
showing that the Lundin-Thompson city hall alliance was
"shaking down" organized vice on the West Side, led to
Grand Jury indictments against a half-dozen insignificant
operators "whose names never appeared before nor later

[11] *Herald-Examiner,* October 29, 1919.

[12] *Chicago Tribune,* September 25, 1919.

[13] *Chicago Daily News,* April 1, 1920.

[14] *Ibid.,* April 27, 1920.

in an underworld expose."[15] Not to be undone the *Tribune* threw the search light on conditions in the South Side levee in August, 1922. Then the *News* again made a new exposure December, 1922, and showed how every form of vice was flourishing in the South Side Black Belt. This was supposed to be the work of the Lundin-Thompson machine, seeking Negro-republican support.

State's Attorney Crowe, who succeeded Hoyne, took up the cudgels against the vice-for-votes policy of the Lundin-Thompson alliance. Crowe in 1922 broke with the Thompson organization. He was quoted as saying: "Any man that is interested in protected gambling and protected vice and protected prostitution I refuse to travel along with, politically or otherwise." Five years later he was back with Thompson.[16]

In 1923 Grand Jury investigations were conducted into syndicated vice and its affiliation with graft. Action under the Kate Adams Law was taken against 75 keepers of disorderly resorts. "It was noticed, however, that certain of the notorious resorts were missing from the list even though evidence was received against them." At the same time that Crowe was beginning his prosecutions, Chief of Police Fitzmorris issued his "vice picket" order and for just two months before the end of the Thompson administration there was partial curtailment of vice in the city.

Dever won the mayoralty election and inaugurated a strict "closed town" policy. The effect of a serious attempt to enforce the action was felt for four years. Organized vice was kept down to the minimum and much of it had to vacate the city and take refuge in the suburbs. But

[15] *Illinois Crime Survey* (1929), p. 858.
[16] *Illinois Crime Survey* (1929), p. 859.

the "closed town" gave way to a more "open town" than ever when Thompson and his machine came back into office May, 1927. From then on organized vice was not merely aligned with city hall politics but Thompson's America First organization imposed tribute upon beer runners, gunmen, gambling kings, and racketeers as no previous organization had ever done.

The murder of Alfred Lingle, *Tribune* reporter, on June 9, 1930, was seen to be the work of Chicago gangs. While Leo V. Brothers, imported St. Louis gangster, was convicted of the murder April 3, 1931, responsibility was never definitely fixed on either the Capone or the Zuta gang. But it was evident that Lingle had come at cross-purposes with the machinations of gangland. A gang informant for the *Chicago Daily News* was also killed.

The rivalry of gangs to control vice, gambling, and liquor traffic in the Chicago territory held the spot light in the more recent developments. Jack Zuta, key member of the North Side gang, composed of Zuta, Aeillo, and Moran, was murdered August 1, 1930, at Delafield, Wisconsin, where he was supposed to be in hiding. It was suspected that this was the work of Capone's gang. Newspaper reports at the time gave out the information that this was the fifty-second gang murder in 1930, already two in excess of the 1929 toll. Further investigation of Zuta's activities showed that he and his North Side gang had controlled 145 saloons, vice dens, and roadhouses.[17] Not long after the Zuta killing, Joe Aeillo, likewise co-leader of the North Side gang was murdered in his hiding place October 23, 1930. The Capone gang had now

[17] See accounts in *Chicago Daily News,* August 2, 1930, and August 22, 1930.

brought about the total capitulation of its principal rival in the Chicago territory. In May, 1931, "Mike de Pike" Heitler West Side vice magnate was burned to death in an old ice-house on the outskirts of Chicago. Later investigation showed that he was threatened by Capone and had dictated a letter before his death in which he named the persons who should be held responsible in event of his being killed. The designated persons were Capone, Jake Guzik (Cusick), Bruno, Manango, Adduci, Belcastro, and "Rocksy."[18] Capone now controlled the whole Chicago area.

While in very recent years there have been exposures of graft and corruption which affected the status of vice and crime in Chicago, the activities of the Capone gang have held the center of attention. The federal government took up the cudgels of battle against gang rule through its internal revenue department in the Chicago district. Cases of income tax evasion were worked up against principal members of the Capone gang. Harry and Sam Guzik were seized by the federal agents for income tax evasion September 25, 1930. Jack Guzik was apprehended September 30, charged with defrauding the government of $222,501.86 back income taxes. He was convicted in November. Al Capone pleaded guilty June 16, 1931, to income tax evasion. The *Tribune* on June 27, 1931, reported that the United States government had indicted 61 members of the Capone gang. Ralph Capone's conviction for income tax evasion was upheld by the United States Circuit Court of Appeals July 24, 1931. He was sentenced to three years in Leavenworth federal penitentiary and fined $10,000. Al Capone was found

[18] *Chicago Daily News*, September 16, 1931.

guilty, October 17, 1931, after having been permitted to enter a plea of not guilty and, according to rumor, after attempting to "fix" the case with the higher officials at a price of $75,000.[19] The alleged amount of back taxes owed by Capone was originally estimated at $1,038,654,[20] although in the course of the trial the estimate was pared down to $266,000 for years 1924 through 1929. It was announced that the federal government had spent $215,-000 in working up the case against Al Capone.[21]

The federal drive against Capone took the edge off of other dramatic campaigns waged against crime in Chicago. The Chicago Crime Commission in 1930 began to publish data on the records of the outstanding criminals, vice mongers, and racketeers. They were called the "Public Enemies." By August, 1931, 56 public enemies had been designated.[22] Judge John H. Lyle in 1930 initiated his drive against these public enemies by issuing vagrancy warrants for their arrest. Some headway was made in this campaign, although there was considerable doubt as to the effectiveness of it when one of the outstanding public enemies introduced movies in court as evidence to show he was a gentleman farmer on the outskirts of Chicago and when it preceded and accompanied Judge Lyle's bid for the primary mayorial nomination.

POLICE GRAFT AND PROTECTION

The affiliations of organized vice with the machine politics and with the police in the localities where the syndi-

[19] *Chicago American,* September 26, 1931.

[20] *Chicago Tribune,* October 12, 1931.

[21] *Ibid.,* July 29, 1931.

[22] *Ibid.,* August 1, 1931.

cates and vice lords ruled have been indicated. For the sake of clarity, however, it is necessary to distinguish between police graft and protection and political protection and tribute, although from 1912 to 1930 they are frequently all interwoven.

The police were charged in 1910 with protecting Van Bever's pandering activities.[23] Mike de Pike was reported in the same year as being collector for Police Inspector McCann in the West Side levee.[24] The same vice lord was said to have paid the police $5,000 for opening the West Side levee on Carpenter Street after he had been driven out of Curtis Street. Police were not to molest keepers in his syndicate but to raid independents who attempted to run without first making arrangements with Heitler.[25]

In 1913, about one year after Wayman's closing of the red light district, Inspector McCann was convicted of accepting bribes from dive keepers. Inspector John Wheeler and Lieutenant John R. Bonfield were suspended on vice-graft charges and November 3, 1913, Chief of Police McSweeney was removed from office by Mayor Harrison for conniving at the open resorts of the vice lords. The levee had evidently been so used to buying, one way or another, police non-interference that it tried to remove the menace of the Morals Squad in 1914 by offering Inspector Dannenberg $2,200 per month.[26]

A *Tribune* exposé (July 18, 1914) of the organized vice situation in the South Side levee, following the murder of Sergeant Birns by vice trust retainers, revealed the fact

[23] *Ibid.*, January 30, 1910.

[24] *Ibid.*, September 25, 1910.

[25] *Chicago Daily Socialist*, July 11, 1911.

[26] *Illinois Crime Survey* (1929), p. 848.

that Captain Ryan of the Twenty-second Street district could not be forced to raid in the levee and that he was put there by the political boss-vice-lord combine.

In the latter part of 1916 Mayor Thompson instituted a Police Civil Service Commission inquiry into vice conditions and police graft as a check mate on State's Attorney Hoyne's investigations. Captain W. P. O'Brien of the Black Belt district was forced to take the blame for conditions. When he was suspended he turned state's witness in Hoyne's investigation and accused Chief of Police Gleason of responsibility for the protection of organized crime.[27]

No sooner had the public recovered from the shock of this exposé when it learned of police exactions of weekly rates for protection of dives on the West Side. Hoyne gave the public Lieutenant White's notebook which was the pocket guide for police handling of resorts in the Lake Street district. The claim was made that the Lieutenant had purchased this little "green book" when he received the Lake Street assignment. Shakedowns from resorts of $150, $50 and $40 were even recorded. The addresses of certain dives bore labels "can be raided" and "can't be raided."[28] Following this expose the Grand Jury investigations returned several indictments. But nothing important happened.[29]

Prompted by his findings at this very time, Hoyne took occasion to tell that innocent bystander, the public, just how police go about to collect tribute from organized vice. He said:

[27] *Illinois Crime Survey,* p. 855.

[28] *Chicago Herald,* January 7, 1917.

[29] *Chicago Examiner,* January 17, 1917.

The conspiracy to collect graft may be initiated, if it is city wide, in one of two ways:

1. By the Chief of Police or Chief of the Detective Bureau. He proceeds to select a confidential man, acquainted with criminal conditions in the city and with criminals and especially with crooked police officers.

2. Or the system may be initiated by some "fixer" with such knowledge, who suggests to the Chief of Police and Chief of Detectives that money is to be made, and that he, the sponsor of the scheme, is the proper man to be trusted.

If the confidential man or "fixer" is competent for the selected task, the next step is to pick out the best fields in the city for exploitation.

Inasmuch as the city is divided into a number of police precincts or districts, these fields are grouped according to such divisions.

The next step is to list all available places or hangouts which may be made to pay tribute.

And the next step is to transfer into each district, to be exploited commanding officers and sergeants who can be relied upon to carry out the conspiracy in consideration of sharing in the graft.

It then becomes necessary to select as collectors such police officers, politicians or others who will compel those operating the places to "kick in."

Incidental to such conspiracy, however, is the making of raids, and arrests of such places as are approached and refuse to pay tribute. These raids may be made on orders from the commanding officer of the district, or such orders may come to him from the chief of police, based on manufactured complaints of pretended citizens.

Such complaints are sent directly to the chief of police, by members of the syndicate or find their way to him through citizen's organizations, or civic organizations designed to eradicate vice.[30]

In October, 1919, charges were brought against Captain Cronnin for levying organized vice in the Warren Avenue district (West Side.) He and five subordinates were sus-

[30] *Chicago Examiner,* January 17, 1917.

pended. Cronnin went on trial before the Civil Service Commission, November 3, 1919, and was dismissed from the police force on November 20, 1919.[31] A few months after the Cronnin episode, indictments were again brought against police on the West Side on the charge of "shaking down" dive keepers. One of the police sergeants was even indicted himself as a panderer.[32]

In April, 1920, State's Attorney Hoyne said, in announcing his candidacy for re-election that "the police force is utterly demoralized. Honest officers who do their duty are punished or terrorized by this vicious machine"[33] —the Lundin-Thompson combine. Police corruption was also announced again in the *Daily News'* exposure of the West Side Lundin-Thompson "hook-up" with dive keepers, October 24, 1921. Police at this time were cast in minor rôles and had very insignificant parts in the "grand scheme" along side the rulers of the 18th Ward William Hale Thompson Men's Club. The *Daily News* a year later resumed its investigations. This time the spot light of publicity was turned on the South Side Black Belt where again the police figured as middle men between the Jackson vice and gambling "hook-up" and the Lundin-Thompson machine (December 19, 1922). Two months later, while Grand Jury investigations of organized vice were in progress, Judge Trude of the Morals Court, made the sensational statement that the profits of vice in Chicago amounted to $13,500,000 per year, part of which went to the police for protection. Incidentally he explained the system of protection.

[31] *Chicago Herald-Examiner,* October 29, 1919.

[32] *Chicago Tribune,* January 31, 1920.

[33] *Chicago Daily News,* April 27, 1920.

The difference between a protected place and one not so favored is best illustrated by these facts: The "Black Four Deuces" at 2222 Dearborn Street if often raided and is about to close up in disgust. Bud Gentry's place, 2222 Indiana Avenue, and the one at 2222 Wabash Avenue never are molested by the police and never will be closed up until some one acts.

In the Des Plaines street police district there are 19 protected places, Warren avenue has ten, and there are 30 each in the Cottage Grove and Stanton Avenue districts. It's a police problem purely and simply. These places are protected against everything except the Morals Court and raids by the Committee of Fifteen.

Chief Fitzmorris said: "Why does he only fine the persons we arrest from $1 to $3? What good does it do for us to raid places if the courts will not aid us?" Judge Trude said: "If the fines go up the rates of protection will go up."[34]

During Dever's administration as Mayor, 1923–27, the closed town policy was conspicuous for its lack of outstanding exposures of police graft and protection. With the newspapers carrying stories on the removal of organized vice to the suburban region, it seemed that the police, led by Chief Collins, were chasing vice out of its old haunts and tracking it to its new ones within the city limits.

With Thompson's return to office in 1927, the wide-open town policy was re-inaugurated and organized vice, gambling, crime, flourished. The exposures of police graft and protection were again current. In September, 1928, the police were implicated in an alleged $5,000,000 fund which organized vice and crime on the South Side paid to the Thompson machine via the America First campaign organization in order to win the primary election. Vice resorts were reported to be paying $100, $250 and $750 per week to the America First faction in return for pro-

[34] *Chicago Tribune*, February 22, 1923.

tection.[35] But in this case it seemed that the city hall rather than the police was the prime mover.

The charge was made in January, 1929, that the police were not only paid off by organized vice but were also used to raid independent dive keepers who dared to stay open after warnings from syndicated vice. This is just what the police were used for by "Mike de Pike" when he opened up the (West Side) Carpenter Street levee in July, 1911.[36]

The October, 1930, Grand Jury charged that the police in Chicago are demoralized and blamed the tolerant attitude of the city hall administration toward vice and gambling. The police department was held to be a tool of politics and protected vice.[37] In a report of the Wickersham Commission before the United States Senate March 3, 1931, the claim was made that as high as $10,000 per week was paid the detective bureau squads in Chicago to "lay off" vice emporia. Chicago was pictured as "a gang ridden city where politicians, gangsters, the police and even the judges conspire to permit every type of crime to flourish."[38] Such charges and allegations have a familiar tone about them and differ very little from the general findings of the many investigations into police corruption during the last twenty years.

AFFILIATIONS WITH MACHINE POLITICS: VOTE TRADING AND TRIBUTE

The record of "machine" politics is no whiter than that of the police—if anything, it is blacker. The Democrats

[35] *Chicago Daily Journal,* September 11, 1928.

[36] *Herald Examiner,* January 17, 1929.

[37] *Chicago Tribune,* November 1, 1930.

[38] *Ibid.,* March 4, 1931.

as well as the Republicans—where political machines have
existed—have thrived off organized vice. If any distinction can be made, it would be that the Democrats seem to
have had the older and the more localized connections
with organized vice—namely, the old First Ward gang
of "Hinky Dink" Kenna and "Bathhouse John" Coughlin.
The Republicans, under the leadership of Lundin and
Thompson, and then Crowe and Thompson, developed
more recently a machine which was charged with taking
tribute from organized vice on the Near West Side, the
South Side Black Belt, and the Lower North Side.

Less than two years after the closing of the segregated
district (July, 1914) the First Ward political machine
had perfected an alignment with the police and the vice
lords. Even Captain Ryan could not be compelled by the
chief of police or the Morals Squad to close up or make
raids on the Twenty-second Street resorts. "Hinky Dink"
placed Ryan as captain in the Twenty-second Street station and he traded protection through Ryan for votes
from the dive keepers.[38] Colosimo at this time was lining
up the Italian vote regularly for "Hinky Dink." But
from the best information at the time no money passed
hands, no tribute was imposed by "Hinky Dink's" machine, only a trade of open vice for votes.

When Jim Colosimo's license was revoked by Mayor
Harrison on August 24, 1914, nominally for violating the
one o'clock closing ordinance, this event was interpreted
as indicating a break between Harrison and Kenna, probably over the reform tendencies of the former. When
Colosimo's license was restored the press reported this
event as follows:

[38] *Ibid.*, July 18, 1914.

A number of politicians saw in the Mayor's step a peace offering to Alderman Michael Kenna and the First Ward forces under him. When the news of the restoration became known the alderman was asked if the new development meant the First Ward was with Harrison. Kenna replied that the First Ward was absolutely neutral and every man was to vote as he chose.[39]

Mayor Thompson assumed office for the first time (May, 1915). His policy with reference to vice was indicated by a liberal interpretation of the one o'clock closing ordinance handed down by Corporation Counsel Ettelson. This was a signal to the saloon-dive keepers that the lid was off. Thompson through his chief of police, Gleason, had already been flirting with the Black Belt for support. Thompson's policy with reference to vice in the Second Ward was embodied in his instructions to Chief of Police Gleason to "lay off" certain dives which had political influence in the Black Belt. Just previous to this (March, 1916) Thompson announced his anti-reform intentions by an offensive directed against the Second Deputy of Police's Office—the one commissioned to look after vice conditions. At this time he discharged Francis D. Hanna, Morals Inspector, under Funkhouser. The next step was the withdrawing of the patrolmen assigned to Funkhouser's vice squad. Two years later Thompson saw to it that the City Council Finance Committee failed to appropriate money for the office, which then died.

In September, 1919, State's Attorney Hoyne made charges that city-wide vice and gambling resorts are "operated under the wing of certain city hall favorites; that through the efforts of someone connected with the city prosecutor's staff, numerous cases against gambling joint

[39] *Ibid.*, January 28, 1915.

owners and operators of disorderly houses are dropped if the defendants 'are in right' with the powers that be in their districts."[40]

In April, 1920, it was reported that the Thompson-Lundin machine had traded with dive keepers and inmates on the Near North Side for support in the coming primary election. Hoyne again told the Grand Jury about the election grab via support of organized vice in return for the "open town." But no outcome—as usual.[41] Less than six weeks later, on May 11, 1920, there was the assassination of Colosimo, king of the vice trust affiliated with Kenna's political machine. This dramatic ending of Chicago's powerful vice lord brought to light the fact that there had been war for control of votes and vice concessions in the old South Side levee district between contending political factions.[42]

Less than a year and a half later the *Daily News* (October 24, 1921) exposed the operations of the Lundin-Thompson machine on the West Side. Instead of trading votes for protection, as had been the time-honored custom, the Thompson machine sold protection to the West Side dive keepers at "antes" of $50 to $100 and at weekly rates of $25 to $200 per week. The *News* reported that collections through the Eighteenth Ward William Hale Thompson Men's Club, which was the means by which protection was sold, amounted to over $1,000,000. So efficient was this organization that it was impossible for a gambling house, dive, or cabaret to open up without first buying the privilege.

[40] *Ibid.*, September 25, 1919.

[41] *Chicago Daily News*, March 30, 1920; April 1, 1920.

[42] *Ibid.*, May 12, 1920.

The political-vice ring in the South Side Black Belt, the beginnings of which were already manifest in 1916 when Captain O'Brien was held responsible for wide-open conditions, took the center of public attention in another *Daily News* exposure on December 19, 1922. The Negro politician, Dan Jackson, was mentioned as the reputed head of this graft-collecting syndicate for the Lundin-Thompson machine. The dives and gambling resorts paying tribute to the grafting political machine, were reported as flourishing in an immunity zone which from the list of addresses published by the *News* seemed to center about Thirty-first Street and Indiana Ave. and extended from State Street to Grand Boulevard, and from Thirty-first to Thirty-fifth Streets.

With the police and the machine suffering at the hands of Grand Jury investigations into organized vice in the early part of 1923, Thompson made his first bow to reform by having his Chief of Police Fitzmorris station officers in front of notorious resorts to prevent patronizing. He retired from office with the vice picket still on. Just how hard the clamp-down affected the owners of vice resorts is not known, but there were indications at least that the picketing made some of the keepers cease operations and wait for announcement of policy from the new administration—a wait of about two months. Thus ended eight years, 1915–23, of an alliance between organized vice and politics, although not without cost to the vice lords themselves, who toward the end were made to pay well for protection. A system at once of protection and control was evolved which was fairly effective against the attacks of the reform organizations.

After a lull of four years (1923–27) during which time

Chicago was run about as "clean" and "closed" as possible under the circumstances, the Thompson machine returned to office on the "open town" platform. The Cusick-Capone combine was at this time struggling for complete control in the old levee, not so much through pull and politics as through guns, gangsters and the profits of beer running.[43]

About ten days after Cooney's immunity had been exposed, a special Grand Jury, probing election crimes found, heard the testimony of over a hundred witnesses—all of them connected with vice and gambling resorts—who admitted that they had paid representatives of the city hall clique for protection but had not received it. The *Herald-Examiner* listed some 52 addresses—all of them dives of one kind or another—to which subpoenas were served for appearance before the Grand Jury.[44]

Less than a month later the *Daily Journal* carried the story of the biggest vice levy ever reported—$5,000,000 extracted from vice, gambling and liquor interests on the South Side to support Thompson's America First Campaign in the primary elections. Two thousand houses of prostitution were said to be paying tribute to the America First organization at $100 to $750 per week. These resorts were said to be on South Parkway (Grand Boulevard) from Thirty-sixth to Fifty-first Streets. Dan Jackson, the Negro boss, was mentioned among others. Al Capone and Jack Cusick, syndicate owner of resorts, were named as contributors as were also the beer joints of Joe Saltis. Eighteen hundred slot machines on the South Side were

[43] *Ibid.*, August 2, 1927. Quoted in the *Illinois Crime Survey*, pp. 862–63 n.

[44] *Herald-Examiner*, August 19, 1928.

reported as paying off one-third to the city hall clique.[45] The special Grand Jury by the end of September had failed to pin the primary election frauds and the vice extortion of America First on any important person in particular.[46]

The claim was made by Frank J. Loesch that Capone had contributed $260,000 to the primary and election campaign of Thompson. The contribution of Capone to the Thompson machine was placed at $150,000 by Judge John H. Lyle.[47] Gangster Jack Zuta was said to have contributed $50,000 to the Thompson campaign. He held a membership card (No. 772, 1927–28) in the William Hale Thompson Republican Club, which membership card was reputed to have cost Zuta $500.[48] He also had a card from the Cook County Sheriff's office extending him the courtesies of all departments for 1927. This meant immunity against arrest at the hands of county officers in the roadhouse territory. These cards were found among Zuta's papers.

More startling than his formal affiliations with the city hall and county administrations was the revelation of his intimate dealings with judges, politicians, and police. Investigation of Zuta's safety deposit vaults brought to light the fact that Judge Joseph W. Schulman of the Municipal Court (rotating on the Morals Court bench); George Van Lent, former state senator; Emanuel Eller, former judge of the Municipal Court; Nate De Lue, assistant business manager of the Chicago Board of Education; Simon Herr, law partner of former Judge Emanuel Eller; Paul W. Rothenberg, Republican Ward Committeeman

[45] *Chicago Daily Journal,* September 11, 1928.

[46] *Herald-Examiner,* September 28, 1928.

[47] *Chicago Tribune,* February 17, 1931.

[48] *Ibid.,* August 16, 1930.

and former chief deputy coroner of Cook County; Harry W. Starr, state senator, former city prosecutor, and former election commissioner, all had received checks from Zuta ranging in amount from $200 to $1,000.[49] Judge Schulman, Richard J. Williams, sergeant of police, and William Freeman, chief of police of Evanston, had signed notes, ranging from $400 to $1,500, which Zuta held. A picture postcard with "greetings from the Maypoles" (Alderman George A. Maypole) sent Zuta from Hot Springs, Arkansas, was found in the gangster's papers.[50]

Such startling exposures made excellent newspaper stories, but, like most exposures of corruption in Chicago, nothing was done about them. Some of the compromised politicians, judges, and policemen hurried to explain publicly their relations with Zuta and with that the matter ended. The intimate relationship between politics and gangland was not disturbed as far as could be discovered.

RESORT TO EVASIVE MEASURES

When, after 1912, Grand Jury investigations, Police Civil Service Commission inquiries and newspaper exposures reported a condition of wide-open, flourishing vice, certain reservations should be made. No matter how well protected the vice lords were, organized vice never flourished as of old. It was persistent with more or less difficulty; but it has never approximated its former abandon of the time of the red light district. In spite of the alliance of machine politics with dives, vice resorts have not had the freedom and security which they formerly had in the segregated district. Resorts nowadays, even

[49] *Ibid.*, August 16, 1930; August 20, 1930; and August 22, 1930.

[50] *Chicago Daily News*, August 22, 1930.

when favored by a "wide-open town" policy, eschew all undue display. The brilliant lights no longer radiate; the echoes of music, boisterousness, and hilarity no longer resound. Solicitation by women at the windows of modern protected resorts is tabu. Carousing patrons are discouraged and the cadets no longer loaf about the premises.

In spite of protection, the necessity of the tunnels for escape, warning buzzer systems, secret panels, trick doors, and the like, indicate that the existence of segregated vice is now precarious. There are still other methods of evasion. Sometimes the modern patron finds himself sent into a dummy smoke shop, from there directed to outside passages, through alleys and yards to the back door of a house or apartment which is absolutely dark. On leaving he is conducted through or directed to take a different route for exit.

Syndicated resorts may be open here today, there tonight, over there tomorrow. One trust has used a daily or a shift assignment scheme. The "brains" tell the subordinates what place to open up; the girls are corralled in cabs not knowing where they will be assigned; the light houses and the ropers are instructed to send patrons to this address. If there is danger the trust can close down on the assignment almost immediately and open up another one.

This system of daily or temporary assignments is dependent on the use of a great deal of slum property—more or less vacated buildings and houses. These properties are bought up by vice syndicates in large numbers, in all sorts of dummy names and owners. On the outside a building may have a "for sale" or a "for rent" sign; it may look entirely vacant; and residents in the neighborhood seldom suspect that their dilapidated, deserted shells harbor vice. The vice syndicates often let the slum families—especially Negroes on the Near South Side—use their houses or buildings for residence or store-front churches. Sometimes there is a poor Negro family or store front church on the ground floor and quarters for a vice assignment on the second or third floor rear.

It is said that Cooney's vice syndicate on the South Side is also a real estate corporation, since it has gone into the wholesale buying up of slum property. It is also rumored that Cooney's organization does much charity work; that the United Charities in budgeting poor Negro families in this section must first find out if they are getting their rent free. This rent-free benevolence has political implications as well. The beneficiaries are potential and actual supporters of the political machine which keeps the vice trust alive and which in turn keeps the beneficiaries alive. And so the vicious circle runs. Under the scheme of wholesale buying of slum property, it is very difficult to catch the vice lords under the Injunction and Abatement Law— where property owners who knowingly allow vice to occupy their premises can be forced to abrogate the use of the property for one year.

SUMMARY: THE RECORD OF ORGANIZED VICE

By the wholesale use of slum property vice has succeeded in evading the Injunction and Abatement Law. By its alliance with politics and the police, organized vice has gained immunity in exchange for votes or by the payment of tribute. Organized vice in co-operation with organized crime has secured the support of gangsters and gunmen, and is contributing to the wealth flowing in from associated illegitimate business, like beer running and racketeering. It has intrenched itself in every way which seems likely to insure its existence in an era of suppression.

CHAPTER IV

CABARETS

The cabaret emerged during the period of vice suppression in Chicago and other American cities, in a new pattern, in which it has gained a wide vogue. In New York and in some other cities cabarets are called "night clubs," but their relation to the old-fashioned saloon with its "family entrance," its beer garden and dance hall connections is evident.

The report of the Vice Commission in 1911, states that its investigators visited 250 saloons in which they counted 928 women whom they identified as prostitutes. These saloons with their family entrances and other conveniences by which they made the transition from commercialized recreation to commercialized vice are described as follows in this report:

Many of these disorderly saloons are under the control of brewery companies as will be seen later in the report. These saloons are frequented by immoral women who openly solicit for drinks and for immoral purposes and receive the protection of the saloon keepers and interests.

In the majority of saloons the entertainment consists of piano playing and singing. In some instances a vaudeville performance is given. The singers usually receive $10.00 per week and a percentage on drinks. These performers mingle with the men at the tables and solicit for immoral purposes.

In many cases public dance halls are located in the same buildings with saloons. While bar permits are usually given for the sale of liquor in the dance halls, the dancers have been seen to frequent the rear rooms of saloons. In other cases the dance halls are in the immediate vicinity of saloons and the dancers go to these.

Aside from solicitation in rear rooms of saloons, women stand in doorways near the end of the bar and ask men to come into rear rooms and buy drinks; then the men are solicited to go upstairs or other places.

It is the common practice for proprietors to protect the girls who frequent their places. By protection is meant the habit of paying the fine or bailing out the girls who are arrested.[1]

There were at this time approximately 275 public dance halls in Chicago which were rented periodically to clubs and societies or were conducted by individuals. Of these the Vice Commission report says:

In nearly every hall visited, investigators have seen professional and semi-professional prostitutes. These girls and women openly made dates to go to nearby hotels or assignation rooms after the dance. In some instances they were accompanied by their cadets who were continually on the lookout for new victims.[2]

ADDITIONAL BACKGROUNDS

The intimate connection of two of the main features of the present-day cabaret—saloon-café life and the public dance—with prostitution was, therefore, already well established before the actual appearance of the cabaret. Even the *revue* and the personal contact of entertainers and patrons which characterize the modern cabaret, were carried over in part at least from levee background—i.e., the exhibition, the "circus," and table solicitation. The other part of the entertainment feature of cabarets was borrowed from the continental cabaret, the beer garden, and the musical comedy revue. Even the exotic jazz had its counterpart in levee "ragtime." The "jazz band,"

[1] *The Social Evil in Chicago* (Vice Commission Report, 1911), pp. 119, 125, 126, 129.

[2] *Ibid.*, p. 185.

which sets the tempo for present-day cabaret dancing, appeared on the American scene about the time when cabarets came into vogue in Chicago. At first the jazz band was a three or four piece orchestra, with the saxophone or clarinet carrying the exotic melody to pulsating drum or banjo beats. Later on it is enlarged to include the brass family of cornets, trombones, and sousaphones, making possible symphonic jazz.

CABARET EXPOSURES

It became very evident by 1916 that all the antecedent forms — revue, beer garden, and public dance — had merged into the cabaret (American style). One indication that a hitherto unrecognized institution had emerged out of the undercurrent of city life was a shock to the public as it learned for the first time, from the newspaper descriptions, of this first new manifestation of the jazz age. If the old saloon and bawdy house seemed tame alongside the cabaret, it was mainly because the combination of saxophone music, fox-trotting, risqué entertainment, open promiscuity, wholesale intoxication and cigarette smoking, prostitutes, shop girls, and slumming society folk was new and unheard of. Even the reporters were shocked.[3]

To a public accustomed to the old and well-recognized pitfalls—the saloon and the brothel—the cabaret was a new and more intriguing form of moral hazard. Stories in the newspapers indicated that cabarets were sending men and girls into destruction.[4]

[3] See for example *Chicago Herald,* February 2, 1916, for an exposure under the heading: "Worst Cabaret in City Found."

[4] *Chicago Tribune,* January 16, 1916; *Chicago Herald,* January 27, 1916.

Naturally enough, this newly emerging institution—the cabaret—was blamed by the public for the demoralization of young men and women, rather than the undercurrent forces and changes in urban life which have been responsible for both. The reason is that a new institution like the jazz-age cabaret gets wide publicity. About ten years later the Chicago public is pointing its finger at another newly evolved institution—the closed dance hall—the locus of taxi dancing, as a prime factor in the demoralization of young girls (see pp. 160–63). At any rate, even if the cabaret was not responsible for the wholesale "fall" of youth, the exposures served to acquaint the public with the pitfalls and thus prepared in advance those who were to meet the conditions first hand.

THE RISE OF THE BLACK-AND-TANS

The newspaper accounts of the freedom, promiscuity, and general impropriety of life and manners in the new phase of city life represented by the cabaret led some of the more notorious of proprietors to seek the freedom and the seclusion of the Black Belt, where public opinion has proverbially been neither vigorous nor vigilant and most of everything has been tolerated. Until recent years in Chicago the Negro has been little tolerated outside of the slum, while the original Negro quarter in Chicago was in the vice area. Once in the Black Belt the cabarets exploited the musical tradition of the Negro who brought with him the "blues" and a new type of jazz. This was the origin of the so-called "Black-and-Tan" where black folk and white met on something approaching the same social level.

To a slumming white patronage the Black Belt location of cabarets offered atmosphere and the colored man's music and patronage added thrill. When the black-and-tan development was noticed, the newspaper reporters, in their characteristic way, described these black-and-tan places as "worse than the worst." The earliest no-color-line cabarets, however, were called the "black and whites."[5]

The black-and-tans were mentioned by the *Chicago Commission on Race Relations* investigating the situation leading up to race friction, following the riots of 1919. The intermingling of the Whites and Negroes in cabarets was looked upon as one factor in the total racial situation.[6]

THE GANG OCCUPATION OF THE CABARET FRONTIER

Some time after discovering the black-and-tan resorts, the Chicago public found that its cabarets had become the hangout of gangsters. The public became aware of this invasion by gangsters when reports of the killing of gangsters by gangsters in these night clubs became noticeably frequent in the press. Cabarets were, it seemed, not only operated and financed by gangsters, but they were important links in the chain of the beer-running operations conducted by different gangs. The cabarets were also the social centers for gangsters, the places where they met the public.

Investigations in the recent murder of Jack Zuta revealed that this gang leader while operating on the West Side in 1926 had an interest in a notorious cabaret in the vicinity, the Liberty Inn, and that Babe Mullaney, notori-

[5] *Chicago Herald*, February 9, 1916.

[6] *The Negro in Chicago* (The Chicago Commission on Race Relations, Chicago, 1922), p. 323.

ous police character, who was shot later in gang turmoils, acted as dummy proprietor for Zuta. But when the case of liquor violation at this cabaret was brought before the Federal Court, Zuta's name was not recorded in the court proceedings. Moreover, the Liberty Inn was known to be operating three months after it had been officially padlocked by the federal government.[7]

Further evidence of the gang control of cabarets is indicated in a newspaper report concerning the re-opening of the Paroquet Club (night club) at 945 North State Street. After the capitulation of the North Side gang, following the murder of Jack Zuta, Ted Newberry, Capone gang representative, was reported as having aligned this cabaret with the South Side gang.[8] When Harry and Sam Guzik (Cusick), important cogs in the Capone machine, were apprehended by the agents of the federal government for income tax evasion, they were seized in a cabaret at 1215 South Wabash, which had a speakeasy in the rear. This establishment was said to be a hang-out for members of the Capone gang.[9]

The Juvenile Protective Association's annual report for 1928 likewise called attention to the fact that "these [cabarets and night clubs] have now become popular resorts for our young gangsters and hold-up men. It is significant that recently our police went to these places when they wished to round up all the criminals."[10]

During Dever's administration many cabaret owners of

[7] *Chicago Tribune*, August 21, 1930.

[8] *Chicago Daily News*, September 12, 1930.

[9] *Chicago Tribune*, September 26, 1930.

[10] *Annual Report of the Juvenile Protective Association of Chicago, 1928*, p. 17.

old vice syndicates betook themselves outside the city walls to run their business unhampered. During the latter part of 1923 the press reported that Roy Jones, of the South Side vice syndicate, was managing the Green Parrot roadhouse on the northern flank of the city's suburban region.[11] In 1923 it was noted that Al Tearney, notorious cabaret owner of the Thirty-fifth Street black-and-tan district, was discomforted so much in town that he retired when Mayor Dever revoked his cabaret license. At this time he was reported as planning to build a "bigger and better" cabaret outside the city where he could hold forth undisturbed.[12] His plans matured into one of the most palatial roadhouses erected during the closed-town interregnum—the "Garden of Allah." When roadhouses came into the possession of vice mongers and beer runners, these underworld magnates did not fail to introduce the large-scale cabaret feature into the general roadhouse business, no matter whether they had been in town cabaret business previously or not.

CABARET AND VICE AREAS

The intimate relation of cabarets with gangland and the vice interest leads us to expect that cabarets and vice resorts will be distributed pretty largely in the same areas of Chicago, so much so that with few exceptions we may say that an area noted as a cabaret district is also an area of commercialized vice and vice versa. Map 2 gives the distribution of licensed cabarets in Chicago from 1923 to 1930.[13]

[11] *Chicago Daily News,* September 25, 1923.

[12] *Ibid.,* May 19, 1923.

[13] Yearly duplications of cabarets were eliminated. If a cabaret at a

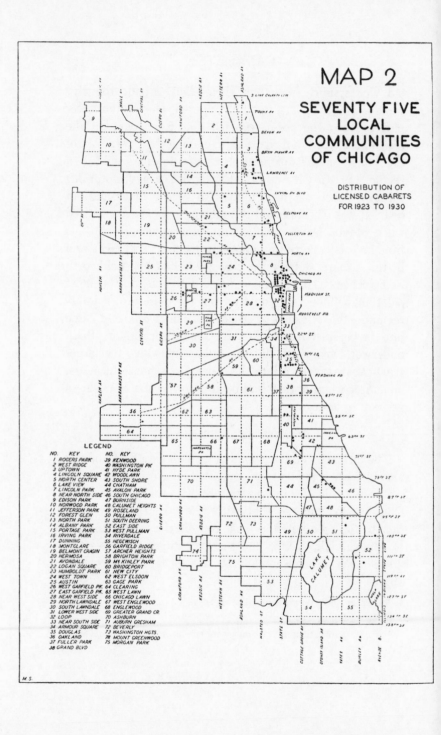

MAP 2

SEVENTY FIVE LOCAL COMMUNITIES OF CHICAGO

DISTRIBUTION OF
LICENSED CABARETS
FOR 1923 TO 1930

LEGEND

NO.	KEY	NO.	KEY
1	ROGERS PARK	39	KENWOOD
2	WEST RIDGE	40	WASHINGTON PK
3	UPTOWN	41	HYDE PARK
4	LINCOLN SQUARE	42	WOODLAWN
5	NORTH CENTER	43	SOUTH SHORE
6	LAKE VIEW	44	CHATHAM
7	LINCOLN PARK	45	AVALON PARK
8	NEAR NORTH SIDE	46	SOUTH CHICAGO
9	EDISON PARK	47	BURNSIDE
10	NORWOOD PARK	48	CALUMET HEIGHTS
11	JEFFERSON PARK	49	ROSELAND
12	FOREST GLEN	50	PULLMAN
13	NORTH PARK	51	SOUTH DEERING
14	ALBANY PARK	52	EAST SIDE
15	PORTAGE PARK	53	WEST PULLMAN
16	IRVING PARK	54	RIVERDALE
17	DUNNING	55	HEGEWISCH
18	MONTCLARE	56	GARFIELD RIDGE
19	BELMONT CRAGIN	57	ARCHER HEIGHTS
20	HERMOSA	58	BRIGHTON PARK
21	AVONDALE	59	Mc KINLEY PARK
22	LOGAN SQUARE	60	BRIDGEPORT
23	HUMBOLDT PARK	61	NEW CITY
24	WEST TOWN	62	WEST ELSDON
25	AUSTIN	63	GAGE PARK
26	WEST GARFIELD PK.	64	CLEARING
27	EAST GARFIELD PK.	65	WEST LAWN
28	NEAR WEST SIDE	66	CHICAGO LAWN
29	NORTH LAWNDALE	67	WEST ENGLEWOOD
30	SOUTH LAWNDALE	68	ENGLEWOOD
31	LOWER WEST SIDE	69	GREATER GRAND CR.
32	LOOP	70	ASHBURN
33	NEAR SOUTH SIDE	71	AUBURN GRESHAM
34	ARMOUR SQUARE	72	BEVERLY
35	DOUGLAS	73	WASHINGTON HGTS.
36	OAKLAND	74	MOUNT GREENWOOD
37	FULLER PARK	75	MORGAN PARK
38	GRAND BLVD		

M.S.

Cursory inspection and comparison with Maps 1 and 4 show that the cabaret and vice areas pretty largely coincide. Eighty-nine per cent of the cabarets on Map 2 fell in the same tracts as 97 per cent of the investigated vice resorts in Chicago for the same period (1923–30).[14] In other words, only 11 per cent of the cabarets were located in areas of Chicago where no detectable vice resorts existed; while only 3 per cent of the resorts for prostitution fell in areas where no cabarets existed. Furthermore, there is a marked indication that the areas containing the largest number of cabarets possess also the largest number of vice resorts and the areas containing few cabarets possess few vice emporia.[15]

THE ATTEMPTS AT LEGAL CONTROL

The principal devices used to control the cabaret in Chicago have included the application of older ordinances governing cafés to cabarets, the framing of new ordinances with additional license regulations, the revocation of licenses, the application of the injunction and abatement

certain address was licensed for the full eight-year period (1923–30), this would be represented by one dot on the map; if a cabaret was licensed for only one year, it would be represented by one dot.

[14] Committee of Fifteen cases for years 1923 through 1930 as given in Table 57 were used for comparison. The number of vice resorts falling in the areas in which the licensed cabarets were located during this period was 3,185, while the number of vice resorts falling within the city limits, exclusive of those outside the city limits and those unclassifiable as to area (because of faulty address), was 3,199.

[15] A correlation according to the rank difference method, the formula being, $\left(p = 1 - \dfrac{\Sigma D^2}{N(N^2 - 1)} \right)$
was run for the number of cabarets and vice resorts for 19 areas of the city of Chicago which contained both cabarets and vice resorts. The coefficient of rank correlation (p) was found to be .65.

act by law-enforcement agencies, and the use of the federal prohibition authorities.

A brief review of the various law-enforcement moves against cabarets in Chicago begins with the out-again-in-again episodes of early cabarets. The license of a certain notorious café or cabaret would be revoked as a pacifying gesture to an indignant public and the place would shut down temporarily until the storm of agitation had blown over. Then the cabaret would get its license returned and reopen. We have already seen the out-again-in-again policy in the case of Freiberg's and Colosimo's. In the case of former 14 months elapsed and in that of the latter 5 months, between closed doors and reopened doors. In the already reported case of the Panama—a black-and-tan cabaret—the pace was set by the Thompson administration for quick out-again-in-again cycles; for it was closed twice and licenses reissued twice within six months (February–August, 1916).[16] But the case of the Rhodes Cafe was, perhaps, still a more spectacular instance of quick-work in the restoration of licenses and this right on top of the startling exposures of sinister cabarets (January–March, 1916) and a movement to legislate against bad conditions surrounding the public dance in Chicago under the Merriams' leadership (both the alderman and his wife).[17] In this case only a few days elapsed between revocation and restoration of the license.

The most vigorous protest against the evils of the public dance took place in 1914 to 1916 under the leadership of Mrs. Charles E. Merriam, wife of the alderman.

After a personal investigation of conditions in public

[16] *Chicago Herald,* August 15, 1916.

[17] *Chicago Tribune,* March 3, 1916.

dance halls, Mrs. Merriam, with the support of the women's clubs of Chicago sought to secure a revocation of the privileges granted to the dance halls to dispense liquor until 3 o'clock in the morning.[18]

The failure of this early movement was evident a few months later when an amendment introduced in the City Council by Alderman Charles E. Merriam, aimed at prohibiting the sale of liquor at dance halls, failed.[19] However, agitation kept on during the first year of Thompson's first administration (in the latter part of 1915). The reform group basing their action on an investigation of open dance halls, proposed the plan of revocation of licenses.[20]

Two months later the city council passed four orders directed at the cabarets and the fox trot clubs. It ordered:

1. Major Funkhouser to investigate the character and conduct of cabarets and submit a weekly report to the council.

2. Ordered City Prosecutor Miller to report at the next meeting why he has failed to prosecute cabarets or fox trot clubs, on evidence given him by the morals inspector and to submit the latter's reports to the council.

3. Ordered Corporation Counsel Ettelson to give a written opinion instead of his oral opinion in which he held that restaurants do not have to close at 1 A. M.

4. Ordered Ettelson to report on the status of the ordinance prohibiting public dancing in restaurants, the validity of which is now being tested in courts.[21]

During the next two years efforts to impose some sort of restrictions on night life in the cabarets were rendered futile by the traditional policy of the police of dealing with

[18] *Chicago Daily News*, March 31, 1915.

[19] *Ibid.*, May 13, 1915.

[20] *Chicago Herald*, November 14, 1915.

[21] *Chicago Herald*, February 8, 1916.

unpopular reforms and reformers. When protests against existing conditions were loud enough to be heard above the noise and confusion of city life the police closed, for a time, one or more of the institutions complained of. Sometimes they did not go as far as that but merely announced that they would be closed. Thus on March 1 it was announced that Corporation Counsel Ettelson would submit to the council the draft of an ordinance that was to be a "death blow" to cabarets.[22]

The cabarets survived these gestures. It appeared that even if the proposed ordinance to close cabarets had gone into effect, the law (according to its draft) would have left the cabaret itself undefined and would have been banished to oblivion because of impossibility of telling legally at what it did or did not aim.[23] After two years of wrangling and delay, the City Council on August 14, 1918, passed an ordinance regulating "dry cabarets." This ordinance was designed to cover places of amusement "where the public is admitted without payment of a fee" and where people "may engage in or witness entertainment, show, amusement, dancing, etc." The license fees were set as follows: $25 for a place of less than 300 seating capacity and 2400 square feet of floor space; $50 for 300–500 seating capacity and 2400–4000 square feet of floor space; $75 for 500–800 seating capacity and 4000–6400 square feet of floor space; $100 for more than 800 seating capacity and 6400 square feet of floor space. In

[22] *Chicago Evening Post,* March 1, 1916.

[23] "Corporation Counsel Ettelson defended the law department's draft of the proposed ordinance to close cabarets. Critics of the ordinance say it won't hold because it doesn't define a cabaret. Mr. Ettelson's answer is that it is up to the [city] council to do the defining." *Chicago Tribune,* March 3, 1916.

the next few years following the 1918 cabaret ordinance certain attempts were made to change definitions as well as the license fees, mainly under the spokesmanship of Alderman Cermak.

On August 3, 1921, the 1918 ordinance was amended to read a "place where food or drink is served to which the public is admitted with or with out a fee" and where the public "may engage in or witness theatrical entertainment, exhibition, show amusement, dance, skating or entertainment, other than musical." Again on December 28, 1921, the 1918 ordinance was modified to eliminate the double license possibility. "In case the business of an ice cream parlor, restaurant, coffee house, retail beverage dealer is conducted (etc.), then only one license shall be required and that shall be the highest license fee under any of the five ordinances." On the same date (December 28, 1921) the 1918 scale of license fees was revised considerably upwards; $250 for a place with a seating capacity not exceeding 150 and a floor space not exceeding 1200 square feet; $375 for 150–300 seating capacity and 1200–2400 square feet floor space; $500 for 300–500 seating capacity and 2400–4000 square feet floor space; $625 for 500–800 seating capacity and 4000–6400 square feet floor space; $750 for 800–1000 seating capacity and 6400–7500 square feet floor space; $1,000 for seating capacity exceeding 1000 and floor space exceeding 7500 square feet. A few months earlier when the City Council was contemplating this upward revision of cabaret license fees and referred the proposed revision to the committee on revenue (April 8, 1921), the press reported this piece of legislative news as follows:

Chicago's cabaret industry was in the dumps today.

The occasion was the ordinance passed yesterday by the city council which fixes licenses varying from $500–$2,000 a year for all cabarets in the city. The ordinance includes every place where food or drinks are served and dancing or entertainment other than merely orchestral entertainment is permitted.

Tom Chamales proprietor of the Green Mill Gardens commented thus: "When it isn't one thing now-a-days, its another. I suppose we can get by but it will make a big hole in the profits. A lot of fellows will have to quit business."[24]

The claim was that the practical effect of much higher licenses would be to favor the survival of the cabarets belonging to the big operators as against those owned by the little, independent fellows and to force cabaret owners to increase their business, legally or illegally, in order to compensate for the high license fees. There was a marked drop on the number of cabarets licensed in 1921, presumably due to the effect of the contemplated and as well as the actual revision of license fees. There was a noticeable recovery in succeeding years but at no time did the yearly number come up to the high water mark of 1918–20. The number of cabarets licensed by the city of Chicago from 1918–30 is given in Table 8 on following page.

On April 24, 1926, a proposed amendment was made in the City Council to take care of a cabaret condition. It was learned that the 1921 cabaret ordinance was not being enforced because the Building Commission refused to approve of many cabaret applications, the point being that the housing of the applicants did not come within the specifications. "If upon refusal of a license there would be no operation of the restaurant as a cabaret, the situation would not be a troublesome one. But the places

[24] *Chicago Daily News*, April 9, 1921.

TABLE 8

NUMBER OF CABARETS LICENSED BY THE CITY OF CHICAGO, 1918–30

Year	Number	Year	Number
1918	76	1924	46
1919	82	1925	40
1920	83	1926	30
1921	16	1927	32
1922	46	1928	65
1923	66	1929	63
		1930	68

run in spite of the fact that they have no licenses."[25] But this matter was placed on file to be considered in connection with the proposed revision of the building code (May 11, 1927).

THE ACTION OF LAW-ENFORCING AGENCIES

While the city fathers settled the cabaret problem by ordinances and rested their case, the law-enforcing agencies did not let the problem rest here. The Committee of Fifteen took up the fight against cabarets, endeavoring to close the vicious ones. In 1922, in collaboration with the police and federal authorities, the Committee was able to close up the black-and-tan Entertainers Café under the Injunction and Abatement Law for one year. It reopened a year later when, however, the place was again padlocked for another year. In 1923 the Committee of Fifteen reported its action against 27 cabarets and vice resorts which were reached through the federal government. After 1924 the Committee of Fifteen dropped its cabaret drive and confined itself solely to the investigation of houses of prostitution. However, the Juvenile Protective

[25] *Journal of the Proceedings of the City Council of the City of Chicago, 1926–27*, p. 3150.

Association from time to time made investigations of cabarets and called the attention of the authorities to the flagrantly violating places.

FEDERAL PADLOCK PROCEEDINGS

The activity of the federal government against cabarets is also noteworthy. In a recent report made by the United States Northern Judicial District of Illinois as to permanent injunctions (i.e. padlock proceedings), we find that 90 cabarets and cafés were closed from September 1, 1925, to March 31, 1930. The yearly report on these two types of places is as follows:

	1925 to (Sept. 1)	1926	1927	1928	1929	1930 to (March 1)	Total
Cabarets......	3	12	1	6	4	2	28
Cafés.........	3	17	3	22	16	1	62
Total.....	6	29	4	28	20	3	90

To get a more accurate idea of how the licensed cabarets of Chicago fared with the prohibition enforcement, a clearance was made of the addresses of cabaret licenses between January 1, 1928, to July 28, 1930, with the addresses at which permanent injunctions were obtained by the federal government during January 1, 1929, to July 1, 1930. Twelve cabarets licensed in the two years and a half (January, 1928, to July, 1930) appeared in the permanent injunction files of the federal government during the year and a half (1929–30). It should be remembered that these 12 padlocked cabarets constituted only 6.7 per cent of the 179 licenses granted from January 1,

1928, to July 28, 1930, and only 1.9 per cent of the 610[26] places padlocked in the city of Chicago by the federal government from January 1, 1929, to July 1, 1930.

REVOCATIONS

Finally, offending cabarets have been dealt with via the revocation power of the mayor of Chicago. This weapon was only used in 32 instances from 1923 to July, 1930, or in 8.4 per cent of the 383 licenses issued during that period.[27] Eighteen of the 32 were revocations in 1923 (Mayor Dever's first year of office and the inauguration of the closed town). Eight of the 32 were revoked in 1924; two in 1925 and none in 1926 making a total of 28 revocations for Dever or 87.5 per cent of the 32. In 1927 there were no revocations; in 1928, 1; in 1929, 2 (but both of these revoked licenses were re-issued), and in 1930 (up to July 28), 1, making a total of 4 revocations for the Thompson administration or 12.5 per cent of the 32.

PERSISTENCE OF CABARETS

For comparison with places of commercialized vice which from the Committee of Fifteen records showed an average life-span of 174 days, the indications are that the life-span of the cabarets is much longer. With the records available for only a time period of eight years 1923–30,

[26] This is an estimated figure and is arrived at in the following way: 847 permanent injunctions were obtained by the federal court (Northern District of Illinois); by a count of 842 cards on which the addresses of these cases were given, it was found that about 72 per cent fell within the limits of Chicago; 72 per cent of 847=610.

[27] Actually the official figures issued by the City Clerk's office for January 1, 1923—July 1, 1930, were 393. However, the record cards which I had to deal with in making the count of revocations amounted to 383.

it was discovered that the 51 cabarets licensed in 1930 (up to July 28) averaged 3.47 years in length of life. If records prior to 1923 had been available, this average figure may have been still higher.

Table 9 reveals the count.[28]

TABLE 9

LIFE-SPAN OF 51 CABARETS LICENSED BY THE CITY OF CHICAGO, JANUARY 1—JULY 28, 1930

No. of Years	No. of Instances	Amount in Years
1.......................	10	10
2.......................	11	22
3.......................	15	45
4.......................	3	12
5.......................	1	5
6.......................	1	6
7.......................	3	21
8.......................	7	56
Total.............	51	177

A check on the cabaret licenses from the other end— that is, from 1923 to 1930—yields a count of 147 cabarets at separate addresses among the 383 licenses for the eight-year period. By this count, the 147 cabarets have averaged 2.6 yearly licenses or a life-span roughly of 2.6 years. Only 7 cabarets or slightly under 5 per cent of the 147 persisted through the entire eight years, while 59 or 40 per cent did not enter the second year of life—a considerable mortality rate. Thirteen, or 9 per cent, of the 147 cabarets showed a gap in between consecutive years

[28] Those cabarets which appeared only in 1930 in the license records were counted as 1 year life-span. Where a cabaret had a skipping life span, the years in which it was licensed were counted only. For the most part the life-span of the cabarets are continuous in successive years where they persist more than one year.

TABLE 10

NUMBER OF YEARLY LICENSES FOR CABARETS LICENSED BY THE
CITY OF CHICAGO, 1923–30*

No. of Years Licensed	No. of Different Cabarets	No. of Licenses
1	59	59
2	31	62
3	24	72
4	11	44
5	5	25
6	5	30
7	5	35
8	7	56
Total	147	383

* Until July 28, 1930.

of license, which means either that they failed to get licenses and continued to operate or closed up the cabaret business and reopened at a later date. The number of years unlicensed (presumably not operating), is given in the diagram below for the 13 irregular cabarets.

	O	NUMBER OF YEARS WITHOUT A LICENSE							No. of Cabarets	Total in Yrs.
		I	II	III	IV	V	VI	VII		
NUMBER OF YEARS WITH A LICENSE I	....	....	....	....	....	....	....	....	0	0
II	....	....	....	....	....	....	....	....	0	0
III	1	1	....	1	1	....	....		4	12
IV	2	....	1	1	....	....	....		4	9
V	1	1	....	....	....	....	....		2	3
VI	....	....	....	....	....	....	....		0	0
VII	3	....	....	....	....	....	....		3	3
No. of Cabarets	7	2	1	2	1	0	0		13	27
Total in Yrs.	37	8	4	7	3	0	0		......	59

The 13 irregular cabarets averaged slightly over 2 years unlicensed ($27 \div 13$) and 4.5 years licensed ($59 \div 13$).

SUMMARY

We have found that (1) the Chicago cabarets emerged out of red-light backgrounds as a new type of pleasure about 1914 (or two years after the closing of Chicago's segregated district); (2) that while prostitution and liquor were affiliated with them to a more or less extent, they have been more critically related to the emancipation of respectable persons (especially women) from the former inhibiting norms of conduct and to the development of new fashions in public behavior; (3) that the fundamental changes in urban life and habits were responsible, in the main, for these radical developments in public behavior of pleasure seekers rather than the cabaret itself; (4) that the black-and-tan type of cabaret was a more or less unpremeditated development in the Black Belt of Chicago; (5) that the recent affiliation of cabarets with gangland is to be explained mainly by the unfavorable position of a dry cabaret in an era of prohibition and by the favorable position of a wet cabaret as an outlet for the rum runners' business and a location for the "big parties," which gangsters were now able to give, partly for their entertainment and partly to advertise the practical annulment of the liquor legislation which their operation had effected; (6) that cabarets like vice resorts have been involved in political-psuedo criminal machinations; (7) that the early anti-cabaret agitation which was directed against the moral conditions resulted in temporary closing of offending places but later resulted in new license ordinances governing cabarets; (8) that the principal method of drastic action against publicly offensive cabarets has come from the arm of the federal government through its padlock proceedings in co-operation with "city" law enforcing agencies and also from revocations of licenses by the mayor although over half of the revocations in the last eight years occurred in 1923 (Dever's first year of office); (9) that the average life span of 51 cabarets licensed in the first half of 1930 was about three and one half years in the eight-year period studied and that 147 cabarets at different addresses obtained on an average of 2.6 licenses in this eight-year period, constituting a persistence rate of slightly over two and one half years.

CHAPTER V

ROADHOUSES

POLITICAL OUTSKIRTS AS REGIONS OF OUTLAWRY

When vice was outlawed, under Dever in Chicago, it took refuge on the borderland outside the city limits.

The political outskirts of the city historically have been regions of outlawry, in which vice and crime have flourished. Modern cities but duplicate, in this respect, cities of ancient and medieval times. Friedlaender, describing the inns of ancient Rome, says: "Inns were often brothels. Jurists are constantly mentioning that the servants at inns, in town or country, consisted of cheap girls, and the inn-keepers were unprofessed panders. As panders and for other reasons, inn-keepers had an ill-repute. On the list of the police-soldiers, they were inscribed with thieves and gamblers."[1]

Not merely the administrative limits of cities,[2] but state and national borders are regions that harbor outlaws. The roadhouses at Burnham, Illinois, just outside

[1] *Roman Life and Manners under the Early Empire* (English transl.), I, 293.

[2] Even the smaller political units within cities have exhibited this same congregation of outlawed elements on the limits. Before the advent of national prohibition, certain districts in American cities had excluded the saloons, which then located just on the other side of the line, as they did in cases where states or counties had turned "dry" under local option. In Chicago, for example, saloons were prohibited in a district one mile square, bounded by Lawrence Avenue on the North, Irving Park Boulevard on the South, Clark Street on the West, and Lake Michigan on the East. A number of saloons were opened at Lawrence and Evanston Avenue (now Broadway), at Lawrence and Clark, at Irving Park and Clark, just across the prohibition line.

Chicago, are on the state line between Illinois and Indiana. There is a legend that whenever the deputies "pull a raid" the inmates and patrons of these resorts step from Illinois over to Indiana, a few feet distant.[3] There they are safe from punishment for offenses committed in Illinois, unless they are apprehended by reason of a special petition to the governor of Indiana.[4]

National borders are notoriously a "no man's land."[5] Smuggling is perhaps the most frequent type of crime characteristic of the nation's boundaries. With the recent national prohibition in the United States, the Mexican and Canadian borders[6] and even the sea coast borders have

[3] According to the evidence (August 1923) concerning commercialized vice at the roadhouse colony of Burnham, submitted to the State's Attorney's office by the Committee of Fifteen, Chicago, it was found, by reference to the county plaques of lots in this section, that the resorts were located about one quarter of a block from the state line.

[4] Between nations there is the more indirect diplomatic process by which extradition is obtained. For interstate extradition see *Corpus Juris* (American Law Book Co., 1921), pp. 254–73. For international extradition, see *ibid.*, pp. 273–960.

[5] It is interesting to note that Ratzel makes an observation concerning the presence of outlawry on the frontiers and in regions of waning influence of the primitive state. "We have examples of frontier points and frontier spaces at every stage. The frontier spaces are clear, and even serve as common hunting-grounds, but they also serve as habitations for forces hostile to civil authority, for desperadoes of every shade of villany." *History of Mankind,* Vol. I, cited in W. I. Thomas, *Social Origins,* 6th ed., p. 761.

[6] "Convinced that narcotics and liquor can be smuggled jointly into the United States, these groups are now in competition with the pioneer drug smugglers. It is estimated that the volume of drugs smuggled into the United States from Canada in 1924 will exceed that of any previous years by approximately 50 per cent, owing to the general participation of liquor smugglers in the 'dope' traffic. There is no section of the international boundary regarded as hazardous by the smugglers of narcotics; the section recognized by all as the safest, however, is that extend-

become the locus for both an organized and an unorganized liquor traffic. Furthermore, certain towns and cities along the international boundary constitute rallying points for agents of this outlawed activity. Tia Juana (Mexico), Montreal (Canada), both just over the border, and Havana (Cuba), not to mention a host of less notorious border towns, have really become "resort cities" for Americans.[7] As city dwellers go out of town for their pleasure trips, so citizens leave the country in their quest for excitement.

A RECENT SURVEY OF CONDITIONS

The roadhouses which harbored criminals have at the same time, in many cases, become nests of vice. The Juvenile Protective Association of Chicago, in co-operation with the American Social Hygiene Association, recently (July–August 1929) investigated the roadhouses in Cook County. The survey revealed that some of the roadhouses were legitimately conducted; but the majority were found to be nothing more than speakeasies which served in some instances as gathering places, and

---

ing from Atlantic westward as far as Rouse's Point. The customs officers are so few that they scarcely attempt to intercept the speeding motor cars which slash by under cover of darkness. The officials realize that murder means very little to black-jacks, loaded clubs, missiles and even red pepper. Scores of customs officers have been assaulted and some will never recover." William J. McNulty, "Drug Smuggling from Canada," *The Current History Magazine* (October. 1924), pp. 93–95.

[7] An interesting parallel to this liquor traffic on the United States border is revealed in medieval Antwerp. "Repeatedly the citizens of Antwerp are charged not to go to Damburgge, Mercexm, Berchem, and other places just outside the town to drink there, for this enabled them to drink without paying excise in the town." Jervis Wegg, *Antwerp*. p. 79.

even regular "hangouts" for a lawless and criminal element.[8]

Of the 171 investigated roadhouses in Cook County, Illinois[9] (outside the corporation limits of Chicago), 142 (52 per cent) sold alcoholic beverages openly or clandestinely. In 89 (33 per cent) intoxicated persons, among them many youths, girls as well as boys, were found. Eleven (4 per cent) sold no alcoholic beverages on the premises, but encouraged guests to bring "their own" by serving "set ups." While most of the 171 resorts had some form of dancing, 47 (17 per cent) were places at which occurred "indecent and suggestive" dancing, by patrons. The chief investigator's summary on this point reads:

In some places it [the dancing] was but slightly indecent; in others it was thoroughly immoral. Young people, some visibly under the influence of liquor, others apparently sober, were repeatedly seen to dance or whirl about the floor with their bodies pressed tightly together, shaking, moving and rotating their lower portions in a way that undoubtedly roused their sex impulses. Some even were seen to engage in "soul" kissing and "biting" one another on the lobes of the ears and upon the neck.[10]

In 32 or 12 per cent of the 171 roadhouses private rooms were available to known guests for immoral purposes. Fourteen or 5 per cent of these roadhouses were resorts

[8] Jessie F. Binford, "Cook County (Illinois) Roadhouses," *Journal of Social Hygiene*, Vol. XVI, No. 5, May, 1930.

[9] This figure does not represent the exact number of places in Cook County which could be classed as roadhouses. But it does include all the noticeably important and most frequented places.

[10] *Juvenile Protective Association Roadhouse Investigation in Cook County, Illinois, July 25—August 31, 1929*, pp. 8–9. On file in typewritten copy. Also given in Jessie F. Binford, *op. cit.*, pp. 3, 6.

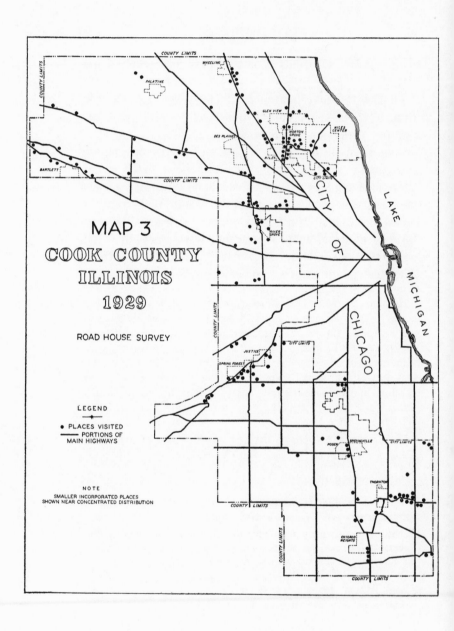

MAP 3

COOK COUNTY
ILLINOIS
1929

ROAD HOUSE SURVEY

LEGEND

• PLACES VISITED
PORTIONS OF
MAIN HIGHWAYS

NOTE
SMALLER INCORPORATED PLACES
SHOWN NEAR CONCENTRATED DISTRIBUTION

of prostitution either in professional or semi-professional form.[11]

It appears from these findings that liquor violation is the greatest problem numerically while prostitution is the smallest (52 per cent vs. 5 per cent).

THE GEOGRAPHY AND TYPES OF ROADHOUSES

The map on page 124 depicts the distribution of road houses in Cook County on the fringe of Chicago's corporation limits, according to the Juvenile Protective Association's survey. This map does not include the whole roadhouse hinterland about Chicago. In some cases the region in which roadhouses are located extends as far as 50 to 60 miles from the center of the city. However, the map includes those resorts most frequently patronized in Chicago's metropolitan area. Attention should be directed to the fact that the roadhouses hug the main highways leading out of Chicago. Notice also should be taken of the distribution of these resorts in reference to the corporation boundaries of Chicago, the state line (between Illinois and Indiana), the county line, and village and township limits.

In an earlier roadhouse study made for the Juvenile Protective Association, Mr. Daniel Russell classifies the types of roadhouses according to the major activity presented by them. He finds that in Chicago's suburban region there are: (1) the saloon roadhouse; (2) the roadhouse of gambling; (3) the roadhouse of prostitution; (4) the roadhouse of dancing; (5) the roadhouse of eating, drinking, and dancing; (6) the picnic grove. These types are separated for convenience, since (1) is likely to be

[11] *Ibid.,* pp. 1–10. Percentages mine.

associated with (2), (3), and (6) and (2) may sometimes be associated with (4).

THE EMIGRATION OF VICE LORDS

Chicago had its city-limits cafés and beer gardens, and a suburban vice resort or two, even prior to the closing of the red light district. But the out-of-town location did not become popular until the active period of suppression in town. As early as 1916 there were indications that the chief owners of the old levee districts were opening up the suburban region. In reviewing the situation since the red light districts were closed (four years previously), Henry M. Hyde in the *Chicago Tribune* (January 14, 1916), calls attention to the outlying quarters of certain familiar levee characters. Commenting on this article, Landesco in the *Illinois Crime Survey* (1929), Page 853, says: "Mr. Hyde disclosed *the earliest venture into suburban areas of members of the old Twenty-second Street Levee Ring. These were the precursors, later to be followed by the Torrio-Capone vice, beer and gambling ring in Burnham, Cicero, Stickney, etc.*"

THE CLOSED TOWN AND THE SUBURBAN OCCUPATION

William C. Dever was elected mayor, April, 1923. Morgan Collins, Dever's chief of police, "within the first year of his incumbency in office, closed two hundred downtown handbook 'joints' that were estimated to produce $364,000 per year to Mont Tennes."[12]

Just prior to Dever's election, the Thompson régime, under pressure of the moral forces of Chicago, and urged by the Grand Jury investigations following a survey of vice

[12] *Illinois Crime Survey* (1929), p. 900.

resorts by the Juvenile Protective Association, made a gesture at law enforcement. Chief of Police Fitzmorris issued a remarkable "vice picket" order (February, 1923). The dive keepers lay low, biding the outcome of the approaching election and the announcement of the new administration's policy. They soon learned that the lid was to be kept on tight.

About the same time that vice and gambling were emigrating to the suburban region of Chicago, consolidated beer runners began to occupy the outer locations. But the occupation of the hinterland by beer racketeers, Torrio's gang in particular, followed more from the large-scale, metropolitan operations of this new illicit traffic, than from law enforcement in the city power. The beer runners discovered "good stands" at the city limits for their expanding business.

The way in which the proprietors of independent roadhouses were forced into line by the invading Chicago syndicates is described by the Juvenile Protective Association.

One proprietor admitted that he paid $55 per barrel for beer and $120 per case for whiskey. The price of the beer to the consumer ranged from 25 to 50 cents per glass; and the whiskey, from 50 to 75 cents a drink. He stated that the amount of beer and whiskey sold netted him a substantial profit, and that the prices which the dispenser or retailer paid were dictated by a so-called "syndicate." He also stated that beer and liquor might be purchased for less elsewhere, but that he and all roadhouse keepers in this section were compelled to purchase their supply from the syndicate in control of the area. Some of the proprietors said that they were told that they could expect to be "blown up" or "taken for a ride" unless they complied with the wishes of the syndicate.

A bartender stated that he had previously operated two roadhouses in a nearby community, and that, in addition to selling intoxicants, he had harbored prostitutes. He said that he was approached by a representative of one of the syndicates who informed him that it had other places in his vicinity, and because he [the then proprietor] had "cut prices," the business of the syndicate's other resorts had markedly decreased. He was advised, under threat, to give up his two places and join the syndicate, being offered a substantial weekly sum for so doing.[13]

This material suggests that gang syndicates have used about the same tactics in the suburban as in the urban field of operation, namely, the intimidation of independent enterprises, the forced "hook-up" with the syndicate, the allocation of territory, the fixing of prices and protection.

While the invasion and occupation of the suburban region is logically the reaction to suppression in the city, this fact alone does not indicate how it is that the contraband activities are able to intrench and maintain themselves outside the city walls.

POLICE CONTROL RELAXES AT THE LIMITS

Police control at the national border and outside city limits is rarely vigorous or effective.[14] First of all, there is a conflict in jurisdiction between the city, county and State.

Governmental agencies in counties for the investigation of crime

[13] *Juvenile Protective Association Roadhouse Investigation in Cook County, Illinois, July 25–August 31, 1929,* pp. 4–6. Report on file in typewritten copy in J.P.A. offices, Chicago.

[14] "Governmental indifference on the part of both Canada and the United States and also lax legislation and inadequate means of enforcing such laws as are already on the statute books are responsible for the present situation. Prompt and effective official action is imperative if the peoples of North America are to be protected from the ever-increasing menace of drug slavery." William J. McNulty, *op. cit.,* p. 97.

and the apprehension of criminals are woefully disorganized. The sheriff, the city police, the prosecutor, and the coroner may all be trying to do the same thing at the same time; each is independent of the other and each officer is apt to be jealous of his own prerogatives. They get in each other's way, they challenge each other's authority, they cast blame on each other for blunders, and altogether they often present a most unedifying spectacle of inefficiency.[15]

Attention has also been called to the fact that, because of the administrative decentralization in the various counties of the state, the state's attorney or public prosecutor may be very liberal in his interpretation and enforcement of law, particularly of statutes dealing with commercialized vice.[16]

The city police force naturally tends to focus its activities upon the center of the city, where are congregated most of the law evaders, requiring surveillance. In suppressing crime and vice and in keeping order in the "bad lands" of the community, the police force has, as it is, a greater load apparently than it can carry. Regulating roadhouses belongs from the point of view of the city police department to the State's Attorney's or sheriff's office.

The county police system in the United States is traditionally weak in both numbers and organization.[17] And especially is this true in counties which include large cities, where a situation is created in which "politics" (i.e., political corruption) may easily enter.

[15] Adapted from *County and Township Government in the United States* by Kirk H. Porter, New York, 1922, pp. 199–200, with permission of The Macmillan Co., publishers.

[16] *Ibid.*, pp. 199–200.

[17] "Some feeble efforts have been made to strengthen the sheriff's arm. In some cases he is provided with a number of deputies, but nowhere has a thoroughly well organized county police force been established." See Porter, *op. cit.*, p. 175.

THE SUBURBAN FRONTIER

The first zone in the metropolitan area beyond the city limits has all the characteristics of a frontier. Here industries that were crowded out of the city are finding new locations; residential suburbs are growing up along the lines of transportation. On the other hand, the original inhabitants are moving out, or preparing to. Everything is new and unsettled. Like the area about the central business area in which the city slums are usually located, it is an "area of transition," an area of demoralization, also.

In both cases an older type of community organization has disintegrated; both areas await the advance of a new type of urban organization, but in the meantime they have become the rendezvous of those who practice vice and crime. In neither case is there a public opinion capable of combating social disorders; nor is there a potential public opinion, which when locally aroused, demands repression and law enforcement. Indeed the underworld at both the center and circumference of the city comprises almost the only well-developed organization for corporate activity in these interstitial areas. The roadhouses outside Chicago, for example, cluster together, forming small communities in a hinterland of sparse population and disintegrating rural settlements.

VICE EVADES CONTROL AT ROADHOUSES

Because of the disorganization on the borders of the city, roadhouses gain a certain freedom, but not complete immunity from control. Prostitution, gambling, and liquor drinking, are three principal forms of commercialized vice which find in the roadhouse a haven of refuge from the police. Raids on roadhouses have occurred time and time again since the contrabands occupied them. But raids have had no greater success in eliminating commercialized vice in the suburban regions than in the city proper.

In the Juvenile Protective Association roadhouse investigation of 1929 the fact is brought out that roadhouse operators are able to evade police control because they have developed an organization which is more powerful than federal, county, and township government.

From many sides statements were made [by operators themselves] that the operators of the resorts do not fear County Police, and are not concerned very much about the activities of the Federal Authorities. One operator said "We get a raid now and then, but that is to be expected in this business. The worst we draw is a $100 fine. The main thing is to keep the joints open."[18]

Statements of this sort, if they may be taken as indicative of prevailing conditions, make it appear that governmental control of roadhouse operations has been reduced to a ceremony.

It appears that most of the measures for evading the laws which vice lords developed as part of their business in the city, have been transferred to the suburbs. Among those most commonly reported in the press are "tip off" systems (i.e., warning of the time of a contemplated raid), tunnels for escape, transferring the place of operation to a new quarter, and local election grabs. Furthermore, intimidation from gang rule and powerless courts have assisted indirectly yet positively evasion of law enforcement.

ROADHOUSE LICENSES AND ABUSES

Besides tip offs, tunnels for escape, gang rule and vil-

---

[18] *Op. cit.*, pp. 6–7.

lage election grabs, another factor has helped to entrench vice in suburban localities. And this is the license system or perhaps the abuse of the system. Local and state governments retain the power to license public places of entertainment, primarily to bring such activities under control and to protect individuals from moral hazards and from community nuisances. Many villages outside Chicago, however, have profited from high license fees imposed on roadhouses. When a small village has a dozen roadhouses paying high license fees, it is likely to be tolerant of the incidental disorder involved. A high license fee means, in short, protection to vice lords.[19]

The limited extent to which licensing was effective after the passing of the state law (approved, June 30, 1925), requiring roadhouses to be licensed by county, village, or township government, can be seen in numbers alone, although we must realize that in American local government a license is not a blue ribbon for good behavior. The Juvenile Protective Association found 271 roadhouses operating in Cook County, Illinois, in the summer of 1926 and the spring of 1927. "During 1926, the first year under this new law, about 103 roadhouses were licensed and in 1927, up to June 1, about 116."[20] According to these figures 38 per cent in 1926 and 43 per cent were licensed in Cook County, considerably under half the total in both instances.

If roadhouses in Cook County are outside town or village limits, they must be licensed by the Cook County Board of Supervisors. The Juvenile Protective Associa-

[19] Jessie F. Binford, "May We Present the Road House?" *Welfare Magazine* (July, 1927), pp. 5–6, 11.

[20] Jessie F. Binford, *op. cit.*, p. 4.

tion found that those places licensed by the Board were much more orderly and law abiding than those licensed by villages and towns.[21]

The number of roadhouses licensed by the Cook County Board, as given out by that office, for years from 1926 to 1930 are as follows:

Year	No.
1926	106
1927	145
1928	140
1929	124
1930	116

One is unable to tell what percentage of the total number of roadhouses in Cook County are licensed by the County Commissioners, due to the fact that their licenses by law only extend to roadhouses outside incorporated villages and townships. And one is also unable to tell what is the proportion of those actually licensed by the county to the total number of roadhouses existing outside incorporated villages and towns, in order to learn the percentage of license evasions.

If we disregard the number of county licensed roadhouses for 1926 (since that was the first year of operation under the new law), we notice that there has been a decline in the number of roadhouses licensed by Cook County from 1927 to 1930 (from 145 to 116). If as years pass there is a steady decline in the number of county licensed roadhouses, this fact may indicate that roadhouses seek the confines of incorporated places in order to escape supervision and to secure freer reign in business operations.

[21] *Ibid.,* pp. 4–5, 11.

THE OUTGOING PLEASURE TRAFFIC

The story of the occupation of the suburban territory by the underworld of the city is incomplete without some account of the patrons of the roadhouse. The point is that the pleasure-seeking public from the city proper, and even from the residential suburbs, has followed the underworld characters in their outward swing beyond the city limits. New patterns of "good time" or "wild party" have developed in keeping with the frontier atmosphere of the outskirts.

While levee characters and pleasure seekers have sought the freedom of the urban frontier, their outlying business and pleasure would have been practically impossible on any large scale without the automobile and paved highways. The easy accessibility has certainly enabled emigrant vice

TABLE 11

REGISTRATION OF MOTOR CARS IN THE UNITED STATES, 1895–1928*

1895	4	1912	902,600
1896	166	1913	1,194,262
1897	90	1914	1,625,739
1898	800	1915	2,309,666
1899	3,200	1916	3,297,996
1900	8,000	1917	4,657,340
1901	14,800	1918	5,621,617
1902	23,000	1919	6,771,074
1903	32,920	1920	8,225,853
1904	54,590	1921	9,346,195
1905	77,400	1922	10,864,128
1906	105,900	1923	13,479,608
1907	140,300	1924	15,460,649
1908	194,400	1925	17,512,638
1909	305,950	1926	19,237,171
1910	458,500	1927	20,219,224
1911	619,500	1928	21,379,125

* Taken from *Facts and Figures of the Automotive Industry* (National Automobile Chamber of Commerce, New York City),' 1929.

lords, inn keepers, gamblers, beer racketeers, slot machine syndicators to play host for the joy-thirsting public which owns or uses automobiles.

A glance at the motor car registrations in the United States will reveal the tremendous increase in the use of automobiles.

The passenger car registrations in Illinois and Chicago within the last decade likewise have far outstripped the growth in population.

TABLE 12

PASSENGER CAR REGISTRATIONS FOR THE CITY OF CHICAGO AND
THE STATE OF ILLINOIS, 1920–28*

Year	Chicago	Illinois
1920		504,250
1921		583,441
1922		682,250
1923	175,000	847,005
1924	218,991	978,428
1925	260,887	1,101,943
1926	289,948	1,195,897
1927	317,433	1,254,521
1928	335,263	1,314,003

* Taken from *Facts and Figures of the Automotive Industry* (National Automobile Chamber of Commerce, Inc., New York City), 1921–29.

The greatest use of the automobile has gone for pleasure and recreation, rather than business. Its increased use has meant that more and more city dwellers are able to seek diversions in the urban hinterland on the frontiers of social control.

SUMMARY

The principal facts from our study of roadhouses may be listed as follows:

1. According to recent investigation liquor violation is

the greatest while commercialized vice is the smallest problem (by numerical count) presented by roadhouses.

2. While the outskirts of cities have been historically regions for outlawed activity, repressive measures inside Chicago in recent years have been accompanied by an emigration of vice lords to the city's borders.

3. Chicago's beer and booze syndicates have extended their activities to the suburban regions, using the same tactics for control of areas there as in the city.

4. The city's hinterland, due to the lack of policing and to the lack of a vigorous public opinion in the sparsely settled outskirts of the city, has become a haven of vice.

5. Attempts at direct methods of control (through raids and prosecutions) have met with dubious success; for the emigrant vice lords have entrenched themselves in local politics and have used evasive measures just as they did in the city proper.

6. The control of roadhouses through license regulation has been beset with difficulties and evasions. Roadhouse keepers can go and have gone into incorporated villages which are favorable to them and where they are able to direct local policy, thus avoiding too much supervision by county commissioners.

7. The study of roadhouses as institutions of commercialized amusement which are able to take advantage of the socio-political situation in the hinterland, is only one part of the total picture of the roadhouse problem. The patronage must also be considered. The pleasure-hunting public has discovered the possibilities for sport in the outlying districts of an urban community where supervision and control over behavior are at the minimum. The increased use of automobiles and the development of good roads have made possible this outgoing pleasure traffic.

CHAPTER VI

UNORGANIZED VICE

One of the recent trends in prostitution has been the rise of an unregimented class of professional, semi-professional, and amateur prostitutes—women who have evolved a scheme of life and found an occupation outside the brothel. They have taken to street walking, rooming houses, hotels, assignation places, and call flats where prostitution is conducted on a more independent, clandestine basis. Brothel prostitution may be said to represent the organized business of vice, i.e., vice regimented by vice lords, panders, keepers, cadets, and political protectors; prostitution by independent and unregimented women may be considered by way of contrast as unorganized vice.

THE MODERN TREND

As clandestine prostitution has developed, the brothel has declined, if not in actual numbers, certainly in pre-eminence of the brothel type. The brothel was the asylum for the exploited, slave and outcast women. Havelock Ellis claims that the growing refinement of life, incident to urban civilization, has been responsible for the decline in this older and cruder system of prostitution.[1]

Whether the decline in brothel prostitution is actually based on the increasing refinements in the expression of sexual desires, or not, it is certain that the modern city with its changes in living conditions, in human relations, and in class attitudes has produced a new type of unregulated prostitution.

[1] Havelock Ellis, *Sex in Relation to Society*, p. 304.

TABLE 13

NUMBER AND PER CENT OF RESORTS IN CENTRALIZED AND DECENTRALIZED AREAS OF CHICAGO AS FOUND BY THE COMMITTEE OF FIFTEEN, 1914–29*

	1914		1915		1916		1917		1918		1919		1920		1921	
	No.	Per Cent	No.	Per Cent	No.	Per Cent	No.	Per Cent	No.	Per Cent	No.	Per Cent	No.	Per Cent	No.	Per Cent
Centralized Vice Areas																
Loop	29	10.7	24	9.3	10	3.5	32	8.4	22	6.6	29	9.6	12	4.1	14	3.7
Near South (22nd St.)	94	34.6	49	18.9	58	20.1	34	8.9	32	9.6	29	9.5	28	9.6	27	7.2
Near West	16	5.9	39	15.1	50	17.4	78	20.5	79	23.8	73	24.1	70	24.1	86	23.0
Lower North	53	19.5	37	14.3	76	26.4	97	25.5	43	13.0	45	14.9	57	19.6	45	12.0
Total	192	70.6	149	57.5	194	67.4	241	63.4	176	53.0	176	58.1	167	57.4	172	46.0
Decentralized Vice Areas																
Douglas	47	17.3	83	32.0	59	20.5	77	20.3	52	15.7	28	9.2	43	14.8	108	28.9
Oakland	5	1.8	8	3.1	7	2.4	13	3.4	18	5.4	14	4.6	12	4.1	6	1.6
Grand Boulevard	9	3.3	6	2.3	9	3.1	23	6.1	17	5.1	18	5.9	21	7.2	33	8.8
Kenwood	1	0.4	0	0.0	2	0.7	1	0.3	3	0.9	3	1.0	5	1.7	1	0.3
Washington Park	1	0.4	0	0.0	0	0.0	0	0.0	3	0.9	6	2.0	4	1.4	3	0.8
Lincoln Park	4	1.5	1	0.4	2	0.7	7	1.8	18	5.4	16	5.3	6	2.1	14	3.7
Lakeview	5	1.8	1	0.4	0	0.0	1	0.3	9	2.7	6	2.0	6	2.1	7	1.9
Uptown	0	0.0	1	0.4	0	0.0	1	0.3	6	1.8	11	3.6	9	3.1	7	1.9
Others	8	3.0	10	3.9	15	4.8	14	4.3	30	9.0	25	8.1	18	6.0	23	6.2
Total	80	29.4	110	42.5	94	32.5	139	36.6	156	47.0	127	41.9	124	42.6	202	54.0

* Based on Table 57.

TABLE 13—*Continued*

	1922		1923		1924		1925		1926		1927		1928		1929	
	No.	Per Cent	No.	Per Cent	No.	Per Cent	No.	Per Cent	No.	Per Cent	No.	Per Cent	No.	Per Cent	No.	Per Cent
Centralized Vice Areas																
Loop	19	4.9	21	6.9	14	5.9	10	2.6	12	2.7	4	0.9	7	1.5	5	1.1
Near South (22nd St.)	30	7.8	16	5.2	17	7.1	21	5.4	16	3.6	11	2.5	13	2.7	9	2.0
Near West	71	18.3	65	21.3	29	12.2	39	10.0	35	7.8	32	7.3	34	7.1	31	6.8
Lower North	29	7.5	30	9.8	15	6.3	27	6.9	32	7.2	68	15.4	64	13.3	33	7.2
Total	149	38.5	132	43.3	75	31.5	97	24.9	95	21.3	115	26.1	118	24.6	78	17.0
Decentralized Vice Areas																
Douglas	163	42.1	75	24.6	65	27.3	127	32.6	132	29.6	68	15.4	67	14.0	50	10.9
Oakland	8	2.1	1	0.3	5	2.1	9	2.3	6	1.3	10	2.3	5	1.0	6	1.3
Grand Boulevard	43	11.1	50	16.4	58	24.4	66	17.0	113	25.3	124	28.1	103	21.5	125	27.2
Kenwood	0	0.0	0	0.7	0	0.0	6	1.5	8	1.8	4	0.9	20	4.2	11	2.4
Washington Park	2	0.5	2	0.7	1	0.4	2	0.5	9	2.0	15	3.4	23	4.8	26	5.7
Lincoln Park	5	1.3	9	3.0	1	0.4	6	1.5	9	2.0	12	2.7	21	4.4	6	1.3
Lakeview	4	1.0	4	1.3	4	1.7	15	3.9	13	2.9	37	8.4	52	10.8	58	12.6
Uptown	5	1.3	12	3.9	19	8.0	39	10.0	47	10.5	45	10.2	60	12.5	96	20.9
Others	8	2.3	20	6.4	10	4.1	22	15.8	14	3.1	11	2.4	11	22.2	3	1.7
Total	238	61.5	173	56.7	163	68.5	292	75.1	351	78.7	326	73.9	362	75.4	381	83.0

Even during the period of brothels and the red light district this unorganized, clandestine vice was also obvious enough. The Vice Commission of Chicago called attention to the social evil outside red light resorts in its investigations of 1910. "New houses, especially in the flat buildings, are being established in residential districts to an alarming extent. In fact, there are more houses of this character in these sections of the city than in the so-called restricted districts."[2]

The closing of segregated vice districts was a spectacular public house cleaning which gave new impetus to changes already in progress. In New York City where suppression of brothel prostitution occurred earlier than in Chicago, there have been for thirty years few open houses of prostitution. Open prostitution has been succeeded by unorganized vice centering in cheap hotels, rooming houses, apartments, night clubs, and unobstructive street walking. In other American cities the immediate effect of closing red light areas has been the invasion of residential neighborhoods.

THE DECENTRALIZED OCCUPATION

In Chicago the steady decentralization of vice resorts is one index of the rise of more casual and less organized forms of prostitution. The addresses of resorts dealt with by the Committee of Fifteen for the last 15 years, shows a steady decline in the percentage of vice resorts in three central vice areas and increasing percentages in the number of resorts in the more outlying neighborhoods. Only the more important areas in which vice resorts have been

[2] *The Social Evil in Chicago* (1911), p. 72.

distributed in the period following public suppression are given in Table 13.[3]

The Committee of Fifteen cases for 1929 as classified by type of building in which resorts operated, indicated (Table 14, p. 142) that the overwhelming majority of resorts located in apartments and apartment hotels occurs in the same dispersed areas. About 99 per cent of the resorts found in apartment buildings (those with over six separate apartments), were distributed in the dispersed areas —9 per cent in the less and 90 per cent in the more decentralized areas of the city. Eighty-three per cent of the resorts discovered in apartment hotels were located in the (more) decentralized areas of Chicago. Seventy-four per cent of the resorts uncovered in flats (buildings with as high as six separate apartments), were distributed in the decentralized locations. The remaining 26 per cent of the resorts in flats were found in the centralized areas, mainly in the Near West Side and Lower North Side, particularly in the flats over business places on West Madison Street and North Clark Street. Sixty-six per cent of the prostitution in the centralized areas was located in hotels. These are the cheap, shady hotels of the Loop, North Clark Street (Lower North Side) and West Madison and Halsted Streets (Near West Side).

A significant point brought out in Table 15 (p. 143) is that the occupancy of "houses" is now about 5 per cent;

[3] The decentralization of vice resorts in neighborhoods on the further West Side, the Northwest, and the Southwest sides has been almost negligible.

TABLE 14

CENTRALIZED AND DECENTRALIZED DISTRIBUTION OF TYPES OF RESIDENCES AT WHICH EVIDENCE OF THE PRACTICE OF PROSTITUTION WAS FOUND BY THE COMMITTEE OF FIFTEEN'S INVESTIGATIONS DURING 1929*

	Hse.		H.		F.		A.		H.A		TOTAL	
	No.	Per Cent	No.	Per Cent	No.	Per Cent	No.	Per Cent	No.	Per Cent	No.	Per Cent
Centralized Areas												
Loop	0	0.0	5	13.9	0	0.0	0	0.0	0	0.0	5	1.0
Near South	0	0.0	6	16.7	3	1.8	0	0.0	0	0.0	9	2.0
Near West	1	4.6	9	25.0	19	11.3	1	0.5	1	8.3	31	6.8
Lower North	5	22.7	4	11.1	22	13.1	1	0.5	1	8.3	33	7.2
Total	6	27.3	24	66.7	44	26.2	2	1.0	2	16.6	78	17.0
Decentralized Areas (less)												
Douglas	12	54.5	2	5.5	20	11.9	16	7.2	0	0.0	50	10.9
Oakland	2	9.1	1	2.8	1	0.6	2	0.9	0	0.0	6	1.3
Lincoln	0	0.0	0	0.0	4	2.4	2	0.9	0	0.0	6	1.3
Total	14	63.6	3	8.3	25	14.9	20	9.0	0	0.0	62	13.5
Decentralized Areas (more)												
Grand Boulevard	0	0.0	0	0.0	50	29.8	75	33.5	0	0.0	125	27.2
Kenwood	0	0.0	0	0.0	1	0.6	10	4.5	0	0.0	11	2.4
Washington Park	1	4.5	1	2.8	13	7.7	11	5.0	0	0.0	26	5.7
Lakeview	0	0.0	2	5.6	10	5.9	45	20.4	1	8.3	58	12.6
Uptown	1	4.5	6	16.6	24	14.3	57	25.8	8	66.7	96	20.9
Others	0	0.0	0	0.0	1	0.6	1	0.5	1	8.3	3	0.7
Total	2	9.1	9	25.0	99	58.9	199	90.0	10	83.3	319	69.5
Grand Total	22	100.0	36	100.0	168	100.0	221	100.0	12	100.0	459	100.0

*Hse.—House, H.—Hotel, F.—Flat, A.—Apartment building, over 6 separate apartments, A.H.—Apartment Hotel. These are the Chicago Committee of Fifteen's definitions.

while the occupancy of flats and apartments has come into the big majority (about 85 per cent).

TABLE 15

NUMBER AND PER CENT OF TYPES OF BUILDINGS OCCUPIED BY
RESORTS IN CHICAGO ACCORDING TO COMMITTEE OF
FIFTEEN INVESTIGATIONS DURING 1929

	No.	Per Cent
House...................	22	4.8
Hotel...................	36	7.8
Flat....................	168	36.6
Apartment.............	221	48.2
Apt. hotel.............	12	2.6
Total.............	459	100.0

In Chicago the decline in the occupancy of "houses" is correlated with the decline in the proportional number of resorts in the centralized areas (since 1912) and a corresponding increase in decentralized areas. When these neighborhoods at the center deteriorated, residences left vacant were occupied by the advancing slum population, and were incorporated in the areas of segregated vice. When the more outlying areas of Chicago began to develop as residential centers, large flat and apartment buildings—the modern residences—were erected. With the growth of the city's business centers these flats and apartments became the havens for unorganized vice.[4]

[4] The fact that Table 14 shows 51 per cent of the "houses" in the decentralized area of Douglas is not contrary to the foregoing conclusions. "Douglas" as well as "Oakland" (see Table 14) are fast becoming centralized areas; for the central business district is moving in their direction and is pushing the slum right on them. When they were built up originally, they were areas of "homes" and consequently we should expect them to rate high in "houses" as against other types of resort occupancy.

The anonymous and mobile populations in large flats and apartment houses in these more outlying areas have favored the existence of unorganized vice resorts.

DIFFERENTIAL RATES IN PERSISTENCE

The growth of unorganized vice in Chicago is not merely indicated by the increase in the number and per cent of resorts found in decentralized neighborhoods, but also by differential rates of persistence, that is, the average number of days resorts have been found to be operating in the centralized as compared with decentralized areas. Mr. Charles E. Miner, general director of the Committee of Fifteen of Chicago, has checked the average number of days which 353 vice resorts have managed to run from the first to last appearance on the Committee's records in the various areas of Chicago. The results are given in Table 16, p. 145. It will be seen that the resorts in the centralized vice areas have an average persistence rate of 603 days; those in the less decentralized areas, 122; those in the still more decentralized areas, 73 days. The average for the whole city was found to be 174 days.

These differentials in persistence of the centralized and of decentralized vice resorts bear out what would be expected of the highly organized as contrasted to the less organized prostitution. The central vice areas in Chicago are the habitat of an organized underworld where the business of vice is conducted on a syndicated basis. The conditions in these areas are thus favorable to greater resistance and consequently greater persistence. The more unorganized prostitution has less resistance and hence a much lower persistence rate.

TABLE 16

PERSISTENCE RATE OF 353 RESORTS CLOSED BY THE COMMITTEE OF
FIFTEEN, CHICAGO, 1929

	No. of Resorts	No. of Days	Average No. of Days
Centralized Areas			
Loop...................	2	9,027	4,514
Near South..............	7	7,988	1,141
Near West..............	18	9,316	518
Lower North............	19	1,406	74
Total..................	46	27,737	603
Decentralized Areas (less)			
Douglas.................	38	4,768	125
Oakland.................	6	1,220	203
Lincoln.................	7	237	39
Total..................	51	6,225	122
Decentralized Areas (more)			
Grand Boulevard..........	136	12,492	92
Kenwood.................	5	274	55
Hyde Park...............	2	188	94
Lakeview................	32	2,330	73
Uptown.................	76	3,122	41
Total..................	251	18,406	73
Not included.............	5	9,014	1,803
Total..............	353	61,382	174

UNREGIMENTED GIRLS

The decentralized vice resorts are the rendezvous of the rising and increasing class of the independent, the emancipated, the clandestine prostitutes who want the "life" without its stigma and hardships. The longest hours, the poorest pay for service, the lowest type of clientele and the most odious working conditions are likewise found in the shops of syndicated vice in the centralized areas. Easier and more refined working conditions and a higher type of patronage can be commanded as an independent in an apartment. The type of girl who maintains the greatest independence and the greatest anchorage with respectability is the "call girl." She works when she pleases; she may have vocational and domestic interests outside her small business of prostitution; she preserves only a telephone connection with the place of resort and lives elsewhere. Such a girl is at best an amateur or a semi-professional.

Even professionals in unorganized resorts live a freer and more independent existence in their apartments and flats. The case of Millicent (given below), is probably typical of the women no longer outcasts, who have assumed a rôle in our pecuniary society, approaching that of the free women of Greece, the *hetaerae*.

AN UNREGIMENTED PROFESSIONAL: MILLICENT'S OWN STORY

Yes, I've been in the game twelve years now. I'm only twenty-eight. Started when I was sixteen in New York City. Met a girl there who put me wise on the hotels and how to play that game. This went on for a year and then I was caught and sent up for a year. So I got out of New York and went South to San Antonio. Set myself up in a fine apartment and had four girls working for me. I made lots of money and saved it too. Then I went to Des Moines. Business was poor and I hooked up with a burlesque troupe doing a specialty number—song and dance skit. I always could sing and sang the Blues numbers like nobody's business. I had sung in cafés in New York. No, I had no training for voice. It just came natural with me. The company left Des Moines and we made a lot of Western towns. Finally I came to Chicago—about six years ago. I booked in as an entertainer and played around a number of cabarets. But that was one awful hard life. It paid fairly well—$75 a week 'cause I was doing high class stuff. That life got me down. The hours were long and tiresome. The worst of it was you smoked yourself to death and inhaled a lot of bad air all night long. And besides they'd expect you to sit down at the tables and that meant a continuous round of highballs and gin. I never made the tables and never collected handouts from the boys. That's the cheap entertainer for you and I never had to make a few paltry dollars a night that way. Oh! Yes, I made a little on the side from a little party or two. All told I netted very little. It costs a lot to keep up a cabaret appearance. Above all else—whether you are good or have a good act—you've got to look like something. And that takes much, much clothes.

So I quit this and went in for myself at my own apartment. No, I never hustled for anyone but my own self. You would never get me into a regular joint. Why do you know there are plenty girls— and good looking ones at that—who hustle at $2 joints. And do you know what they get? Ninety cents a trick. A dollar ten goes to the house. Imagine it! Not me. Three years of that life would make an old woman out of anybody. Look at me! I don't look worn out, do I? How old do you think I am? No, I'm twenty-eight. Would you believe it? A few years ago I was getting a few gray hairs for some reason or other. And so I had it dyed blonde. I think it becomes me. I had dark auburn hair before I changed.

For the last eighteen months I had my own apartment up on X.X. avenue [North Side—near Sheridan Road in the Lakeview district]. I ran it all alone and had nobody else with me except Buddy. Made money and saved it. I was in with the cabbies. They knew my number and sent me up a lot of tricks. They get $2 out of every $5 spent, you know. If they don't trust you, they will stick around and collect then and there. But I always had them come back in the morning and get their money. I didn't want them ringing the bell any more than was necessary. But they're a dumb lot. They send up just anybody. They're just as liable to send up some spy, reformer or plain clothes man. They can't tell the difference. I'm through with them now. I won't take business that way any more. It's too risky.

I've been in the Morals Court 11 times here in Chicago. Got picked up here and there. Never much trouble though. And I was in my last flat eighteen months and did not have a bit of trouble from police. No, I paid no cop to lay off. I'd rather take the "pinch" than pay one of the rotters. I never paid for any protection and I don't intend to. You've got to be intelligent at this game just like in any other business. And if you can keep just one step ahead, you can beat the game hands down.

I gave up the apartment. I didn't have to get out, mind you, but thought it best in the end. One night I had a high class trick from New York. He had a well-to-do friend with him—a lawyer and an attorney from the East somewhere—I guess it was New York. I served them up some good drinks and they asked me to call in some girls. They evidently thought I was just a "hostess." The first man took the one to the room twice and I collected $3 each time. The attorney just wanted to talk to the girl. He gave her a break though —$25 she got for sitting on the sofa listening to him talk. Well, the girl who did business thought I held out money on her and got sore at me. I didn't know it at the time 'cause I play fair with everybody. Anyway one evening she got pinched and squealed on me. Told one of the plain clothes men and he came over. I didn't know him. He came up and I looked at him thru the open door—I had the chain bolt on. I thought there was something wrong with him. He said that Bob sent him. He said you know Bob—the cab starter over here. I knew him, of course, but thought the fellow was a cop and said no you've got the wrong place I don't know no Bob. Well, he said that's funny. Isn't your name Gerry—that's my other name. I said well what if it is or what if it ain't? What's that got to do with you? What do you want, anyhow? So I got hauled into court and sent down to the Health Department. And those darn fools reported back positive on a smear. Imagine it. Well, they shipped me to Lawndale for two weeks. I had to wait until I showed 6 negative slides in succession. I knew I had no active infection. Oh, how I hate that place. They poke at you in a way that would make anyone come due and they call themselves doctors. God what a foul place.

I'm not anxious to have a quantity of business. It's the quality that counts—men who pay well. I had an old papa, worth a lot of jack, who used to come up to see me. Took a likin' to me, I guess. He was about 58. The first party he gave me $50. After that when he used to come up—that's when I was in the apartment where I was squealed on—I would disconnect the door bell. I needed no more business that night. The next party, he gave me $61. He came up for dinner the next time and stayed until 4 A. M. and left me $50. That's the kind to get. Quality.

Charity! Hm! Well this is what I think about that. It's for green girls who want to be shown a good time. Not for me. You'd starve to death. I picked up a fellow in a beautiful car awhile back and he said "Let's go out to the Lincoln Tavern." I sized him up as another one of these guys who wants it for nothing or expects something for buying a girl a little food and dancing her around a bit. So I said "Look here, baby, let's you and I talk the same language." I said, "I have to make my living. I get much food at home and if I want to dance, I turn on the radio. No, no Lincoln Tavern for me. If you're interested in my kind of party, it's O. K. with me." Well he said, "I'd spend 50 bucks on having a good time but as for paying for it—I'm through with that." And then I said, "That's where you and I part, so leave me out and God bless you."

I don't mind keeping house. I do all my own work. No, no maids. I wouldn't have one. They're too nosey and talk too much on the outside. I have a lot of pretty things at home and keep them well. I do everything at home except the laundry and I send that out. And I rather enjoy it. I like to cook, and can I cook? You should ask Buddy. When I met him he only weighed 118 pounds and now you should see him—160. He's had a lot of good food, you see. I've lived with Buddy for some time now and we get along fine. No, he doesn't bring me tricks. I don't want that kind of a man. He makes his living and I make mine. He gives me $10 a week toward the food and a little on the rent. But he's got it hard and makes very little in commissions. He drives a yellow cab and it's pretty darn hard to make much. There's too many cabs and not enough people who use them in Chicago. He eats his meals at home and he works the night shift—gets off about 3 A. M. He'll drop home for his supper about 7:30. Tonight I've made him some good bean soup. Buddy's about 37 and he's a good kid. He used to work around 3X St. when it was white. He entertained a little, ran a few errands and later opened up a smoke shop with a little game in the rear. Well his health broke down from all that bad air and the doctor said he'd have to work outside or it would be just too bad. So he quit and is now driving a cab. I got a letter from his mother the other day. She writes "Dear Kids, I'm comin' on to see you." It's O. K. with me. I invited her. She'll only stay a couple of days and I'll manage fine.

I've been married twice and divorced both of them. The first one batted me around too much. The second was an oil man down in Texas. He was just a "farmer" at first and then got "wised up" all of a sudden. He got running around and then started to take dope. I put him in the hospital twice and I paid for it myself. The last time he got down on his knees and said he would lay off forever. But he went right back on. So I left him. Oh, I might get married again, if I could find the right man to keep me.

No, I have never had syphilis. It pays to be clean. Thank God. Never had anything in the blood and don't expect to. I look at every man I see. If they don't look right, I give him his money back and say this is where you and I stop.

When I got out of Lawndale I found out who squealed. I called that girl up—and did I land into her. She said she'd get her husband after me. Her husband—imagine. Why he's a thin consumptive bozo. I said let him talk to Buddy and they did over the phone. Buddy said he'd meet him anywhere with the fists. He said it'd be guns or nothing. So the matter dragged along until one evening Buddy and I were sitting with a party in the lobby of the hotel (an apartment hotel), playing rummy. And who should come in but that consumptive man of the squealer. He called Buddy out. Buddy fanned him on the right side but he forgot to fan him on the left hip. They went out and Buddy knocked him for a row. When he came to he pulled out the gat. And I ran between it and Buddy. And so he hauled off and hit Buddy with the butt end over the eye. It left a big scar. She and her man got away in a hurry. I never could find them after that.

After coming out of Lawndale I came up for my booking at court and was dismissed. I decided to move. If I had stayed on at the old place I was sure they would get me 'cause the police now had the number. So I got completely out. Changed my name and telephone number. And now no more cab drivers bringing in tricks. I'm through with that game. I'll build up my trade alone and keep all my profits instead of splitting 2 out of 5. It's going to be a little

slow at first but it'll come all right. I called up some of my old reliable friends and told them where they could get me. And no more
business in the flat. I take the trick to another place I know that's
safe as a church. No more business at home. If I get caught, I can
give my address as any place. And they can't get me for running a
house. And another thing. No more selling of liquor. I never did
like to drink. I just had it around 'cause the men would always be
asking for some and I could make extra money. But no more liquor.
It's too risky. It's all right if the "city" pinches you but if you are
taken by the federal, goodbye!

Millicent is, no doubt, for one in her profession, an unusual woman. But she is, at the same time, a type—a new
type—intelligent, sophisticated, independent, a product of
the emancipation and the individualization of women; of
the abolition of the segregated vice district and the caste of
the painted lady.

She is quite aware that she is playing a desperate game,
but she is cautious, takes no unnecessary risks, guards her
health, and expects to beat it. She is not without some
domestic interests; she saves her money and above all
preserves her individual freedom.

Lillian, whose story is told in the following pages, is a
woman of a different sort. She is neither as intelligent
nor as sophisticated as Millicent, and she does not expect
as much of life. At any rate she is not exploited. Her
"cadet" makes his own money.

Lillian was born in Detroit. She came to Chicago to get a job.
She was a waitress in Detroit and also in Chicago, working in first
class restaurants. She was 22 at the time she came to Chicago. Lillian went to live in a small West Side Hotel. It was at this hotel
that she met Charley and Charley was a pimp. He gave her the
usual line: Why should an attractive girl wear herself out all day
long when there's an easier and better way? And so Lillian started
living with Charley. This was her first time for money. She wasn't

a "good" girl when she met Charley. She had men in Detroit. But I give you her exact words: She said, "I gave thousands of dollars away before I knew it was worth a dollar."

Two weeks after she met Charley, he got her placed with Isabelle who was hustling for Joe in a little flat on the West Side.

Lillian went to high school but she did not graduate. She is not what one would call a bright girl. In fact, she is just a little dull. She is tall, blonde and very pleasing to look at. She reads the Motion Picture Magazine and all the heavily illustrated periodicals and once in a while a detective story. She has read The Well of Loneliness. (Most of these girls like books dealing with sex problems.)

Lillian and Charley get along well together. He seldom beats her. Once after an argument he struck her with a curtain pole on the leg. She threatened to leave him and he made up to her by giving her a fur coat and everything went along lovely after that.

The flat Lillian works in is a $2 joint and gets largely a Jewish trade. She has laid off from work only 23 days in the 7 months she has been hustling. This is exclusive of her disabilities which last 3 days. That makes an additional 21 days. So out of the 7 months she has been off work 44 days. During this time she has earned $1,365. She showed me her book in which she keeps pretty accurate account of her earnings.

Now let's figure her expenses because I think they indicate something very significant. She pays $18 per week for their room and bath at the hotel. That would make $504 for 7 months. The rest we will figure at the very minimum.

Lillian pays very little for breakfast and lunch. She eats lunch at the flat and this costs her very little. Then at night she and Charley eat dinner together at a dollar restaurant. She finishes work at 9 o'clock at night and he meets her. Let's say she spends $3 per day on food which takes care of very little more than the evening meal they have together. That would make $630. She must buy one pair of stockings a week, say at $1.50 a pair. That would make $42 for 7 months. And underwear is even more important. Let's say she spends $1 per week for undergarments. This is all much lower than I believe a girl like Lillian really spends on clothes and finery. $1 per week would make $28 for 7 months. She must have a lot of nice dresses for the street—let's say she bought 4 dresses at

$15 per. I think it would be 6 during that time (they're extravagant, you know) but let's say 4. That would be $60 for 7 months. And this is exclusive of the cheap house dresses and aprons but we won't count them. We'll allow her 4 pairs of shoes at $5 ($20). Then her beauty parlor bill must be included. She's had one permanent wave ($10) and goes to the beauty parlor once a week— (she has told me all this)—and gets a manicure and shampoo and all the other things. Let's say this comes to $2 a week or $56. Then she must ride in cabs at the slightest provocation, especially in rainy weather and to come to town (which is about twice a week). We'll say she spends $3 per week on cabs which is probably very much lower than a girl like Lillian spends on cabs. That would make $84. And then, I forgot hats. She likes lots of them, but we'll allow her 3 for the 7 months at $5 each or $15. And let's put in $25 for paint, powder and perfume which she likes in great quantities and expensive varieties. And then I haven't figured in magazines, doctor's bills, cigarettes and other trifles which a luxury-loving woman must always be buying. Let's allow $125 for these.

Well, there you are, $1,095 for her own expenses and I said she only took in $1,365 in 7 months. Add to this the $100 for the fur coat which Charley gave her and which undoubtedly came out of her earnings she turns over to him. And she also told me today she had just sent $20 home to her mother for Christmas. That's $1,215.

Well now, what's left for Charley out of the $1,365? His expenses are high. I know these fellows. They must dress well and they drink a lot. I know Charley consumes plenty of liquor. You know a pimp is a man of leisure and his kind of man must have money to support his style. It must take at least $5 a day over and above his food and shelter which he gets from her to keep him going. So you see he can't really live off her and her earnings. Where do you suppose he gets it from? I know one thing he doesn't get it from any other girl. He's only got Lillian. I know many more cases of girls and their men who come to me who live just about the same. I would call this a marriage of convenience—yes, even a companionate marriage. She makes her expenses and he makes his. And together they get along better than separate.[5]

[5] The physician who relates this case treats a great many prostitutes and their men in Chicago. He knows their lives well; he is a confidant

CAB DRIVERS AS RUNNERS

In the days of the red light districts hack drivers and "cabbies"—both horse and automobile—who were expected to know the town, frequently acted as guides to visitors in the segregated areas. After the period of suppression, cab drivers assumed a new and important rôle. They became runners and steerers for resorts which were on the move so frequently that their exact whereabouts were no longer known. Especially was this true in the decentralized areas, where the unorganized business of prostitution had to rely on personal connections with cabbies, hotel clerks, and café and cabaret attachés and waiters. During the last ten years in Chicago the usual commission to a cab driver who delivered a customer was $2.00.

Taxicab running for the unorganized prostitution seems to have reached its height about 1923 in Chicago and has been declining since then. The main reason seems to be that cab drivers did not exercise the proper caution and discrimination and frequently exposed these unregulated women to the investigators of law-enforcing agencies. Sometimes there were misunderstandings about commission and cab drivers became reformers.

A minor reason for the decline in taxicab running is the danger to cab drivers themselves of exposure involving as it does the risk of having their numbers turned in to the company or in the case of an independent driver of being haled into court. A partial check-up on the cab situation was made by the Committee of Fifteen during the week

---

and father confessor to many of them. They tell him their stories and the every-day incidents in their lives. He is interested in their sociology.

ending December 7, 1929. A number of cab men including Yellows, Checkers, Deluxe, and independents were approached by investigators at cab stands throughout the city. Sixty-five answers were obtained; 31 (48 per cent) had no information as to resorts; 5 (8 per cent) had merely general locations; 1 (1 per cent) had a specific address; 5 (8 per cent) mentioned specific addresses, but suggested that the parties may have moved; 3 (5 per cent) knew of specific addresses which were closed; 8 (12 per cent) claimed "it was a tight town" which answer should be added to 31 (48 per cent) "no information" to make the latter 39 (60 per cent); 10 (15 per cent) suggested riding about for a street pick up; 2 (3 per cent) insisted they did not run for resorts at all. It should be remembered that these findings were obtained during the wide-open-town régime of Mayor Thompson.

STREET WALKERS AS INDEPENDENTS

In the past "street walkers" have been mainly those prostitutes whom the brothels for one reason or another had rejected. Often they were the "hags" of the streets. Often they were lonely individualists of the underworld, who preferred to make their own way.

Next to beckoning from doorways and windows, street walking was the most obvious form of solicitation. When prostitutes were "painted ladies" whose caste was obvious even if their street conduct had been modest and discreet, street walking, from the police standpoint, was easy to detect and easy to curb.

The status of street walkers in contrast to that of the women in established houses was precarious. At any moment they might be ordered off the streets, rounded up for vagrancy and disorderly conduct, or induced to make contributions to police benefits or political campaigns. During the red light days, before the World's Fair and after, a fairly consistent policy was maintained by police administration in order, as far as possible, to keep street walkers out of the "Loop." This measure was based on the same principle as the police measure which attempted to curb soliciting from doorways and windows of houses on the routes of the principal street car lines running to and from the Loop. While street walking was, on the grounds of public decency, more or less suppressed in Chicago's central business district, it was also supervised and controlled in the areas in which organized vice had its brothels. Sometimes this control was a mere political gesture; at other times, the street walking was suppressed in the interest of organized vice, since street walking was regarded as unfair competition.[6]

In any case, in Chicago, before the inauguration of suppression of houses of prostitution, street solicitation constituted the bulk of the "vice" cases in the municipal courts of Chicago. Since that time (1912) it has become an almost negligible factor in the total sum of cases in this category.

It appears that street walking, in the technical sense, at least, has diminished during the period covered in this record. From 1908 to 1912, when the arrests of street walkers were most numerous, segregated brothels were tolerated, more or less, by both public and police. Street walking was irregular and efforts were made to suppress it. After 1912 the cases against houses of prostitution, both inmates as well as keepers, grew in number.

[6] *Illinois Crime Survey* (1929).

TABLE 17

STREET SOLICITING: NUMBER OF ARRESTS BY POLICE AND CASES
DISPOSED OF BY MUNICIPAL COURT, CHICAGO. 1906–29

Year	S.F.P.†	Total Arrests	Per Cent	N.W.†	Total Cases Disposed	Per Cent
1906..........	2437	91,554	2.7	....	....	....
1907..........	897	63,132	1.4	....	....	....
1908..........	1731	68,220	2.5	1664	‡74,930	2.2
1909..........	1778	70,575	2.5	1665	78,371	2.1
1910..........	1619	81,269	2.0	1619	87,922	1.8
1911..........	1730	84,838	2.0	1633	92,730	1.8
1912..........	1516	86,950	1.7	1659	106,369	1.4
1913..........	1645	109,764	1.5	1846	121,333	1.5
1914..........	2006	116,895	1.7	2093	134,048	1.6
1915..........	2079	121,714	1.7	2254	130,971	1.7
1916..........	742	111,527	0.7	834	123,873	0.7
1917..........	537	137,910	0.4	502	149,268	0.3
1918..........	476	110,819	0.4	613	124,397	0.5
1919..........	202	96,676	0.2	210	111,276	0.2
1920..........	167	94,453	0.2	195	103,150	0.2
1921..........	597	125,843	0.5	571	162,190	0.4
1922..........	549	143,185	0.4	536	184,362	0.3
1923..........	387	192,278	0.2	429	219,705	0.2
1924..........	498	256,345	0.2	575	279,960	0.2
1925..........	97	282,260	*	29	317,352	*
1926..........	115	281,268	*	52	324,444	*
1927..........	794	223,848	0.4	677	296,082	0.2
1928..........	745	168,784	0.4	713	251,370	0.3
1929..........	319	212,426	0.2	288	224,725	*

* Less than one-tenth of 1 per cent.
† S.F.P. is "soliciting for prostitution," which is the classification containing street soliciting as used in the police reports. N.W. is "night walker" which is the classification under which are put the street soliciting cases in the Municipal Court Reports. It may be that night walker harks back to a time when "vagrant" women primarily walked the streets at night plying their trade.
‡ The Municipal Court was not organized prior to this time.

Throughout the whole period from 1908 to 1929, there was this inverse relation between the number of street walking cases in court, and the number of cases against persons in houses of prostitution. In any given year as street walking goes up, the brothels go down; if the latter drops off, the former rises.

Note also the decreasing percentage which street walking cases comprise of the total number of quasi-criminal cases disposed of in the Morals Court as well as for all branches of the Municipal Court (1914–29).[7]

TABLE 18

NUMBER AND PER CENT OF STREET SOLICITING AMONG THE QUASI-CRIMINAL CASES DISPOSED OF IN THE TOTAL MUNICIPAL COURT AND MORALS COURT OF CHICAGO, 1914–28

YEAR	N.W.	QUASI-CRIMINAL	PER CENT	N.W.	QUASI-CRIMINAL	PER CENT
	Municipal Court (all branches)			Morals Branch		
1914..........	2,093	104,115	2.0	2,085	12,007	17.3
1915..........	2,254	99,134	2.3	2,016	11,828	17.0
1916..........	834	91,271	0.9	579	5,765	10.0
1917..........	502	109,759	0.5	308	5,940	5.2
1918..........	613	91,041	0.7	395	5,044	7.8
1919..........	210	76,480	0.3	203	3,754	5.4
1920..........	195	69,719	0.3	182	4,099	4.4
1921..........	*	111,882	....	*	5,474	....
1922..........	536	122,792	0.4	525	6,322	8.3
1923..........	429	149,742	0.3	392	6,135	6.4
1924..........	575	197,956	0.3	547	8,913	6.1
1925..........	61	223,617	†	55	4,792	1.1
1926..........	52	233,684	†	40	5,553	0.7
1927..........	677	205,736	0.3	408	9,002	4.5
1928..........	713	166,790	0.4	595	8,608	6.9
Total......	9,744	1,941,816‡	0.5	8,330	97,762‡	8.5

* Not included because inaccurately reported in the Municipal Court report for 1921.
† Less than one-tenth of 1 per cent.
‡ Total is exclusive of the figure for 1921.

That cases of "night walkers" should show a decreasingly yearly percentage of the total number of quasi-criminal cases disposed of in the Municipal Court as a whole was, perhaps, to be expected. But the fact that

[7] It will be noted that the Morals Court disposed of the great bulk of cases against street walkers. This particular branch of the Municipal Court of Chicago was established to handle vice cases principally.

this trend is equally apparent in the Morals Court—the branch of the Municipal Court expressly established to deal with cases of commercialized prostitution—indicates clearly that street walking is becoming less and less a police and court problem. In fact, there are certain factors in the present situation which tend to make it disappear as an obviously detectable form of prostitution. One of these is the changed street manners and public life of women in general. The "painted lady" is no longer so obvious as she was. The dress and manners of street walkers no longer distinguishes them as they once did from the rest of the female population. Respectable women do not have to be accompanied downtown. The unescorted girl is no longer suspected. The increase in street flirtations shields the street walker from public detection. Modern women conduct themselves in public in ways that a few years ago were permitted only to the demi-monde. On the other hand, the "original" women of the streets have also refined their manners and subtilized their approach to men.

PUBLIC DANCE HALLS: THEN—NOW.

One of the principal rendezvous of the unregimented prostitutes in the red light days was the public dance hall. Since 1910, the social agencies and law-enforcement bodies have improved the character of, and more or less legitimized, public dancing. Changes in manners which have permitted greater freedom in public to women and girls have contributed. No doubt this new freedom and the new promiscuity have their demoralizing consequences, but acts which do not involve loss of status, but merely physical damage or economic waste, are not as disastrous as they would otherwise be if they wrecked the career of the person involved.

Only recently (during April, 1930) the Committee of Fifteen made a survey of 118 dance halls in response to the statement "that several dance halls are being used to promote commercialized prostitution."

Investigation was made during April, at such times as might be available, at all the 118 addresses listed in the winter (1930) issue of the *Chicago Red Book* [classified telephone directory] as dance halls, dance academies, etc. Seven of these addresses were found to be large ball rooms, 52 were private schools for dancing instruction, stage dancing, including ballet dancing, and 4 were taxi dance halls in which girls were employed to dance with any men who might visit the premises in return for compensation of 50 per cent of the charge to the patron which in each instance was 10 cents for each dance. While several leads were secured there was no immediate securing of competent evidence of commercialized prostitution at any of the 118 addresses visited during this investigation. It seems clear that opportunities for public dancing are not widely used for the direct promotion of commercialized prostitution in Chicago.[8]

THE TAXI-DANCE HALL

Most public dance halls in Chicago would probably be given a clean bill of health by most social agencies, so far as concerns the charge that they encourage prostitution or allow prostitutes on the premises. On the other hand, social welfare workers have suspected the "closed" dance hall—the taxi-dance hall—of being organized in the interest of commercialized vice. But a recent investigation of these places by the Committee of Fifteen (made May 20 to June 15, 1930) was entirely negative

[8] From a *Memorandum to the Directors,* "A Report on Current Activities," dated May 27, 1930, submitted by Charles E. Miner, general director of the Committee of Fifteen, Chicago.

for evidence of prostitution. Not a single instance of a solicitation from any of the dancing instructresses was obtained, although the investigators let it be known with every girl they danced (and they danced with all of them) that they were looking for a "party." This particular investigation covered six taxi-dance halls—each of which was visited three times by investigators. Four of the six operated continuously, while two skipped Sunday nights. The first two visits were of an hour to an hour and a half duration. At the third and last visit the investigator stayed from opening to closing time.

Mr. Cressey in his study of *The Taxi-Dance Hall* lists 21 successful and 15 unsuccessful taxi-dance halls, which operated at one time or another in Chicago from 1927 to 1930. The number operating at any given time was much smaller than these totals for the four years. In 1927 there were 15 successful closed dance halls and by successful is meant that they did not go out of business during the year. In 1930 there were only 6 dance halls of this type.[9] This decline in number is accounted for in part by competitive elimination and integration among the halls themselves and in part by the pressure of law-enforcing bodies to bring them under close supervision and control.

In view of the investigations of the Committee of Fifteen the popular impression that the closed dance hall is a place where young girls are exploited for prostitution or where they even practice prostitution seems to be

[9] Paul C. Cressey, *The Taxi-Dance Hall* (University of Chicago Press, 1932), map opposite p. 224; see also his earlier statement of this problem, "The Closed Dance Hall." M. A. Thesis, University of Chicago, August, 1929, pp. 109–10.

mistaken. This conclusion is likewise borne out by the data collected by Cressey, who says:

> The marked similarity between the social situation of the taxi-dancer and the prostitute is at least a partial explanation for the universal belief that much regular prostitution is to be found in the taxi-dance hall. Actually, however, the professional prostitute is seldom discovered in a taxi-dance hall. While promiscuous sex behavior and extra-marital alliances of varying types are all too frequent, prostitution of the older forms is not common.[10]

No doubt the taxi-dancer, like the chorus girl, succeeds by her sex appeal, but she is at any rate a free agent. She is not exploited or forced to play the sex game by the dance hall operators. The fact that young girls can dance professionally and promiscuously in public places whose patrons are limited to men, without totally losing caste and without sinking to the level of a common prostitute, is some indication of the profound changes in manners and habits which thus came about since the red light districts were wiped out and women achieved in their sex relation something of the freedom of men. The same changes have enabled young girls to frequent the business places of men, their barber shops, their race tracks, gambling parlors, cigar stores, and share with them rough sports formerly permitted to men only. The important thing is that women now can enter this man's world and return. In the red light days many entered but few returned. Cressey, who has studied the taxi-dance hall intensively, indicates that the instructresses, no matter how young and tender, do not inevitably become outcasts. They are not enslaved or doomed to continue the career,

[10] *Cressey, The Taxi-Dance Hall* (Chicago, 1932), pp. 264–65.

no more than the woman who occasionally and casually sells her favors.[11]

SUMMARY

In this chapter we have presented pertinent material on vice conditions as they exist today in Chicago outside the realm of syndicated brothels. Attention has been called to the following facts:

1. There has been a tendency towards the decline of brothel prostitution in modern times.

2. Unorganized prostitution (outside of brothels) has developed in flats and apartments of Chicago's decentralized areas.

3. The operation of independent flats and apartments is in keeping with the trend away from brothel exploitation and the avoidance of identification with a prostitute class.

4. Recent check-ups have shown that cab running for flats or any resorts for that matter is not very prevalent.

5. Street walking, which in the past has represented the *modus operandi* of unregimented prostitutes, has become a much less obvious and detectable form of law violation.

6. Dance halls, which used to be the stamping grounds for professional and semi-professional prostitutes, are practically free from prostitutes and solicitation for commercialized vice.

7. Contrary to popular impression, studies have shown that the taxi-dance halls are not agencies for the exploitation of prostitution and that the sex problems of instructresses at taxi-dance halls in the main lie outside the realm of commercialized vice.

[11] *Ibid.*, p. 84.

CHAPTER VII

THE COMPOSITION OF THE POPULATION IN THE VICE AREAS

Human beings tend to find somewhere in the urban environment the particular milieu which conforms to their interest, temperament, or condition. Urban areas tend to achieve, therefore, a distinct sociological character because they attract persons who subscribe to the same scheme of life or are subject to the same conditions. Hobohemia, Greenwich Village, ghettoes, black belts, bright light areas, dormitory suburbs are cases in point. Vice areas are no exception to the rule.

A vice area not only attracts kindred spirits but also converts over to the scheme of life those individuals who fortuitously find their way there.

A NOTE ON SEGREGATION

Any well-defined area of the city gets to be what it is and where it is through the sifting and sorting of population in the process of urban growth. Even the old red light district of Chicago was much more a product of natural than artificial (i.e., police) segregation. The Twenty-second Street vice district was a district of tolerated vice—tolerated within recognized boundaries. But commercialized vice had located there before the policy of toleration and "compulsory" segregation was applied. In fact, vice pushed out of its earlier habitat in the old Customs House Place section by expanding business, had invaded Twenty-second Street and became notorious as *the* red light district. Twenty-second Street at the height of its reputation was not the only center of vice—even on the South Side, not to mention the vice areas on the Lower North and Near West Sides.

THE GEOGRAPHY OF VICE RESORTS

In order to locate the distribution of commercialized vice in Chicago, a study was made of the records of the Committee of Fifteen by years from 1910–29. Only those places at which investigators in any given year found evidence of commercialized prostitution, were studied. It was found that there were 5,895 such places within the corporation limits of Chicago. Dividing the city of Chicago into 70 communities convenient for the purpose of statistical analysis, it appears that vice resorts existed in 38 of these tract communities during the last twenty years. Table 19 and Map 4 show this twenty-year vice distribution as obtained from the Committee of Fifteen's cases. The 38 tracts which contained vice resorts during 1910–29 are indicated on Map 4. This total area portrays the widest distribution of commercialized vice, for, in any given year of the period covered, vice was not found in all of the 38 tracts. The average number of tracts per year in which vice was located was 16. The highest number for any given year was 24 and the lowest, 5.

It appears that in 1910 vice resorts were confined largely to 5 areas in Chicago. A more or less steady rise in the number of areas housing vice resorts is manifest thereafter, until the peak of 24 areas is reached for the years 1919 and 1921. From then on a slight decline in the number of tracts harboring commercialized vice is apparent. One concludes that during the first ten years of public suppression in Chicago vice reached its greatest

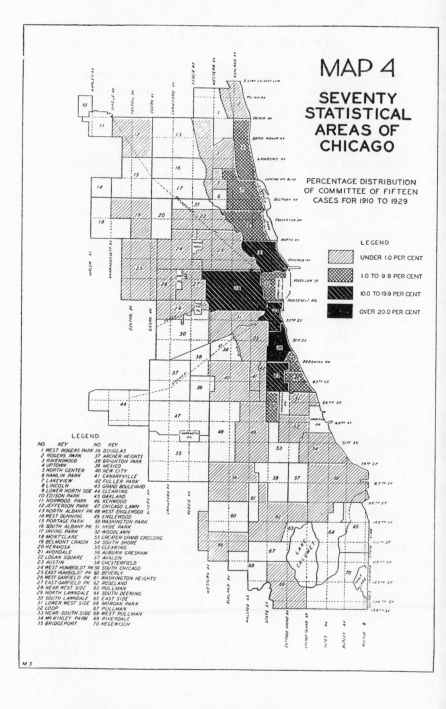

MAP 4

SEVENTY
STATISTICAL
AREAS OF
CHICAGO

PERCENTAGE DISTRIBUTION
OF COMMITTEE OF FIFTEEN
CASES FOR 1910 TO 1929

LEGEND

UNDER 1.0 PER CENT

1.0 TO 9.9 PER CENT

10.0 TO 19.9 PER CENT

OVER 20.0 PER CENT

LEGEND

NO.	KEY	NO.	KEY
1	WEST ROGERS PARK	36	DOUGLAS
2	ROGERS PARK	37	ARCHER HEIGHTS
3	RAVENSWOOD	38	BRIGHTON PARK
4	UPTOWN	39	MEXICO
5	NORTH CENTER	40	NEW CITY
6	HAMLIN PARK	41	CANARYVILLE
7	LAKEVIEW	42	FULLER PARK
8	LINCOLN	43	GRAND BOULEVARD
9	LOWER NORTH SIDE	44	CLEARING
10	EDISON PARK	45	OAKLAND
11	NORWOOD PARK	46	KENWOOD
12	JEFFERSON PARK	47	CHICAGO LAWN
13	NORTH ALBANY PK.	48	WEST ENGLEWOOD
14	WEST DUNNING	49	ENGLEWOOD
15	PORTAGE PARK	50	WASHINGTON PARK
16	SOUTH ALBANY PK.	51	HYDE PARK
17	IRVING PARK	52	WOODLAWN
18	MONTCLARE	53	GREATER GRAND CROSSING
19	BELMONT CRAGIN	54	SOUTH SHORE
20	HERMOSA	55	CLEARING
21	AVONDALE	56	AUBURN GRESHAM
22	LOGAN SQUARE	57	AVALON
23	AUSTIN	58	CHESTERFIELD
24	WEST HUMBOLDT PK.	59	SOUTH CHICAGO
25	EAST HUMBOLDT PK.	60	BEVERLY
26	WEST GARFIELD PK.	61	WASHINGTON HEIGHTS
27	EAST GARFIELD PK.	62	ROSELAND
28	NEAR WEST SIDE	63	PULLMAN
29	NORTH LAWNDALE	64	SOUTH DEERING
30	SOUTH LAWNDALE	65	EAST SIDE
31	LOWER WEST SIDE	66	MORGAN PARK
32	LOOP	67	PULLMAN
33	NEAR SOUTH SIDE	68	WEST PULLMAN
34	McKINLEY PARK	69	RIVERDALE
35	BRIDGEPORT	70	HEGEWISCH

M 5

dispersion in contrast with its confined location in 1910 and before, i.e., in the days of tolerated prostitution; while during the second decade of suppression there seems to be a slight tendency back toward concentration, i.e., away from extreme dispersion.

It should be remembered that vice resorts do not cover the entire space of any one tract. In the spot map of places of commercialized prostitution for 1930 (see Map 1), there was a bunching at certain points and scattering at other locations.

Many of the 38 tracts which contained vice resorts during 1910–29 do not show an average of 1 resort per year (as Table 19 will indicate). We may assume that when a tract does not harbor one vice resort a year, it should be eliminated from the ranks of the constant quantities. Such an elimination removes 22 tracts from the total vice distribution and leaves only 16 vice-infested tracts.

THE POPULATION COUNT

In terms of population, the widest, all-inclusive tract distribution of vice (38 all told) embraced a count of 2,163,358 inhabitants or 80 per cent of the total population for Chicago in 1920 (which was 2,701,705). The 16 non-eliminated tracts contained a count of 1,229,561 persons or 45.5 per cent of Chicago's 1920 population. At the same time these 16 tracts possessed, as would be expected, the lion's share of the vice resorts in the twenty year period, viz., 98.3 per cent (see Table 20, p. 169).

On closer inspection we discover that the first 12 of the 16 tracts (which harbored 98 per cent of the vice resorts) contained 96.3 per cent of the total number of places of commercialized vice from 1910–29, and 29.8

TABLE 19*

DISTRIBUTION OF VICE RESORTS BY LOCAL COMMUNITY TRACTS,
CHICAGO, 1910–29

Tract† Number	Name	Population	No. of Vice Resorts	Per Cent	Average 1 Year	Rate per 100,000
2....	Rogers Park	26,857	4	.07	.20	0.7
3....	Ravenswood	45,195	7	.12	.35	0.8
4....	Uptown	74,211	358	6.07	17.90	24.1
5....	North Center	17,343	1	.02	.05	0.3
7....	Lakeview	99,749	223	3.80	11.15	11.2
8....	Lincoln Park	94,247	136	2.31	6.80	7.2
9....	Lower North	83,936	778	13.20	38.90	46.3
12....	Jefferson Park	6,449	1	.02	.05	0.8
19....	Belmont Cragin	11,945	1	.02	.05	0.4
22....	Logan Square	82,180	8	.14	.40	0.5
23....	Austin	69,350	1	.02	.05	0.1
24....	West Humboldt	69,986	3	.05	.15	0.2
25....	Lower North West	237,492	27	.46	1.35	0.6
26....	West Garfield Park	44,122	4	.07	.20	0.5
27....	East Garfield Park	65,858	41	.70	2.05	3.1
28....	Near West	194,259	873	14.81	43.65	22.5
29....	North Lawndale	75,910	3	.05	.15	0.2
31....	Lower West	85,680	7	.12	.35	0.4
32....	Loop	13,140	287	4.87	14.35	109.2
33....	Near South	17,389	632	10.72	31.60	181.7
35....	Bridgeport and Armour Square	78,755	23	.39	1.15	1.5
36....	Douglas	64,453	1,267	21.49	63.35	98.3
40....	New City	87,303	2	.03	.10	0.1
41....	Canaryville	13,602	2	.03	.10	0.7
42....	Fuller Park	14,377	2	.03	.10	0.7
43....	Grand Boulevard	73,555	824	13.98	41.20	56.0
45....	Oakland	16,540	135	2.29	6.75	40.8
46....	Kenwood	30,976	65	1.10	3.25	10.5
49....	Englewood	114,429	15	.25	.75	0.7
50....	Washington Park	41,359	98	1.66	4.90	11.8
51....	Hyde Park	32,967	12	.20	.60	1.8
52....	Woodlawn	62,751	16	.27	.80	1.3
54....	South Shore	33,425	2	.03	.10	0.3
56....	Auburn-Gresham	13,566	1	.02	.05	0.4
59....	South Chicago	43,642	29	.49	1.45	3.3
62....	Roseland	17,086	2	.03	.10	0.6
66....	Morgan Park	5,959	4	.07	.20	3.4
69....	Riverdale	3,315	1	.02	.05	1.5
	Total	2,163,358	5,895	100.00	295.75	13.7

* Based on Table 57.
† According to 70 statistical communities.

TABLE 20

DISTRIBUTION OF COMMERCIALIZED VICE IN 16 POPULATION
TRACTS OF CHICAGO, 1910–29

Name of Tract	No. of Resorts	Per Cent (5,895)	Population 1920
Douglas......................	1267	21.49	64,453
Near West..................	873	14.81	194,259
Grand Blvd.................	824	13.98	73,555
Lower North................	778	13.20	83,936
Near South.................	632	10.72	17,389
Uptown.....................	358	6.07	74,211
Loop........................	287	4.87	13,140
Lakeview....................	223	3.80	99,749
Lincoln.....................	136	2.31	94,247
Oakland.....................	135	2.29	16,540
Washington Park............	98	1.66	41,359
Kenwood....................	65	1.10	30,976
East Garfield...............	41	0.70	65,858
South Chicago (with Calumet Heights)..................	29	0.49	43,642
Lower Northwest............	27	0.46	237,492
Armour Square-Bridgeport....	23	0.39	78,755
Total..................	5796	98.34	1,229,561

per cent of the 1920 population in Chicago. These 12
tracts not merely showed the highest percentage figures
for vice but also the highest 12 per capita figures.

THE DISTRIBUTION OF VICE IN 1920 AND 1930

While in the twenty-year period (1910–29) 98 per
cent of the vice resorts were concentrated in 16 tracts as
local communities which contained approximately 46
per cent of Chicago's 1920 population, it is necessary to
discover how these vice resorts are distributed throughout
the city according to per capita tract population and what
differences in the location and concentration of vice
resorts have occurred between 1920 and 1930.

Since the 1920 census for Chicago was taken in 1919

and the 1930 census was made in 1929, it was decided to use places at which the Committee of Fifteen found legal evidence of the practice of prostitution in the years 1918–20 and 1928–30. Tables 21 and 22 give the tracts or areas of Chicago in which vice resorts were located during the specified periods according to rates per 100,000 tract population.

In the 1918–20 series, vice resorts were found to be distributed in 27 tracts of the city, 8 of which had less than one resort per year. The total population of the 19 remaining tracts was 1,488,921 or 55 per cent of Chicago's entire 1920 population. In the 1928–30 series, vice resorts were distributed in 19 tracts, 4 of which contained less than one resort per year for the three-year period. The combined population of the remaining 15 tracts amounted to 1,152,951 or 34 per cent of Chicago's total population for 1930. It is apparent that in 1930 vice resorts were distributed in fewer areas which constituted a much smaller proportion of the total city population than ten years earlier.

In 1920 the areas, having the highest number of vice resorts per 100,000 population, were those of a central or near central location—Near South, Loop, Oakland, Douglas, Near West Side, Near North Side, in ranking order. The areas in 1920 having the highest two rates of vice resorts per 100,000 population—rates almost twice as high as the third ranking area—occupy the most central location of Chicago. (See Near South Side and the Loop in Table 21.)

In 1930 the situation was quite different. A decentralized area, Grand Boulevard, had the highest rate of vice resorts per 100,000 population. Douglas, the Loop, and

TABLE 21

NUMBER OF VICE RESORTS PER 100,000 POPULATION BY
TRACTS FOR CHICAGO, 1920

Name of Tract	Tract Number	1920 Population	No. of Vice Resorts, 1918–20	Average for 1 Year	Rate per 100,000
Near South........	33	17,389	89	29.67	171
Loop..............	32	13,140	63	21.00	160
Oakland..........	45	16,540	44	14.67	89
Douglas..........	36	64,453	123	41.00	64
Lower North.......	9	83,936	145	48.33	58
Near West Side....	28	194,259	222	74.00	38
Grand Boulevard...	43	73,555	56	18.67	25
Lincoln Park.......	8	94,247	40	13.33	14
Uptown...........	4	74,211	26	8.67	12
Kenwood..........	46	30,976	11	3.67	12
Washington Park...	50	41,359	13	4.33	10
South Chicago.....	59	43,642	11	3.67	8
Lakeview..........	7	99,749	21	7.00	7
East Garfield Pk...	27	65,858	10	3.33	5
Beverly Hills-Washington Hts.-Roseland.........	60-61-62	18,104	2	0.67	4
Edison-Norwood-Jefferson Park....	10-11-12	9,917	1	0.33	3
North Center......	5	17,343	1	0.33	2
West Garfield Pk...	26	44,122	2	0.67	2
Bridgeport-Armour Square....	35	78,755	4	1.33	2
Fuller Park........	42	14,377	1	0.33	2
Englewood........	49	114,429	7	2.33	2
Woodlawn.........	52	62,751	4	1.33	2
Ravenswood (Lincoln Square)..	3	45,195	2	0.67	1
Logan Square......	22	82,180	3	1.00	1
Lower Northwest (West Town)....	25	237,492	4	1.33	1
Austin............	23	69,350	1	0.33	*
Humboldt Park....	24	69,986	1	0.33	*
Total	....	1,777,315	926	303.65	11

* Less than 0.5 per 100,000.

the Near South Side, all of them centralized areas, occupy
second and third places. Lakeview, Uptown, Washington
Park, and Kenwood, decentralized tracts, are found in

TABLE 22

NUMBER OF VICE RESORTS PER 100,000 POPULATION
BY TRACTS FOR CHICAGO, 1930

Name of Tract	Population	No. of Vice Resorts, 1928–30	Average for 1 Year	Rate per 100,000
Grand Boulevard.............	87,005	301	100.33	115
Douglas....................	50,285	148	49.33	98
Loop and Near South Side.....	18,267	51	17.00	93
Lakeview...................	114,872	230	76.67	67
Uptown....................	121 637	220	73.33	60
Washington Park.............	44,016	77	25.67	58
Kenwood...................	26,942	47	15.67	58
Oakland....................	14,962	23	7.67	51
Near North Side.............	79,554	121	40.33	51
Near West Side.............	152,457	86	28.67	19
Lincoln Park................	97,873	51	17.00	17
Hyde Park.................	48,017	7	2.33	5
Lincoln Square..............	46,419	3	1.00	2
East Garfield Park...........	63,353	3	1.00	2
West Town..................	187,292	3	1.00	1
Rogers Park................	57,094	2	0.67	1
Montclare and Belmont Cragin.	68,721	1	0.33	*
Humboldt Park..............	80,835	1	0.33	*
Englewood.................	89,063	1	0.33	*
Total..................	1,448,664	1,379	459.66	14

* Less than 0.5 per 100,000.

fourth to seventh places. In 1930 areas like the Near North Side and the Near West Side, contiguous to the central business and notorious in the past for their concentrated vice emporia, have slipped back to ranks nine and ten; whereas in 1920 these very same areas occupied fifth and sixth places. While vice resorts in 1930 still linger to a diminishing extent in their oldest locations, i.e., in the near central slum regions, they concentrate more and more in decentralized neighborhoods in Uptown, Lakeview, Kenwood, Grand Boulevard, Washington Park.

With the general vice area or areas in Chicago delimited, it is possible to discover the sociological conditions in the various tracts contained therein. Such conditions like age and sex disproportions, racial and foreign-born concentrations, the extent of home ownership, and problems like venereal diseases, prohibition violation, juvenile delinquency, adult crime, poverty, suicide, divorce, desertion, etc., may be thought of as indexes of the presence of factors causing social disorganization. In this chapter we shall confine ourselves to the composition of the population in the tracts of the city which contained the vice distribution, while in the succeeding chapter we shall consider how vice is related to and associated with other social problems.

DEVIATIONS FROM THE IDEAL POPULATION DISTRIBUTION

In Western civilization the most effective family-community controls—other factors being held constant—can be brought to bear on individual conduct when the pro-

TABLE 23

IDEAL POPULATION DISTRIBUTION
PERCENTAGE BY AGE GROUPS FOR EITHER SEX

Age Group	Per Cent	Age Group	Per Cent
0– 4	5.40	45–49	2.62
5– 9	5.09	50–54	2.31
10–14	4.78	55–59	2.00
15–19	4.47	60–64	1.70
20–24	4.17	65–69	1.39
25–29	3.86	70–74	1.08
30–34	3.55	75–79	0.77
35–39	3.24	80–84	0.46
40–44	2.93	85–89	0.15*
		Total	49.97

* The method of computing these percentages was obtained from Mr. Charles Newcomb, research fellow in sociology, University of Chicago. The mid-point of each of the 18 age groups is taken and multiplied by .3086. Hence 5.40 per cent for age group 0–4 is obtained by multiplying .3086 by 17.5; 5.09 per cent (for 5–9) = .3086×16.5; 0.15 per cent (for 85–89) = .3086×.5.

portion between the sexes is equal and when the percentage of individuals gradually diminishes in age level from infancy to the zero point of old age. Such an ideal population distribution has been computed as follows for either sex from infancy to 90 years by five-year age periods. If a community's population in Western countries shows marked deviations from this ideal distribution of sex and age, these irregularities would lead one to suspect that such a community is being disturbed by factors causing the deviations in its population distribution. The foreign-born white population in the United States for example, shows marked irregularities in its percentage distribution. For purposes of brevity the 1920 foreign-born whites in the United States may be compared with the ideal population for combined age periods.

TABLE 24

AGE GROUP DISTRIBUTION OF FOREIGN-BORN
WHITE POPULATION

AGE GROUP	PERCENTAGE EITHER SEX	PERCENTAGE MALES	PERCENTAGE FEMALES
	Ideal Population*	Foreign-born Whites†	
Under 15....................	15.27	2.0	2.0
15–19.......................	4.47	1.9	2.0
20–44.......................	17.75	29.3	23.2
45–69.......................	11.10	20.2	16.4
Total..................	48.59	53.4	43.6

* Based on percentages given in Table 23.
† Population (U.S.) 1920. Based on figures given in foreign-born white pyramid (1920) in "Immigrants and Their Children, 1920," *U.S. Census Monograph*, VII (1927), 155.

Chicago shows marked deviation in its 1920 population from the ideal distribution, although not as marked as the foreign-born whites in the United States. Com-

parisons for significant grouped age periods are listed
as follows:

TABLE 25

AGE GROUP DISTRIBUTION BY SEX
CHICAGO, 1920

AGE GROUP	PER CENT EITHER SEX	PER CENT MALE	PER CENT FEMALE
	Ideal Population	Chicago, 1920	
Under 15....................	15.27	14.0	13.9
15–19......................	4.47	3.6	3.9
20–44......................	17.75	22.95	22.1
Above 45...................	12.48	10.0	9.3
Total..................	49.97	50.5	49.2

In 1920 Chicago's population was below the standard
or the ideal in proportion of children under 15 and much
above the norm in percentage of adults 20–44.

The available 1930 census data at present writing do
not separate the population of age groups by sex and do
not list the age group 15 to 19. For comparison with the
ideal population and the 1920 Chicago population, we
must be content with the groupings as given in Table 26.

TABLE 26

AGE GROUP DISTRIBUTION
CHICAGO, 1920 AND 1930

AGE GROUP	IDEAL POPULATION	CHICAGO POPULATION	
	Per Cent	Per Cent, 1920	Per Cent, 1930
Under 15....................	30.54	27.9	24.1
15–44......................	44.44	52.5	54.5
45 and over.................	24.96	19.3	21.4

The percentage of the population of Chicago under 15 years of age in 1930 is lower than in 1920 and still lower than the ideal standard, while the proportion of inhabitants 15–44 years of age in Chicago in 1930 is higher than in 1920 and still higher than the ideal figure. In ten years, Chicago's child population has fallen proportionately still further under the normal, while its adult population has proportionately risen further above the standard. In other words, Chicago has become less a haven for children and more a city for adults in the productive ages of life. This disproportionate concentration of adults in Chicago is in large part due to the non-family adults who, seeking opportunity, have migrated to Chicago from Europe or from Chicago's American hinterland. The persistence of a social problem like commercialized vice, as well as the existence of other sex problems, must be interpreted in the light of the effect of urban conditions on an adult or a young adult population, a large segment of which lives in furnished rooms or apartments.

It so happens that in Chicago we find neighborhoods which are characterized by a preponderance of males, females, adults of both sexes and by the shortage of children. Offhand it seems that such areas show up with problems of sex, sex delinquency, and commercialized vice more so than areas which contain a more normal (ideal) distribution of sex and age groupings, primarily because of the absence of a vigorous family-community life. The West Madison Street hobo area, the Lower North Side rooming-house area, the Wilson Avenue furnished-apartment area are cases in point.

It will be impossible in the limitations of this study to

give the specific population pyramids for each local community in Chicago, in order to check against the vice distribution. As a substitute, we must rest content with giving the relationship of commercialized vice to salient features of a disturbed type of population pyramid, as may be represented in the disproportion of the sexes, the percentage of persons under 15, and the percentage of adults 20 to 44 years of age.

VICE AREAS AND TRACT CENSUS DATA

The population data for 1920 are available for 70 tracts or areas in Chicago, several of which were under 10,000 inhabitants. By combination of contiguous tracts in the city so as to eliminate tracts with small populations, we have remaining 55 tracts or combinations of tracts. The vice resorts investigated by the Committee of Fifteen in Chicago for 1918–20 were thrown into the tracts according to street address and their incidence and rate were then compared with the main population features of the various tracts. The same procedure was followed for the 1928–30 series of vice resorts. However, the 1930 census for Chicago is given by 75 tracts or local areas of Chicago, some of which had to be combined in order to group tracts under 10,000 with contiguous areas. As a result there remain 62 tracts or combined tracts. (See Tables 27 and 28.)

THE DISPROPORTION OF SEXES

The claim has been made that vice resorts tend to concentrate in areas of marked disproportion of the sexes, especially of men. In areas where men greatly outnumber women, so the argument runs, vice resorts fit into a man's

TABLE 27

Tract Population Features and Distribution of Vice Resorts, Chicago, 1920

Community Area*	Population	Per Cent	Sex† Ratio	Per Cent Children Under 15	Per Cent Adults 20–24	Per Cent Foreign-Born	Per Cent Colored	Per Cent Home Ownership	No. Cases 1918–20‡	Average for 1 yr.	Rate per 100,000
1–2	35,203	1.70	—113	25.3	46.4	17.1	0.3	29.1			
3	45,195	1.67	—103	25.2	46.1	23.5	0.0	32.1	2	0.67	1
4	74,211	2.75	—118	15.6	52.8	18.3	0.4	15.7	26	8.67	12
5	17,343	.64	—104	23.6	45.4	23.9	0.1	38.9	1	0.33	2
6	21,036	.78	+100	27.3	43.3	27.9	0.0	34.9			
7	99,749	3.69	—111	20.6	47.2	27.7	0.2	19.8	21	7.00	7
8	94,247	3.47	+101	24.5	46.1	33.7	0.3	16.1	40	13.33	14
9	83,936	3.11	+122	20.8	49.6	34.8	0.2	9.6	145	48.33	58
10–11–12	9,917	.37	+101	34.4	38.2	28.2	0.03	60.2	1	0.33	3
13	11,069	.41	+103	28.7	48.6	24.9	0.7	37.1			
14–15	25,189	.93	+101	33.4	43.2	26.3	0.1	60.5			
16	40,908	1.51	—103	27.5	45.5	24.3	0.0	44.6			
17	33,562	1.24	—101	30.5	43.0	24.8	0.1	45.8			
18–19	17,478	.65	+108	40.9	39.9	33.6	0.05	59.1			
20	21,741	.80	+103	30.0	43.6	28.2	0.0	42.8			
21	27,321	1.01	+101	31.6	40.7	26.8	0.0	35.9			
22	82,180	3.04	—101	28.4	43.6	31.1	0.0	30.6	3	1.00	1
23	69,350	2.57	—107	24.3	45.0	20.1	0.2	41.3	1	0.33	
24	69,986	2.59	+102	28.4	43.7	28.8	0.1	34.0	1	0.33	
25	237,492	8.79	+106	36.1	41.9	44.3	0.1	18.4	4	1.33	
26	44,122	1.63	—109	22.3	46.4	20.6	0.0	27.2	2	0.67	2
27	65,858	2.44	—104	23.9	45.9	25.6	0.2	18.6	10	3.33	5
28	194,259	7.19	+121	29.9	42.6	38.5	4.3	13.6	222	74.00	38
29	75,910	2.81	+102	31.7	43.2	43.0	0.2	25.1			
30	88,378	3.27	+103	33.0	43.0	35.2	0.3	38.1			
31	85,680	3.17	+110	37.2	42.1	44.3	0.0	18.3			
32	13,140	.49	+347	4.8	54.4	27.2	3.3	1.7	63	21.00	160
33	17,389	.64	—124	15.3	54.3	18.9	24.9	30.8	89	29.67	171
34	22,016	.81	—108	36.1	40.5	30.8	0.1	35.9			
35	78,755	2.92	+112	35.3	40.9	35.9	1.2	23.2	4	1.33	2
36	64,453	2.39	+108	15.0	60.1	7.3	73.5	7.5	123	41.00	64
37–38	24,488	.91	—112	37.4	41.9	33.7	0.06	45.9			
39	14,420	.54	+108	43.3	41.4	37.4	0.0	49.7			
40	87,303	3.23	+112	37.1	42.3	40.0	0.2	30.5			
41	13,602	.50	+113	31.0	40.3	27.0	0.0	25.9			
42	14,377	.53	+105	32.9	40.5	36.6	0.2	32.2	1	0.33	2
43	73,555	2.72	—108	16.4	54.3	15.4	33.0	8.9	56	18.67	25
44–47–55	22,672	.84	+103	35.2	42.3	24.1	0.04	69.2			
45	16,540	.61	—107	14.1	54.6	15.7	17.7	8.5	44	14.67	89
46	30,976	1.15	—131	15.7	55.7	18.6	9.5	15.1	11	3.67	12
48	52,373	1.94	+102	30.5	42.0	24.4	2.3	50.5			
49	114,429	4.24	—104	24.8	44.0	20.6	1.3	30.2	7	2.33	2
50	41,359	1.53	—106	19.0	50.2	18.5	17.5	8.1	13	4.33	10
51	32,967	1.22	—121	17.8	48.9	20.7	0.3	10.4	4	1.33	4
52	62,751	2.32	—110	18.8	49.8	16.3	2.6	13.4	4	1.33	2
53	25,973	.96	—100	28.3	40.5	23.9	0.5	44.6			
54	33,425	1.24	—107	22.0	50.2	28.3	0.5	33.5			
56	13,566	.50	+122	28.8	42.8	20.5	0.2	56.3			
57–58	13,664	.51	+114	36.8	41.5	35.7	0.02	52.3			
59	43,642	1.62	+112	38.0	40.0	35.5	0.4	34.1	11	3.67	8

* Based on 70 statistical communities.
† —=female: +=male.
‡ Based on Table 57.

TABLE 27—*Continued*

TRACT POPULATION FEATURES AND DISTRIBUTION OF
VICE RESORTS, CHICAGO, 1920

Commu-nity Area*	Popula-tion	Per Cent	Sex† Ratio	Per Cent Chil-dren Under 15	Per Cent Adults 20–24	Per Cent For-eign-Born	Per Cent Colored	Per Cent Home Own-er-ship	No. Cases 1918–20‡	Aver-age for 1 yr.	Rate per 100,000
60–61–66	18,104	.67	−104	31.2	38.1	17.6	4.2	71.6	2	0.67	4
62–63...	19,681	.73	+109	35.6	40.8	39.2	1.1	50.7	.....	.....	.....
64–65–70	25,551	.95	+120	36.3	41.1	35.4	0.01	46.2	.....	.....	.....
67......	26,557	.98	+115	31.0	42.4	37.2	0.5	51.0	.....	.....	.....
68–69...	12,657	.47	+116	38.1	39.4	37.7	0.02	50.8	.....	.....	.....
Outside .	....	....	....	....	....	....	....	.....	15	5.00	.....
Total	2,701,705	99.79	.....	.....	.....	.....	....	.....	926	308.67	11

* Based on 70 statistical communities.
† −=female; +=male.
‡ Based on Table 57.

world—perhaps homeless man's world—atmosphere. On inspection, however, it was found that several vice-ridden neighborhoods of Chicago showed disproportions in favor of women. In order to test out the relationship of the distribution of vice resorts in Chicago to disproportion of sexes, either male or female, it was necessary to compute the ratios of men to women or of women to men in terms of 100. Column 3 of Tables 27 and 28 indicate the tract ratios of the sexes. The + sign indicates males in excess; the —, females in preponderance.

The 55 combined tracts for 1920 were classified according to the highest 14 ratios of sexes, the next highest 14, the next lowest 14 and the lowest 13, corresponding roughly to a quartile distribution or division of the 55 tracts (since each quarter contains 25 per cent of the total number of tracts). Having classified the tracts into quarters according to the array of ratios, a count was made of the number of vice resorts which were located in each quarter. Almost 62 per cent of the vice resorts

TABLE 28

Tract Population Features and Distribution of
Vice Resorts, Chicago, 1930

Community Area*	Population	Per Cent	Sex Ratio†	Per Cent Children Under 15	Per Cent Adults 25-44	Per Cent Foreign-Born White	Per Cent Colored	No. of Vice Resorts 1928-30‡	Average No. for 1 yr.	Rate per 100,000
1	57,094	1.7	−115	17.8	42.2	15.8	0.2	2	0.67	......
2	39,759	1.2	−106	26.5	40.4	17.5	0.1	......	......	......
3	121,637	3.6	−108	13.2	42.6	20.4	0.4	220	73.33	60.3
4	46,419	1.4	−106	19.8	38.7	22.5	*	3	1.0	2.2
5	47,651	1.4	+101	21.3	35.6	27.3	*	1	0.33	......
6	114,872	3.4	−105	16.9	40.6	28.8	0.2	230	76.67	66.7
7	97,873	2.9	+106	20.8	37.7	33.8	0.1	51	17.00	17.4
8	79,554	2.4	+114	16.1	40.1	26.4	0.5	121	40.33	50.6
9-10	19,778	0.6	−103	30.7	36.0	16.5	*	......	......	......
11-12	24,597	0.7	+103	30.7	35.7	23.2	*	......	......	......
13	11,052	0.3	−106	24.9	41.2	27.2	0.6	......	......	......
14	55,577	1.6	−104	22.9	35.8	32.2	*	......	......	......
15	64,203	1.9	+101	26.1	35.3	23.7	*	......	......	......
16	66,783	2.0	−102	23.0	36.5	23.9	*	......	......	......
17	19,659	0.6	+107	34.2	35.8	23.3	*	......	......	......
18-19	68,721	2.1	−104	30.4	35.2	26.9	*	1	0.33	......
20	23,518	0.7	+102	24.1	36.7	26.5	*	......	......	......
21	48,433	1.4	−101	26.1	36.3	25.4	*	......	......	......
22	114,174	3.4	+101	25.3	34.4	29.7	*	......	......	......
23	80,835	2.4	−104	25.6	34.3	31.4	*	1	0.33	......
24	187,292	5.5	+108	31.0	31.2	38.6	0.4	3	1.00	0.5
25	131,114	3.9	−105	21.0	37.6	19.6	0.1	......	......	......
26	50,014	1.5	−101	20.5	35.7	25.9	*	......	......	......
27	63,353	1.9	+105	21.9	35.6	23.9	2.9	3	1.00	1.6
28	152,457	4.5	+127	26.4	33.4	25.1	16.6	86	28.67	18.8
29	112,261	3.3	+104	25.4	31.1	45.0	0.3	......	......	......
30	76,749	2.3	+107	26.5	34.5	31.5	0.9	......	......	......
31	66,198	2.0	+112	30.4	30.8	36.6	*	......	......	......
32-33	18,267	0.5	+206	7.5	39.2	22.6	14.1	51	17.00	93.1
34	21,450	0.6	+122	31.5	32.0	25.0	18.9	2	0.67	......
35	50,285	1.5	+103	18.3	45.2	2.9	88.8	148	49.33	98.1
36	14,962	0.4	+105	16.3	40.3	13.9	28.7	23	7.67	51.3
37	14,437	0.4	+108	31.6	30.2	28.1	7.6	......	......	......
38	87,005	2.6	−104	17.9	48.5	1.4	94.6	301	100.33	115.3
39	26,942	0.8	−120	12.4	40.4	18.4	0.7	47	15.67	58.2
40	44,016	1.3	−104	19.3	46.6	2.0	91.9	77	25.67	58.3
41	48,017	1.4	−118	14.1	38.9	20.1	1.1	7	2.33	4.9
42	66,052	2.0	−103	15.0	39.7	14.9	13.0	......	......	......
43	78,755	2.3	−114	18.6	30.0	16.6	0.2	......	......	......
44	36,228	1.1	−102	24.0	41.2	19.3	*	......	......	......
45	10,023	3.0	+101	27.2	39.1	16.4	*	......	......	......
46	56,683	1.7	+114	31.2	33.0	23.6	1.3	......	......	......
47-48	10,826	0.3	+111	33.7	31.3	27.0	0.2	......	......	......
49	43,206	1.3	+106	27.0	34.2	27.0	2.9	......	......	......
50-51	14,603	0.4	+124	32.8	31.5	34.5	0.0	......	......	......
52-55	24,729	0.7	+115	31.6	31.5	28.1	0.0	......	......	......
53-54	29,960	0.8	+111	31.2	30.0	31.1	0.6	......	......	......
56-57	14,170	0.4	+110	37.4	28.2	31.0	*	......	......	......
58	46,552	1.4	+108	32.5	31.9	30.3	*	......	......	......

* Based on 75 Census Tracts of Chicago for 1930.
† − = female; + = male.
‡ Based on Table 57.

TABLE 28—*Continued*

TRACT POPULATION FEATURES AND DISTRIBUTION OF
VICE RESORTS, CHICAGO, 1930

Community Area*	Population	Per Cent	Sex Ratio†	Per Cent Children Under 15	Per Cent Adults 25-44	Per Cent Foreign-Born White	Per Cent Colored	No. of Vice Resorts 1928-30‡	Average No. for 1 yr.	Rate per 100,000
59.......	22,032	0.7	+107	32.9	30.5	23.0	*	......	......	......
60.......	53,553	1.6	+108	31.5	29.9	28.7	*	......	......	......
61.......	87,103	2.6	+110	32.8	30.8	29.3	*	......	......	......
62-63....	34,396	1.0	+106	30.2	33.9	26.1	0.0	......	......	......
64-65....	14,353	0.5	+111	33.0	33.6	21.1	*	......	......	......
66.......	47,462	1.4	+101	25.8	37.2	21.4	*	......	......	......
67.......	63,845	1.9	+102	27.3	16.9	22.9	3.1	......	......	......
68.......	89,063	2.6	+101	22.6	33.6	21.8	1.3	1	0.33	......
69.......	60,007	1.8	+101	22.6	35.7	21.4	0.4	......	......	......
70-71....	58,114	1.7	−102	25.0	37.4	18.5	*	......	......	......
72-74....	17,103	0.5	−108	27.7	32.5	13.8	0.3	......	......	......
73.......	17,865	0.5	−100	29.2	37.6	16.0	0.2	......	......	......
75.......	12,747	0.4	−105	28.0	31.7	9.1	34.9	......	......	......
Outside..	......	......	......	......	......	......	......	1	0.33	......
Total	3,376,438	......	+102.6	24.1	36.2	24.9	6.9	1380	460.00	13.6

* Based on 75 Census Tracts of Chicago for 1930.
† − =female; + =male.
‡ Based on Table 57.

fell in the quarter containing the highest 25 per cent of
the sex ratios, namely, in Quarter 4. The vice rate per
100,000 for the tracts in Quarter 4 is almost 3 times as
high as that for entire Chicago (31.8 vs 11.2). The
smallest number of vice resorts and the lowest rate per
100,000 population were found in Quarter 1, which contained the tracts showing the lowest 13 sex ratios or the
lowest 25 per cent of the sex ratios. (See Table 29.)

In 1930, however, the greatest number of vice resorts
(56.9 per cent) were located in tracts showing the next
to lowest 25 per cent of the sex ratios. Those tracts with
the lowest ratios were practically free of vice, while 43
per cent of the vice emporia were located in the tracts
possessing the highest 50 per cent of the sex ratios (see
Table 30). The reason why the greatest proportion of

TABLE 29

QUARTER DISTRIBUTION OF VICE RESORTS ACCORDING TO
TRACT SEX RATIOS, CHICAGO, 1920*

Quarter	Population	Per Cent	No. Vice Resorts, 1918–20, Average 1 Year	Per Cent	Rate per 100,000
4	587,678	21.7	186.67	61.5	31.8
3	738,093	27.3	73.67	24.3	10.0
2	825,430	30.6	28.32	9.3	3.4
1	550,504	20.4	14.99	4.9	2.7
Total	2,701,705	100.0	303.65	100.0	11.2

* Based on Table 27.

TABLE 30

QUARTER DISTRIBUTION OF VICE RESORTS ACCORDING TO
TRACT SEX RATIOS, CHICAGO, 1930*

Quarter	Population	Per Cent	No. of Vice Resorts, 1928–30	Per Cent	Rate per 100,000
4	699,888	20.7	105.34	22.9	15.1
3	921,940	27.3	92.33	20.1	10.0
2	957,227	28.4	261.33	56.9	27.3
1	797,383	23.6	.66	0.1	....
Total	3,376,438	100.0	459.66	100.0	13.6

* Based on Table 28. Less than 0.5 per 100,000.

the vice resorts is not in Quarter 4 in 1930, as it was in 1920, is partly that the business of vice has decentralized itself into areas, away from the center of the city, which do not show marked disproportion of the sexes.

The coefficient (p) of correlation by the rank-difference method for tract vice rates and sex ratios in 1920 was 57; in 1930, 21.[1] In 1920 there was a tendency for tract vice

[1] The formula for obtaining the coefficient of correlation by the rank-difference method is $p = 1 - \dfrac{6 \Sigma D^2}{N(N^2 - 1)}$. Only the tracts containing vice re-

rates to vary in magnitude as the tract sex ratios increased or decreased. In 1930 this tendency is not apparent from the low coefficient. The reason for this change has already been partially explained. Vice resorts in seeking more decentralized locations no longer concentrate in the near central regions of the city where the high sex disproportions are found. Besides, the business of vice was even less associated in 1930 than in 1920 with foreign born residence areas where the high disproportions of sex frequently occur.

THE PREPONDERANCE OF ADULTS

The percentage of adults 20–44 years of age in the total population of Chicago in 1920 was 45.1; in the total population of the 19 tracts containing an average of 1 or more vice resorts per year for 1918–20, 46.5; for the 36 remaining non-vice tracts, 43.4; in the ideal population, 35.5. While the percentage of Chicago's adult population is considerably above the standard population, the proportion of adults in the 19 vice tracts is the highest of all, higher than the figure for Chicago generally and still higher than that for the non-vice tracts.

In 1930, the percentage of adults 25–44 years of age in the total population of Chicago was 36.2; in the total population of 15 tracts containing an average of 1 or more vice resorts per year for 1928–30, 38.6; in the 47 remaining non-vice tracts, 34.9; in the ideal population, 27.2. Here again, the proportion of adults in the vice tracts of 1930

sorts were used in the correlation. The p's have not been converted into r's with probable errors because the data, as given by tract rates and percentages for such a small number of instances (28 tracts in 1920 and 21 in 1930) are not adapted to the statistical assumptions behind $r = \dfrac{\Sigma xy}{N \sigma_x \sigma_y}$.

is markedly higher than the ideal figure, and is noticeably higher than the corresponding figures for Chicago generally and the non-vice tracts specifically.

In those tracts which had the highest 14 or 25 per cent of the percentages of adults 20–44 in Chicago in 1920, practically two-thirds of the vice resorts were located (see Quarter 4 in Table 31). The vice rate for these tracts with the highest percentage of adults was 3 times as high as that for Chicago as a whole.

TABLE 31

QUARTER DISTRIBUTION OF VICE RESORTS ACCORDING TO TRACT
PERCENTAGE OF ADULTS 20–44 YEARS OF AGE
CHICAGO, 1920*

Quarter	Population	Per Cent	No. Vice Resorts, 1918–20, Average 1 Year	Per Cent	Rate per 100,000
4	655,520	24.3	199.67	65.8	30.5†
3	746,787	27.6	22.32	7.3	3.0
2	970,324	35.9	75.33	24.8	7.8
1	329,074	12.2	6.33	2.1	1.9
Total	2,701,705	100.0	303.65	100.0	11.2

* Based on Table 27.
† Actually 30.45. Not to be converted to 31.0.

In 1930, the situation is even more pronounced. Almost 89 per cent of the vice resorts were located in those tracts which possessed the highest 15 percentages of adults 25–44, i.e., the highest 25 per cent of the 62 tract percentages (see Quarter 4, Table 32). The vice rate for these tracts is almost 4 times as high as that for Chicago as a whole.

The coefficients of correlation by the rank-difference method for tract vice rates and tract percentages of adults were .64 in 1920 and .76 in 1930. It may be concluded

TABLE 32

QUARTER DISTRIBUTION OF VICE RESORTS ACCORDING TO TRACT
PERCENTAGES OF ADULTS 25–44 YEARS OF AGE,
CHICAGO, 1930*

Quarter	Population	Per Cent	No. Vice Resorts, 1928–30, Average 1 Year	Per Cent	Rate per 100,000
4................	777,748	23.0	406.67	88.5	52.3
3................	815,230	24.1	20.33	4.4	2.5
2................	990,949	29.4	31.66	6.9	3.2
1................	792,511	23.5	1.00	0.2	0.1
Total.........	3,376,438	100.0	459.66	100.0	13.6

* Based on Table 28.

that tract vice rates show a marked tendency to increase
or decrease positively with the magnitude of the tract
proportions of adults.

THE SHORTAGE OF CHILDREN

Sociologically we should expect commercialized vice to
thrive best in areas where child shortage is manifest. For,
as the percentage of children under 15 decreases, the
percentage of adults increases. Since commercialized vice
is an adult problem, it should tend to locate in those tracts
which possess relatively low proportions of children and
high proportions of adults. Besides, a high tract percentage of children—other things being equal—usually
signifies a type of family-community life in which commercialized vice has no quarter or cannot maintain quarter.

In 1920, 27.9 per cent of Chicago's population was
under 15 years of age. The 19 vice tracts contained only
25.5 per cent children under 15; while the 36 non-vice
tracts possessed 30.8 per cent. The percentage under 15

years of age for the ideal population is 30.5. In 1930, the vice tracts as well as Chicago as a whole had even a lower proportion of children as compared with the standard figure. For the whole city the percentage was 24.1; for the 15 vice tracts, 20.6; for the 47 non-vice tracts; 25.4. It is clear that in 1920 as in 1930 the proportion of children under 15 in the vice areas was markedly lower than the proportion for Chicago generally and the non-vice areas in particular; while the percentages in the vice tracts for both census years were conspicuously lower than those in the ideal population.

Almost two-thirds of the vice resorts in Chicago for the period 1918–20 were located in the tracts showing the lowest 25 per cent of the tract percentages of children under 15 (see Quarters 1 and 4 of Table 33). The rate of the vice resorts in Chicago in 1920 was 30 times as high in Quarter 1 as in Quarter 4; while the rate in Quarter 1 was about 3 times as high as that for the total city (31.0 as compared with 11.2).

TABLE 33

QUARTER DISTRIBUTION OF VICE RESORTS ACCORDING TO TRACT
PERCENTAGES OF CHILDREN UNDER 15, CHICAGO, 1920*

Quarter	Population	Per Cent	No. Vice Resorts, 1918–20, Average 1 Year	Per Cent	Rate per 100,000
4	705,499	26.1	6.33	2.1	0.9
3	614,856	22.8	75.33	24.8	12.3
2	736,899	27.3	22.32	7.3	3.0
1	644,451	23.8	199.67	65.8	31.0
Total	2,701,705	100.0	303.65	100.0	11.2

* Based on Table 27.

In 1930, 89 per cent of the vice resorts were concentrated in the tracts having the lowest 25 per cent of the tract percentages of children under 15; while less than 1 per cent of the resorts was found in the tracts containing the highest 25 per cent of the tract percentages of children under 15 (see Quarters 1 and 4 of Table 34). The vice rate for Quarter 1 in 1930 was 45.4 per 100,000 and for Quarter 4, 0.3. This rate for Quarter 1, where child shortage is most evident, is almost three and a half times as high as that for Chicago as a whole (45.4 as compared with 13.6).

TABLE 34

QUARTER DISTRIBUTION OF VICE RESORTS ACCORDING TO TRACT
PERCENTAGES OF CHILDREN UNDER 15, CHICAGO, 1930*

Quarter	Population	Per Cent	No. Vice Resorts, 1928–30, Average 1 Year	Per Cent	Rate per 100,000
4	617,402	18.3	1.67	0.4	0.3
3	760,080	22.5	29.00	6.3	3.8
2	1,095,065	32.4	19.00	4.1	1.7
1	903,891	26.8	410.00	89.2	45.4
Total	3 376,438	100.0	459.67	100.0	13.6

* Based on Table 28.

The coefficients of correlation by the rank-difference method for tract vice rates and tract percentages of children were −.60 in 1920 and −.66 in 1930. Tract vice rates accordingly show a strong tendency to vary inversely with the size of the tract proportions of children.

HOME OWNERSHIP

In 1920, 26.6 per cent of the total number of families owned their own homes in Chicago. Only 17.7 per cent of the families in the 19 vice tracts owned their own homes. But in the 36 non-vice tracts the percentage of home ownership was 37.5. Thus, the percentage of home ownership was over twice as low in the vice areas as in the non-vice neighborhoods of Chicago.[2] And yet this great difference in amount of home ownership existed in spite of the fact that the 19 vice tracts contained 55 per cent of the total 1920 family count in Chicago; while the 36 non-vice tracts housed only 45 per cent of the total number of families in Chicago in 1920.

Just as vice resorts were concentrated in areas having the highest proportions of adults and the lowest percentages of children, so the majority of them were found in the tracts with the lowest percentages of home ownership. Low percentages of home ownership vary directly with high percentages of adults and indirectly with low percentages of children. They indicate areas of non-family or loosely knit family life—areas in which commercialized vice can thrive. In 1920, almost 83 per cent of the vice resorts for 1918–20 were housed in tracts possessing the lowest 25 per cent of the tract percentages of home ownership, while less than 1 per cent of the resorts was located in the quarter of the highest tract percentages of home ownership. The number of resorts per 100,000 population was 28.8 for Quarter 1, which was two and a half times as high as the rate for Chicago as a whole. The rate for Quarter 4, on the other hand, was only 0.3 per 100,000 (See Table 35).

The coefficient of rank correlation for tract vice rates and tract percentages of home ownership was −.61 in

[2] The 1930 home ownership data for Chicago by tracts are not available at present writing.

TABLE 35

QUARTER DISTRIBUTION OF VICE RESORTS ACCORDING TO TRACT
PERCENTAGES OF HOME OWNERSHIP, CHICAGO, 1920*

Quarter	Population	Per Cent	No. Vice Resorts, 1918–20, Average 1 Year	Per Cent	Rate per 100,000
4................	296,317	11.0	1.00	0.3	0.3
3................	525,750	19.5	4.66	1.5	0.9
2................	1,011,564	37.4	47.66	15.7	4.7
1................	868,074	32.1	250.33	82.5	28.8
Total.........	2,701,705	100.0	303.65	100.0	11.2

* Based on Table 27.

1920. Vice resorts, therefore, show a tendency to be less concentrated in tracts with high proportions of home ownership and to be highly concentrated in tracts with low percentages of home ownership.

FOREIGN-BORN WHITES

The relationship of the location of commercialized vice resorts to foreign-born white residence areas in Chicago goes somewhat contrary to popular belief, which identifies the aggravated social problems of American city life with concentration of persons of alien extraction. In 1920, 29.8 per cent of Chicago's population consisted of foreign-born whites. But 29.6 per cent of the population in the 19 vice tracts were foreign-born whites; while 30 per cent of the population in the 36 non-vice tracts were alien-born whites. In 1930, the foreign-born white population of Chicago constituted 24.9 per cent of the total. Of the total number of persons in the 15 vice tracts, 23.6 per cent were of alien white nativity; while 25.6 per cent of the inhabitants of the 47 non-vice tracts of Chicago were foreign-born whites. Both in 1920 and 1930 the percentage of foreign-born whites residing in the vice tracts was practically the same as the percentage of them residing in the non-vice areas. From this conclusion it appears that the general location of vice resorts in Chicago cannot be characterized by a higher foreign-born white concentration than that which holds for the areas free of prostitution.

In 1920, only 26.6 per cent of the vice resorts for 1918–20 were concentrated in the areas containing the highest 25 per cent of the percentages of foreign-born whites in the tract populations, while 40.7 per cent of the resorts were found in the tracts with the lowest 25 per cent of the percentages of alien-born whites. On the other hand, the highest rate of vice resorts per 100,000 population was found in the tracts with the lowest percentages of foreign-born white population. This vice resort rate (22 per 100,000 in Quarter 1) was twice as high as the rate for Chicago as a whole in 1920 (See Table 36).

According to the 1930 population, only 20.7 per cent of the resorts for 1928–30 were located in the tracts with the highest 25 per cent of the tract percentages of foreign-born whites, while 43.4 per cent of the resorts concentrated in areas of the smallest proportions of foreign-born whites. The highest vice rate per 100,000 occurred in Quarter 1 or the tracts with the lowest percentages of the immigrant whites; whereas the lowest rate existed in Quarter 4 or the tracts with the highest 25 per cent of the percentages of alien-born whites. The vice rate for Quarter 1 was about two and a half times as high as the rate for Chicago as a whole (See Table 37).

Contrary to general opinion, it is clear that the highest

TABLE 36

QUARTER DISTRIBUTION OF VICE RESORTS ACCORDING TO TRACT
PERCENTAGES OF FOREIGN-BORN WHITES, CHICAGO, 1920*

Quarter	Population	Per Cent	No. Vice Resorts, 1918–20, Average 1 Year	Per Cent	Rate per 100,000
4	929,948	34.4	80.66	26.6	8.7
3	681,717	25.2	91.32	30.1	13.4
2	528,461	19.6	7.99	2.6	1.5
1	561,579	20.8	123.68	40.7	22.0
Total	2,701,705	100.0	303.65	100.0	11.2

* Based on Table 27.

TABLE 37

QUARTER DISTRIBUTION OF VICE RESORTS ACCORDING TO TRACT
PERCENTAGES OF FOREIGN-BORN WHITES, CHICAGO, 1930*

Quarter	Population	Per Cent	No. Vice Resorts, 1928–30, Average 1 Year	Per Cent	Rate per 100,000
4	1,141,425	33.8	95.00	20.7	8.3
3	770,927	22.8	71.33	15.5	9.3
2	863,586	25.6	93.99	20.4	10.9
1	600,500	17.8	199.34	43.4	33.2
Total	3,376,438	100.0	459.67	100.0	13.6

* Based on Table 28.

concentration and rates of vice resorts both in 1920 and 1930 were not located in the tracts with the highest percentages of immigrants but rather in those with the lowest.

The coefficients of rank correlation for tract vice rates and tract percentages of foreign-born whites were −.26 in 1920 and −.50 in 1930. The high vice rates are more associated with the low tract percentages of foreign-born whites in 1930 than in 1920. In the ten-year interval the business of vice has located to a greater extent in neighborhoods of primarily native born population.

THE NEGRO POPULATION

The fact that Negroes in the past had to take up residence in or about the vice areas of Chicago was due to the natural segregation of poor, colored immigrants in the sections of least desirability in the city. In addition to this we find also that as the South Side Black Belt expanded southward as a result of the increase in the Chicago Negro population incident to the northern migration of Negroes from the southern states, commercialized vice was also spreading southward in Chicago at about this time in consequence of the efforts at public suppression. The disorganized condition of the poor colored neighborhoods enabled white vice resorts to hide from law enforcement. And later on Negro prostitution itself developed alongside the white commercialized vice just as the black-and-tan cabarets developed alongside the white night clubs which already had sought concealment in the Black Belt. When Negroes betook themselves to the Near West Side of Chicago they found themselves again among white vice resorts. It is only within the last few years that Negroes have been able to shake loose from their residential association with vice resorts.

The Negroes in 1920 comprised only 4.1 per cent of the total population of Chicago. In the 19 vice tracts they constituted 7.1 per cent of the population; while in the 36 non-vice tracts they composed only 0.4 of the total number of inhabitants. In 1930, the Negroes in Chicago comprised 6.9 per cent of the total population, 18 per cent of the total in the 15 vice tracts, and 1.2 of the total in the 47 non-vice tracts. The percentage of colored people in the vice tracts is, therefore, much greater than in the non-vice areas for both 1920 and 1930 census years.

The quarter distribution of vice resorts in 1920 shows that 70 per cent of them were located in the areas with the highest 25 per cent of the tract percentages of the Negro population in Chicago, while less than 1 per cent of the vice emporia was found in the lowest quarter of the tracts. The number of resorts per 100,000 population was 26.7 for Quarter 4 and 0.5 for Quarter 1. Thus, the rate for Quarter 4 was over twice as high as that for entire Chicago in 1920.

TABLE 38

QUARTER DISTRIBUTION OF VICE RESORTS ACCORDING TO TRACT
PERCENTAGES OF NEGRO POPULATION, CHICAGO, 1920*

Quarter	Population	Per Cent	No. Vice Resorts, 1918–20, Average 1 Year	Per Cent	Rate per 100,000
4................	797,764	29.5	212.67	70.0	26.7
3................	677,300	25.1	82.66	27.2	12.2
2................	778,564	28.8	5.98	2.0	0.7
1................	448,077	16.6	2.34	0.8	0.5
Total.........	2,701,705	100.0	303.65	100.0	11.2

* Based on Table 27.

In 1930, 50 per cent of the vice resorts in Chicago concentrated in the tracts with the highest 25 per cent of the tracts arranged according to percentage of Negro population; while less than 1 per cent was located in Quarter 1 of the tracts. The fact that the Negroes between

1920 and 1930 spread over a wider area of Chicago accounts for the reason why Quarter 4 in 1930 has a much smaller percentage of the vice resorts than in 1920. Indeed, Quarter 3, containing the next to highest 25 per cent of the tracts classified by percentage of Negro population, possessed almost as many resorts as Quarter 4 in 1930. The vice rate per 100,000 for Quarter 4 in 1930 was 28.9; for Quarter 3 it was 20; for Quarter 1, 0.2; for Chicago as a whole, 13.6.

TABLE 39

QUARTER DISTRIBUTION OF VICE RESORTS ACCORDING TO TRACT
PERCENTAGES OF NEGRO POPULATION, CHICAGO, 1930*

Quarter	Population	Per Cent	No. Vice Resorts, 1928–30, Average 1 Year	Per Cent	Rate per 100,000
4	797,828	23.6	230.67	50.2	28.9
3	1,049,986	31.1	210.00	45.7	20.0
2	865,092	25.6	17.66	3.8	2.0
1	663,532	19.7	1.33	0.3	0.2
Total	3,376,438	100.0	459.66	100.0	13.6

* Based on Table 28.

The conclusion is evident that the greatest concentration of vice resorts both in 1920 as well as in 1930 has occurred in the tracts possessing the highest percentages of Negro population. The reasons for this are primarily historical and sociological and are to be found in those factors which have determined the location of Negro residence and the business of vice in Chicago.

The coefficients of rank correlation for tract vice rates and tract percentages of Negro population were .73 in 1920 and .56 in 1930. There was tendency for vice to vary in its tract concentrations with the size of the tract percentages of colored population. This tendency was more noticeable in 1920 than in 1930. The reason for this is partly that the vice resorts have found a thriving habitat on the decentralized North Side where few Negroes reside and partly that the Negroes in claiming more residential space in the city have moved into neighborhoods which are too inaccessible or too well organized for vice emporia.

SUMMARY

A study of 5,895 cases of vice resorts for a twenty-year period reveals a 100 per cent distribution in 38 tracts or local communities of Chicago, which segment of the city included 80 per cent of the population count in 1920. Ninety-eight per cent of these resorts were found in 16 tracts, which held 46 per cent of Chicago's 1920 population; while 96 per cent were located in 12 tracts, which contained 30 per cent of the total number of inhabitants in Chicago in 1920.

The average number of tracts in which vice resorts were located was 16.6 for the entire twenty-year period. There was considerable dispersion in the location of houses of prostitution in Chicago during the first decade of public suppression, although a retrenchment was found in the second decade of law enforcement. A three-year distribution of vice resorts showed that the problem was located in tracts comprising 55 per cent of Chicago's 1920 population and 34 per cent of the total 1930 population count.

In 1920, the areas with the highest number of vice resorts per 100,000 population were located in the central or near central regions of Chicago. In 1930 the highest rates of vice concentration were divided between the areas of centralized and decentralized locations. The greatest concentration of vice resorts, consequently, no longer is found in the traditional near central areas where resorts thrived unimpeded before the dawn of public suppression.

The vice tracts showed a lower percentage of children, a higher percentage of adults, a lower percentage of home ownership, and higher percentage of Negroes than the non-vice tracts for 1920 and 1930.

The great majority of houses of prostitution were invariably concentrated in those tracts showing the most exaggerated population features, that is, in that quarter segment of Chicago showing the highest 25 per cent of the tract ratios between the sexes (1920 only), the lowest 25 per cent of the tract percentages of children under 15, the highest 25 per cent of the tract percentages of adults, the lowest 25 per cent of the tract percentages of home ownership, and the highest 25 per cent of the tract percentages of Negro population. The number of resorts per 100,000 in these quarter segments of the tracts with the extreme population features was over twice as high as the rates for Chicago as a whole in 1920 and 1930.

The vice tracts both in 1920 and 1930 did not indicate an appreciably different proportion of foreign-born white population than the non-vice tracts. The highest percentage and rate of vice resort concentration were found in that quarter (Quarter 1) of the population tracts having the lowest 25 per cent of the tract percentages of foreign-born white inhabitants. Contrary to general belief, the location of vice resorts in Chicago does not fall within the areas of greatest immigrant density.

Tract vice rates showed a marked tendency to vary in

magnitude with the magnitude of tract sex ratios for 1920 only, of tract percentages of adults for 1920 and 1930, and of tract percentages of Negro population for 1920 and 1930. The tract vice rates, however, showed a noticeable tendency to vary inversely with the tract percentages of children for 1920 and 1930, the tract percentages of home ownership for 1920, and the tract percentages of foreign-born whites in 1930.

CHAPTER VIII

PROBLEMS ASSOCIATED WITH VICE

It appears that sexual vice occurs ordinarily in association with other forms of social and personal disorganization. This relationship can be tested by finding to what extent vice occurs in those areas of the city characterized by a heavy incidence of prohibition violations (federal padlock cases), venereal diseases, adult male offenders (county jail cases), juvenile delinquency (Juvenile Court cases), poverty (United Charity cases), and divorce. These particular items are selected rather than some others because the data in regard to them are comparable.

FEDERAL PADLOCK CASES

About six years after American cities began their experiment in suppression of commercialized vice, the United States inaugurated its nation-wide ban on intoxicating liquors and beverages. While the saloon and liquor interests were closely associated with commercialized vice heretofore, it is of interest to see to what extent they are related at the present time—when both are under attack by law enforcement agencies.

For this comparison with vice, we have taken the federal padlock cases in the Chicago district (of northern Illinois) for 1926 and 1929. The comparison grows in significance when we realize that both the vice and prohibition violations have been hunted with about the same weapons of law enforcement. While the Committee of Fifteen of Chicago (from which agency the vice cases were obtained) is a private law-enforcing agency, it sends investigators into the field to collect competent legal evidence and then proceeds against the offending places under the arm of the State Injunction and Abatement Law. Likewise the federal office in Chicago sends its investigators into the field to collect evidence and prosecutes the offending places under the Federal Injunction and Abatement Law—padlocks them—under civil action, besides instituting criminal proceedings against the law breakers themselves. As in the case of commercialized vice in Chicago, it often happens that the business of law violation at a given stand or place can be closed by legal measures, although the owner of the business or the party actually responsible for the illicit traffic cannot be reached because he was not on the premises and taking part in the illegal sale when the investigations and raid took place.

During the calendar year of 1926, 701 places in the Chicago region were padlocked by the federal court. In 1929 (calendar year), 542 cases were reported as padlocked. In transcribing these cases in order to get their distribution by tracts within the corporation limits of Chicago, it was found that 695 and 540 cases in 1926 and 1929 respectively had been transcribed, resulting in an error of less than 0.9 per cent in the first instance and less than 0.4 per cent in the second instance. These cases were sorted first with reference to location within and without the corporation limits of Chicago.

	No. 1926	Per Cent	No. 1929	Per Cent
Inside............	589	84.7	389	72.0
Outside.........	106	15.3	151	28.0
Total.......	695	100.0	540	100.0

The lion's share of padlock cases falls within the city limits, although a much higher percentage fell outside in 1929 than 1926 (which was the first complete calendar year for padlock proceedings). It would appear that the urban liquor interests are reacting to law enforcement drives in much the same way that organized vice did—by an exodus to the outskirts of the city.

Clearing the addresses of the padlock cases for the periods January 1, 1926, to July 1, 1927, and January 1, 1929, to July 1, 1930, with the places at which the Committee of Fifteen found evidence of prostitution (in those years), only two actual duplications (that is, cases where the business management in both liquor and vice could be connected) were discovered. There were four likely duplications although not legally substantiated. And there were two instances where vice and liquor cases were in the same building but on different floors with no known or suspected business connection, and four instances where vice and liquor cases were found in adjoining buildings without evidence of any business connection between the two illegal trades. Interestingly enough only one instance of association was found in the 1929–30 series and that of actual duplication. All other instances of duplication or of propinquity occurred in 1926–27. It is clear that vice and liquor do not run hand in hand at the same address as interlocking businesses. On the other hand, it appears that they keep apart at separate addresses. This may be due to the fact that entrepreneurs of vice realize that greater risk is incurred by a partnership with liquor than by plying one trade. And the liquor proprietors have probably discovered that a combination with vice would be even more fatal to their illicit business.

While liquor and vice are generally conducted as separate businesses, they still have some semblance of proximity in general location throughout the city. In 1926, 50.6 per cent of the padlock cases were concentrated in the areas which contained 100 per cent of the Committee of Fifteen's cases (the vice resorts). In 1929, 47.0 per cent of the padlock cases were located in the areas containing 100 per cent of the vice resorts. The padlock cases, therefore, have a much more scattered distribution throughout the city than vice resorts. The reasons for this are probably the following (assuming vice and liquor to be equally matched in gaining protective legal and political favor). There is a wider and more general demand for liquor. Since prohibition women as well as men, contrary to the situation in commercialized vice, patronize night clubs, and even speakeasies. The scheme of life of most individuals which tabus association with bawds, does not stop fraternizing at speakeasies. For the majority of people —those with middle class manners and morals—liquor-drinking and speakeasy-frequenting are matters of public confession and bragging, while bawd-chasing (although confined to men who are still generally excused for their morals) is vulgar, low, common. Immigrant family groups, with their strong notions of familial virtue and female chastity, sanction home brewing, toping, speakeasies, but condemn sexual lapses and patronage of vice resorts. Whether American or immigrant, family neighborhoods are more likely to resist and complain about the intrusion of a disorderly house than to get indignant over the presence of a speakeasy.

In 1926 the tracts of Chicago with the highest 25 per cent of the padlock rates contained practically 66 per cent

MAP 5

SEVENTY FIVE LOCAL COMMUNITIES OF CHICAGO

DISTRIBUTION OF
FEDERAL PADLOCK CASES
WITHIN CORPORATION LIMITS
FOR 1929 AND FIRST SIX
MONTHS OF 1930

LEGEND

NO.	KEY	NO.	KEY
1	ROGERS PARK	39	KENWOOD
2	WEST RIDGE	40	WASHINGTON PK
3	UPTOWN	41	HYDE PARK
4	LINCOLN SQUARE	42	WOODLAWN
5	NORTH CENTER	43	SOUTH SHORE
6	LAKE VIEW	44	CHATHAM
7	LINCOLN PARK	45	AVALON PARK
8	NEAR NORTH SIDE	46	SOUTH CHICAGO
9	EDISON PARK	47	BURNSIDE
10	NORWOOD PARK	48	CALUMET HEIGHTS
11	JEFFERSON PARK	49	ROSELAND
12	FOREST GLEN	50	PULLMAN
13	NORTH PARK	51	SOUTH DEERING
14	ALBANY PARK	52	EAST SIDE
15	PORTAGE PARK	53	WEST PULLMAN
16	IRVING PARK	54	RIVERDALE
17	DUNNING	55	HEGEWISCH
18	MONTCLARE	56	GARFIELD RIDGE
19	BELMONT CRAGIN	57	ARCHER HEIGHTS
20	HERMOSA	58	BRIGHTON PARK
21	AVONDALE	59	Mc KINLEY PARK
22	LOGAN SQUARE	60	BRIDGEPORT
23	HUMBOLDT PARK	61	NEW CITY
24	WEST TOWN	62	WEST ELSDON
25	AUSTIN	63	GAGE PARK
26	WEST GARFIELD PK.	64	CLEARING
27	EAST GARFIELD PK.	65	WEST LAWN
28	NEAR WEST SIDE	66	CHICAGO LAWN
29	NORTH LAWNDALE	67	WEST ENGLEWOOD
30	SOUTH LAWNDALE	68	ENGLEWOOD
31	LOWER WEST SIDE	69	GREATER GRAND CR.
32	LOOP	70	ASHBURN
33	NEAR SOUTH SIDE	71	AUBURN GRESHAM
34	ARMOUR SQUARE	72	BEVERLY
35	DOUGLAS	73	WASHINGTON HGTS.
36	OAKLAND	74	MOUNT GREENWOOD
37	FULLER PARK	75	MORGAN PARK
38	GRAND BLVD.		

M. S.

TABLE 40

TRACT DISTRIBUTION OF FEDERAL PADLOCK CASES AND VICE RESORTS,
CHICAGO, 1926

Community Area*	Population	1926 Padlock Cases	Per Cent	Rate per 100,000	1926 Vice Resorts†	Per Cent	Rate per 100,000
1	57,094	6	1.0	11			
2	39,759						
3	121,637	13	2.2	11	47	10.5	39
4	46,419	1	0.2				
5	47,651	7	1.2	15			
6	114,872	29	4.9	25	13	2.9	11
7	97,873	14	2.4	14	9	2.0	9
8	79,554	53	9.0	67	32	7.2	40
9–10	19,778						
11–12	24,597						
13	11,052						
14	55,577	2	0.3	4			
15	64,203						
16	66,783	1	0.2	1			
17	19,659	2	0.3	10			
18–19	68,721	3	0.5	4			
20	23,518						
21	48,433	4	0.7	8			
22	114,174	18	3.1	16			
23	80,835	6	1.0	7			
24	187,292	25	4.2	13			
25	131,114	1	0.2	1			
26	50,014	1	0.2	2			
27	63,353	11	1.9	17	8	1.8	13
28	152,457	92	15.6	60	35	7.8	23
29	112,261	7	1.2	6	1	0.2	1
30	76,749	10	1.7	13			
31	66,198	34	5.8	51			
32–33	18,267	45	7.6	246	28	6.3	153
34	21,450	12	2.0	56			
35	50,285	11	1.9	22	132	29.6	263
36	14,962	2	0.3	13	6	1.3	40
37	14,437	16	2.7	12			
38	87,005				113	25.3	130
39	26,942				8	1.8	30
40	44,016	3	0.5	7	9	2.0	20
41	48,017	3	0.5	6			
42	66,052	3	0.5	5	4	0.9	6
43	78,755	5	0.8	6			

* Based on 75 Census Tracts of Chicago.
† Based on Table 57.

TABLE 40—*Continued*

Community Area*	Population	1926 Padlock Cases	Per Cent	Rate per 100,000	1926 Vice Resorts†	Per Cent	Rate per 100,000
44	36,228	5	0.8	14			
45	10,023						
46	56,683	8	1.3	14			
47–48	10,826	3	0.5	28			
49	43,206	2	0.3	5			
50–51	14,603	6	1.0	41			
52–55	24,729	3	0.5	12			
53–54	29,960	4	0.7	13			
56–57	14,170	2	0.3	14			
58	46,552	10	1.7	21			
59	22,032	4	0.7	18			
60	53,553	10	1.7	2			
61	87,103	47	8.2	54			
62–63	34,396	4	0.7	12			
64–65	14,353						
66	47,462	4	0.7	8			
67	63,845	6	1.0	9			
68	89,063	15	2.5	17	1	0.2	1
69	60,007	14	2.3	23			
70–71	58,114	1	0.2	2			
72–74	17,103						
73	17,865	1	0.2	6			
75	12,747						
Total	3,376,438	589		17	446		

* Based on 75 Census Tracts of Chicago.
† Based on Table 57.

of the padlock cases and 56 per cent of the vice resorts. The padlock rate for this quarter (4) segment of tracts was 43 per 100,000; while the vice rate was 28 per 100,000 for the same tracts, as compared with rates of 17 and 13 per 100,000 respectively for the city as a whole. Twenty-seven per cent of the vice resorts were located in the tracts with the lowest 25 per cent of the tract rates, while less than 1 per cent of the padlock cases fell in this quarter as may be seen in Table 42.

In 1929 the tracts with the highest quarter of the rates

TABLE 41

TRACT DISTRIBUTION OF FEDERAL PADLOCK CASES AND OF
VICE RESORTS, CHICAGO, 1929

Community Area*	Population	1929 Padlock Cases	Per Cent	Rate per 100,000	1929 Vice Resorts†	Per Cent	Rate per 100,000
1	57,094	4	1.0	7	1	0.2	2
2	39,759	1	0.2	3	.....	.....	.....
3	121,637	7	1.8	6	96	20.9	79
4	46,419	1	0.2	2	.....	.....	.....
5	47,651	2	0.5	4	.....	.....	.....
6	114,872	14	3.6	12	58	12.6	50
7	97,873	7	1.8	7	6	1.3	61
8	79,554	34	8.7	43	33	7.2	41
9–10	19,778	.....	.....	.....	.....	.....	.....
11–12	24,597	.....	.....	.....	.....	.....	.....
13	11,052	.....	.....	.....	.....	.....	.....
14	55,577	1	0.2	2	.....	.....	.....
15	64,203	.....	.....	.....	.....	.....	.....
16	66,783	1	0.2	1	.....	.....	.....
17	19,659	.....	.....	.....	.....	.....	.....
18–19	68,721	4	1.0	6	.....	.....	.....
20	23,518	.....	.....	.....	.....	.....	.....
21	48,433	6	1.5	12	.....	.....	.....
22	114,174	6	1.5	5	.....	.....	.....
23	80,835	6	1.5	7	.....	.....	.....
24	187,292	16	4.1	9	.....	.....	.....
25	131,114	6	1.5	5	.....	.....	.....
26	50,014	2	0.5	4	.....	.....	.....
27	63,353	6	1.5	9	.....	.....	.....
28	152,457	33	8.5	22	31	6.8	20
29	112,261	1	0.2	1	.....	.....	.....
30	76,749	3	0.8	4	.....	.....	.....
31	66,198	10	2.6	15	.....	.....	.....
32–33	18,267	42	10.8	230	14	3.1	77
34	21,450	4	1.0	19	.....	.....	.....
35	50,285	16	4.1	32	50	10.9	99
36	14,962	3	0.8	20	6	1.3	40
37	14,437	1	0.2	7	.....	.....	.....
38	87,005	12	3.1	14	125	27.2	144
39	26,942	2	0.5	7	11	2.4	41
40	44,016	3	0.8	7	26	5.7	59
41	48,017	6	1.5	12	2	0.4	4
42	66,052	12	3.1	18	.....	.....	.....
43	78,755	1	0.2	1	.....	.....	.....

* Based on 75 Census Tracts of Chicago.
† Based on Table 57.

TABLE 41—*Continued*

Community Area*	Population	1929 Padlock Cases	Per Cent	Rate per 100,000	1929 Vice Resorts†	Per Cent	Rate per 100,000
44	36,228	3	0.8	8			
45	10,023						
46	56,683	1	0.2	2			
47–48	10,826	2	0.5	18			
49	43,206	1	0.2	2			
50–51	14,603	1	0.2	7			
52–55	24,729	2	0.5	8			
53–54	29,960						
56–57	14,170						
58	46,552	4	1.0	9			
59	22,032	3	0.8	14			
60	53,553	5	1.3	9			
61	87,103	22	5.7	25			
62–63	34,396	1	0.2	3			
64–65	14,353						
66	47,462	5	1.3	11			
67	63,845	28	7.2	44			
68	89,063	23	5.9	26			
69	60,007	4	1.0	7			
70–71	58,114	4	1.0	7			
72–74	17,103	4	1.0	23			
73	17,865						
75	12,747	1	0.2	8			
Wrong Address		2	0.5				
Total	3,376,438	389		12	459		14

* Based on 75 Census Tracts of Chicago.
† Based on Table 57.

TABLE 42

QUARTER DISTRIBUTION OF VICE RESORTS ACCORDING TO TRACT RATES OF PADLOCK CASES, CHICAGO, 1926*

Quarter	Population	Per Cent	No. Padlock Cases	Per Cent	Rate per 100,000	No. Vice Resorts	Per Cent	Rate per 100,000
4	896,622	26.6	386	65.5	43.1	249	55.8	27.8
3	947,694	28.1	139	23.6	14.7	62	13.9	6.5
2	936,726	27.7	61	10.4	6.5	14	3.2	1.5
1	595,396	17.6	3	0.5	0.5	121	27.1	20.3
Total	3,376,438	100.0	589	100.0	17.4	446	100.0	13.2

* Based on Table 40.

for padlock cases held 64 per cent of the padlock cases
and 56 per cent of the vice cases. The rates per 100,000
for the two series of cases were 29 and 31, as contrasted
with the rates of 12 and 14 for Chicago as a whole. Twenty-
seven per cent of the vice cases were concentrated in the
tracts with the next to lowest quarter of the tract padlock rates (see Table 43). While the majority of the vice
resorts were found in the quarter with the highest concentration of padlock cases, slightly under 30 per cent of
the vice cases were located in tracts with the lowest or
next to lowest padlock concentration.

TABLE 43

QUARTER DISTRIBUTION OF VICE RESORTS ACCORDING TO TRACT
RATES OF PADLOCK CASES, CHICAGO, 1929*

Quarter	Popula-tion	Per Cent	No. Padlock Cases	Per Cent	Rate per 100,000	No. Vice Resorts	Per Cent	Rate per 100,000
4........	846,202	25.1	248	64.1	29.3	259	56.4	30.6
3........	960,419	28.4	88	22.7	9.2	78	17.0	8.1
2........	1,006,157	29.8	47	12.2	4.7	122	26.6	12.1
1........	563,660	16.7	4	1.0	0.7	0	0.0	0.0
Total	3,376,438	100.0	387	100.0	11.5	459	100.0	13.6

* Based on Table 41.

The coefficients of correlation by the rank-difference
method for tract vice and padlock rates were .05 in 1926
and .23 in 1929.[1]

It is clear that there is practically no tendency for vice
rates to vary in magnitude with padlock rates by tracts.
This bears out the previous conclusions that vice resorts

[1] See note 1, p. 184. Thirteen tracts of Chicago had vice rates in 1926;
15, in 1929.

and places violating the federal prohibition law are not closely associated in the same tracts of the city. High vice rates are likely to occur in areas with low padlock incidence; while areas of high padlock rates are likely to occur in areas of low vice resort incidence or areas free of commercialized vice.

VENEREAL DISEASES

Venereal diseases, especially syphilis, have invariably in recent times been incident of sex promiscuity. We should like to know, particularly, whether the incidence of venereal disease has been affected by the suppression of commercialized vice in American cities. Even with the best-recorded statistical data this factor would be hard to isolate due to the great mobility of individuals, the extent of sex promiscuity in non-commercialized relations, and the increased use of preventive measures through the spread of sex hygiene education. Most medical authorities, in spite of more adequate venereal disease reporting in the last few years, as compared with the 1910 era, believe that the social diseases are showing a tendency to decline. They assign it, however, less to increased public morality than to the increased use of precautionary measures, and to the greater inclination toward, and facilities for, medical attention. Though it is not practicable to treat the effect of vice suppression on the incidence of venereal disease, it is possible to discover the extent to which vice resorts and venereal disease cases are related in the areas of the city.

For the comparison we shall take the venereal disease cases and vice data of 1928 in Chicago. The venereal disease data comprise a sample of 18.1 per cent of the total number of reported cases[2] in Chicago in 1928. The sample was taken from the 1928 records in the files of four free clinics—one on the Lower North Side, one on the Near South Side, one on the Near West Side and one (the largest of the four) in the downtown location.[3] The sample is limited to those persons who cannot or are unwilling to pay for private medical care either by private physicians or by the Public Health Institute (of Chicago). It represents, for the most part, the charity cases (although this might not be always a sign of low economic status) and, in the minority, conscripted cases (especially from the Morals Court). It lacks the paying cases which according to the reported cases from all sources would constitute about 47 per cent of the total number reported for 1928.[4]

[2] Cases of 4,682 individuals who appeared for treatment one or more times in 1928 at four clinics in Chicago and who resided within the corporation limits of the city at an identifiable address, were found in the files of these four clinics. Due to the migratory character of persons under venereal disease treatment (i.e. their tendency to shift from one clinic to another in process of treatment) and due to the fact that an individual who was treated for a new or reinfection in 1928 was only counted once (but would be reported twice), the 4,682 individuals would probably mount up to a slightly higher figure if translated into mere cases reported. But taking these 4,682 as they are, we find that they comprise 18.1 per cent of the total of 25,931 venereal disease cases reported to the Health Department of the City of Chicago from all reportable sources.

[3] The sample of 4,682 cases was distributed in the four clinics as follows: the downtown clinic, 3,142; the Lower North Side clinic, 696; the Near South Side clinic, 477; the Near West Side clinic, 517. Geographically, this distribution does not favor any one of the three sides of the city of Chicago.

[4] This percentage figure is arrived at as follows: 7,023 cases reported from the Public Health Institute and 5,096 from private physicians, making a total of 12,119 paying cases reported out of 25,931 total cases reported for 1928.

VICE IN CHICAGO

TABLE 44

TRACT DISTRIBUTION OF VENEREAL DISEASE CASES
AND VICE RESORTS, CHICAGO, 1928

Community Area*	Population	1928 V.D. Cases	Per Cent	Rate per 100,000	1928 Vice Resorts†	Per Cent	Rate per 100,000
1	57,094	10	.21	16	1	0.2	2
2	39,759	8	.17	20	.....	.....	.....
3	121,637	107	2.29	88	60	12.5	49
4	46,419	8	.17	17	2	0.4	4
5	47,651	13	.28	27	.....	.....	.....
6	114,872	82	1.75	71	52	10.8	45
7	97,873	106	2.26	108	21	4.4	21
8	79,554	301	6.43	378	64	13.3	80
9–10	19,778	3	.06	15	.....	.....	.....
11–12	24,597	6	.13	24	.....	.....	.....
13	11,052	2	.04	18	.....	.....	.....
14	55,577	4	.09	7	.....	.....	.....
15	64,203	13	.28	20	.....	.....	.....
16	66,783	17	.36	25	.....	.....	.....
17	19,659	1	.02	5	.....	.....	.....
18–19	68,721	11	.23	16	1	0.2	1
20	23,518	1	.04	4	.....	.....	.....
21	48,433	14	.30	29	.....	.....	.....
22	114,174	51	1.09	45	.....	.....	.....
23	80,835	33	.70	41	1	.02	1
24	187,292	210	4.49	112	1	.02	1
25	131,114	23	.49	18	.....	.....	.....
26	50,014	28	.60	56	.....	.....	.....
27	63,353	83	1.77	131	1	0.2	2
28	152,457	1017	21.72	667	34	7.1	22
29	112,261	59	1.26	53	.....	.....	.....
30	76,749	25	.53	33	.....	.....	.....
31	66,198	83	1.77	125	.....	.....	.....
32–33	18,267	132	2.82	723	20	4.2	109
34	21,450	54	1.15	252	1	0.2	5
35	50,285	778	16.62	1547	67	14.0	133
36	14,962	83	1.77	555	5	1.0	33
37	14,437	31	.66	215	.....	.....	.....
38	87,005	524	11.19	602	103	21.5	118
39	26,942	18	.38	67	20	4.2	74
40	44,016	258	5.51	586	23	4.8	52
41	48,017	22	.47	46	3	0.6	6
42	66,052	82	1.75	124	.....	.....	.....
43	78,755	11	.23	14	.....	.....	.....

* Based on 75 Census Tracts of Chicago.
† Based on Table 57.

TABLE 44—*Continued*

Com- munity Area*	Popula- tion	1928 V.D. Cases	Per Cent	Rate per 100,000	1928 Vice Resorts†	Per Cent	Rate per 100,000
44.........	36,228	13	.28	36			
45.........	10,023	1	.02	10			
46.........	56,683	17	.36	30			
47–48......	10,826	2	.04	18			
49.........	43,206	18	.38	42			
50–51......	14,603	6	.13	41			
52–55......	24,729	6	.13	24			
53–54......	29,960	11	.23	37			
56–57......	14,170	8	.17	56			
58.........	46,552	23	.49	49			
59.........	22,032	16	.34	73			
60.........	53,553	45	.96	84			
61.........	87,103	58	1.24	67			
62–63......	34,396	7	.15	20			
64–65......	14 353	5	.11	35			
66.........	47,462	11	.23	23			
67.........	63,845	28	.60	44			
68.........	89,063	50	1.07	56			
69.........	60,007	22	.47	37			
70–71......	58,114	5	.11	9			
72–74......	17,103	1	.02	6			
73.........	17,865	1	.02	6			
75.........	12,747	16	.34	126			
Total...	3,376,438	4682	99.97	142	480	100.0	14

*Based on 75 Census Tracts of Chicago.
†Based on Table 57.

When this 1928 sample of venereal disease cases with its superabundance of non-paying patients is distributed by tracts in the city, it is found that 82 per cent of the 4,682 individuals in the sample were located in the areas covered by 100 per cent of the 1928 vice cases. It seems, therefore, that while most of the venereal disease cases fell in the same general location of Chicago as commercialized vice, 18 per cent of them fell in areas of the city untouched by vice resorts. The charity-conscripted venereal distribution is slightly more widespread than commercialized vice itself. If in the sample of 4,682 venereally infected individuals there had been 47 per cent paying patients, the venereal distribution would have been less concentrated in the areas containing the vice resorts. This would follow providing the paying cases show a higher economic status than the non-paying ones, so as to increase the quota of infected individuals from neighborhoods outside the vice tracts.

In 1928, 71 per cent of the vice resorts fell in the tracts of Quarter 4 (see Table 45), while 28 per cent fell in Quarter 3. On the other hand, 80 per cent of the venereal disease cases fell in Quarter 4, while 13 per cent fell in Quarter 3. In other words, practically 99 per cent of the vice resorts and 93 per cent of the venereal disease cases were concentrated in those tracts with the highest 50 per cent of the rates for venereal disease, which tracts contained 59 per cent of Chicago's total population. It is significant to note that the vice rate per 100,000 in Quarter 4 was almost two and a half times that for the city as a whole.

The coefficient of rank correlation for tract vice and

TABLE 45

QUARTER DISTRIBUTION OF VICE RESORTS ACCORDING TO TRACT
RATES OF VENEREAL DISEASE CASES, CHICAGO, 1928*

Quarter	Population	Per Cent	No. V.D. Cases	Per Cent	Rate per 100,000	No. Vice Resorts	Per Cent	Rate per 100,000
4........	975,948	28.9	3,758	80.3	385.0	340	70.8	34.8
3........	1,022,044	30.3	619	13.2	60.6	135	28.1	13.2
2........	752,828	22.3	221	4.7	29.4	1	0.2	0.1
1...,....	625,618	18.5	84	1.8	13.4	4	0.8	0.6
Total	3,376,438	100.0	4,682	100.0	138.6	480	99.9	14.2

* Based on Table 44.

venereal disease rates in 1928 was .68.[5] There is a marked tendency for the vice rates to increase or decrease with the tract variations in the rates for venereal disease cases. Offhand it might be concluded that commercialized vice and venereal disease stand in relation to one another as cause to effect. But sociologically the venereal disease incidence is to be thought of as an indicator of the presence of maladjusted individuals, who may or may not have reached their condition by contact with commercialized vice.

ADULT MALE OFFENDERS

Urban vice areas in the past—those which contained the concentration of brothels—were reputed havens for criminals and criminal activities. While the police in justification of their policy of "segregation" have argued to the contrary, no vice area has ever been as orderly as painted by official police statements. The break-up of the caste of the criminal, the partial lifting of stigma from a criminal "record," the indulgence in outlawed activity by "respectable" people, the devices for transportation and communication have undoubtedly operated to diffuse adult male offenders throughout the city rather than to confine them in the slums. Furthermore the slum no longer is the sole refuge of crime and vice. Vice in assuming milder and less obvious forms has spread out over a larger area; so crime in taking new forms has become more widely dispersed.

How about the distribution of adult male offenders throughout the city? Is it more widespread than vice? And how much overlapping occurs? In order to get the

[5] Nineteen tracts with vice rates were used in running the rank correlation with tract venereal disease rates.

social geography of adult male offenders in Chicago, it was necessary to take the addresses of males in the county jail in 1920. The ordinary inhabitants of this penal institution are bound over to the criminal court awaiting trial, men who were not granted or could not make bond, as well as men who had been sentenced for short-term misdemeanors which did not carry "penitentiary offense." It appears that the tracts of Chicago, which contained 100 per cent of the commercialized vice distribution in 1920, included 71.7 per cent of the Chicago males in the county jail. While adult male offenders have a more widespread location throughout Chicago than vice resorts, yet in terms of the percentage contained within the tracts possessing 100 per cent of the vice resorts adult male offenders do not fall outside the vice tracts as much as padlock cases and are not as confined to them as much as the venereal disease cases.

In 1920, 85 per cent of the vice resorts were concentrated in the tracts of the highest quarter of reported residence for males in the county jail. The vice rate in this quarter (i.e., Quarter 4) was almost two and a half times that for entire Chicago. Besides containing the overwhelming majority of houses of prostitution, the tracts in Quarter 4, which held 36 per cent of the total population of Chicago in 1920, contained 67 per cent of the male offenders. It seems clear that the neighborhoods which housed the majority of vice resorts in 1920 were at the same time the reported residence of the adult male offenders. The conditions of community life which favor the existence of vice emporia are, undoubtedly, the same ones which either foster criminality or attract the adult criminal population (See Table 47).

TABLE 46

TRACT DISTRIBUTION OF MALES IN THE COUNTY JAIL AND
VICE RESORTS, CHICAGO, 1920

Community Area*	Population	1920, No. of Males, Co. Jail†	Per Cent	Rate per 100,000	1920 Vice Resorts‡	Per Cent	Rate per 100,000
1–2.......	35,203	15	0.20	43	......	......	......
3..........	45,195	36	0.48	80	1	0.34	2
4..........	74,211	104	1.40	140	9	3.09	12
5..........	17,343	17	0.23	98	......	......	......
6..........	21,036	30	0.40	143	......	......	......
7..........	99,749	106	1.42	106	6	2.06	6
8..........	94,247	224	3.01	238	6	2.06	6
9..........	83,936	492	6.61	586	57	19.59	68
10–11–12....	9,917	4	0.05	40	......	......	......
13..........	11,069	4	0.05	36	......	......	......
14–15.......	25,189	27	0.36	107	......	......	......
16..........	40,908	33	0.44	81	......	......	......
17..........	33,562	35	0.47	104	......	......	......
18–19.......	17,478	25	0.34	143	......	......	......
20..........	21,741	21	0.28	97	......	......	......
21..........	27,321	29	0.39	106	......	......	......
22..........	82,180	83	1.12	101	1	0.34	1
23..........	69,350	42	0.56	61	......	......	......
24..........	69,986	88	1.18	126	......	......	......
25..........	237,492	597	8.03	251	1	0.34	......
26..........	44,122	48	0.65	109	1	0.34	2
27..........	65,858	142	1.91	216	2	0.69	3
28..........	194,259	1,292	17.37	665	70	24.06	36
29..........	75,910	136	1.83	179	......	......	......
30..........	88,378	110	1.48	124	......	......	......
31..........	85,680	278	3.74	324	......	......	......
32..........	13,140	270	3.63	2,055	12	4.12	91
33..........	17,389	223	3.00	1,282	28	9.62	161
34..........	22,016	52	0.70	236	......	......	......
35..........	78,755	180	2.42	229	......	......	......
36..........	64,453	860	11.56	1,334	43	14.78	67
37–38.......	24,488	63	0.85	257	......	......	......
39..........	14,420	29	0.39	201	......	......	......
40..........	87,303	238	3.20	273	......	......	......
41..........	13,602	71	0.95	522	......	......	......
42..........	14,377	51	0.69	355	......	......	......
43..........	73,555	346	4.65	470	21	7.22	29
44–47–55....	22,672	31	0.42	137	......	......	......
45..........	16,540	84	1.13	508	12	4.12	73

* Based on 70 statistical communities of Chicago for 1920.
† Obtained from data collected by Clifford R. Shaw, Behavior Research Fund, Chicago.
‡ Based on Table 57.

TABLE 46—*Continued*

Community Area*	Population	1920, No. of Males, Co. Jail†	Per Cent	Rate per 100,000	1920 Vice Resorts‡	Per Cent	Rate per 100,000
46.........	30,976	51	0.69	165	5	1.72	16
48.........	52,373	109	1.47	208	......	......	......
49.........	114,429	194	2.61	170	......	......	......
50.........	41,359	137	1.84	331	4	1.38	10
51.........	32,967	41	0.55	124	2	0.69	6
52.........	62,751	85	1.14	135	2	0.69	3
53.........	25,973	24	0.32	92	......	......	......
54.........	33,425	16	0.22	48	......	......	......
56.........	13,566	17	0.23	125	......	......	......
57–58......	13,664	29	0.39	212	......	......	......
59.........	43,642	103	1.38	236	7	2.41	16
60–61–66....	18,104	13	0.17	72	1	0.34	6
62–63......	19.681	17	0.23	86	......	......	......
64–65–70....	25,551	46	0.62	180	......	......	......
67.........	26,557	32	0.43	120	......	......	......
68–69......	12,657	9	0.12	71	......	......	......
Total...	2,701,705	7,439	100.00	....	291	100.00	......

* Based on 70 statistical communities of Chicago for 1920.
† Obtained from data collected by Clifford R. Shaw, Behavior Research Fund, Chicago.
‡ Based on Table 57.

TABLE 47

QUARTER DISTRIBUTION OF VICE RESORTS ACCORDING TO TRACT
RATES OF ADULT MALE OFFENDERS, CHICAGO, 1920*

Quarter	Population	Per Cent	No. Males in Co. Jail	Per Cent	Rate per 100,000	No. Vice Resorts	Per Cent	Rate per 100,000
4........	967,573	35.8	5,002	67.2	517.0	248	85.2	25.6
3........	670,355	24.8	1,350	18.2	201.4	20	6.9	3.0
2........	703,211	26.0	836	11.2	118.9	21	7.2	3.0
1........	360,566	13.4	251	3.4	69.6	2	0.7	0.5
Total..	3,376,438	100.0	7,439	100.0	275.3	291	100.0	10.8

* Based on Table 46.

The coefficient of rank correlation for tract vice rates
and tract rates for adult male offenders was .78.[6] There

[6] Twenty-one tracts with vice rates were used in correlation with
the tract rates for adult male offenders.

was a strong tendency for tract vice rates to vary directly with the size of the tract rates for adult male offenders. In other words, a high incidence of adult male delinquents was associated in areas with a high vice resort incidence. While the vice areas in the past attracted a criminal or pseudo-criminal male population, there was perhaps less of a parasitic attachment of a criminal element with houses of prostitution in 1920 than in 1910. This was due in large part to the changes in the form and location of the business of prostitution in Chicago. The association of the two problems in the same areas should not be thought of as cause and effect but rather as problems related to the same background conditions. The conditions of neighborhood life which enable vice resorts to thrive are undoubtedly the same ones which foster the development and maintenance of adult male criminals.

JUVENILE DELINQUENCY

Vice areas have been said to have a demoralizing effect on the youth and young adults who must live in their environs. Any direct and immediate effect of this factor on behavior (especially on sex delinquency) would be unlikely to occur and at best the vicious environs and bad companions associated with commercialized vice nowadays would be registered more as a secondary background cause than a primary causative factor in juvenile delinquency. Even this secondary relationship of the presence of commercialized vice in the neighborhood to delinquency must be discovered in the individual case rather than assumed because it is there in the local community background.

Without assuming any necessary relation of cause and

TABLE 48

TRACT DISTRIBUTION OF JUVENILE COURT GIRLS' CASES AND VICE RESORTS, CHICAGO, 1917–23

Community Area*	Population	No. of J.C. Girls 1917–23 †	Per Cent	Av. No. for 1 Year	Rate per 100,000	Vice Resorts 1917–23 ‡	Per Cent	Av. No. for 1 Year	Rate per 100,000
1–2	35,203	7	0.24	1.00	3	1	0.04	0.14	.....
3	45,195	24	0.83	3.43	8	4	0.17	0.57	1
4	74,211	23	0.80	3.29	4	51	2.17	7.29	10
5	17,343	8	0.28	1.14	7	1	0.04	0.14	1
6	21,036	12	0.42	1.71	8	.....	.....	.....	.....
7	99,749	64	2.23	9.14	9	37	1.58	5.29	5
8	94,247	103	3.58	14.71	16	75	3.19	10.71	11
9	83,936	150	5.22	21.43	26	346	14.74	49.43	59
10–11–12	9,917	5	0.17	0.71	7	1	0.04	0.14	1
13	11,069	3	0.10	0.43	4	.....	.....	.....	.....
14–15	25,189	20	0.30	2.86	11	.....	.....	.....	.....
16	40,908	23	0.80	3.29	8	.....	.....	.....	.....
17	33,562	26	0.90	3.71	11	.....	.....	.....	.....
18–19	17,478	13	0.45	1.86	11	.....	.....	.....	.....
20	21,741	13	0.45	1.86	9	.....	.....	.....	.....
21	27,321	19	0.63	2.71	10	.....	.....	.....	.....
22	82,180	60	2.09	8.57	10	4	0.17	0.57	1
23	69,350	21	0.73	3.00	4	1	0.04	0.14	.....
24	69,986	53	1.84	7.57	11	1	0.04	0.14	.....
25	237,492	415	14.43	59.29	25	8	0.34	1.14	.....
26	44,122	17	0.59	2.43	6	3	0.13	0.43	1
27	65,858	45	1.57	6.43	10	15	0.64	2.14	3
28	194,259	353	12.28	50.43	26	522	22.23	74.57	38
29	75,910	40	1.39	5.71	8	.....	.....	.....	.....
30	88,378	70	2.43	10.00	11	.....	.....	.....	.....
31	85,680	89	3.10	12.71	15	6	0.26	0.86	1
32	13,140	6	0.21	0.86	7	149	6.35	21.28	162
33	17,389	42	1.46	6.00	35	196	8.35	28.00	161
34	22,016	13	0.45	1.86	8	.....	.....	.....	.....
35	78,755	95	3.30	13.57	17	17	0.72	2.43	3
36	64,453	238	8.28	34.00	53	546	23.25	78.00	121
37–38	24,488	38	1.32	5.43	22	.....	.....	.....	.....
39	14,420	23	0.80	3.29	23	.....	.....	.....	.....
40	87,303	108	3.76	15.43	18	2	0.09	0.28	.....
41	13,602	20	0.70	2.86	21	2	0.09	0.28	2
42	14,377	15	0.52	2.14	15	2	0.09	0.28	2
43	73,555	128	4.46	18.28	25	205	8.73	29.28	40

* Based on 70 Statistical Communities.
† Obtained from data collected by Clifford R. Shaw, Behavior Research Fund, Chicago.
‡ Based on Table 57.

TABLE 48—*Continued*

Community Area*	Population	No. of J.C. Girls 1917-23 †	Per Cent	Av. No. for 1 Year	Rate per 100,000	Vice Resorts 1917-23 ‡	Per Cent	Av. No. for 1 Year	Rate per 100,000
44-47-55	22,672	14	0.49	2.00	9	......	.....	.....	....
45......	16,540	25	0.87	3.57	22	72	3.07	10.29	62
46......	30,976	16	0.56	2.29	7	13	0.55	1.86	6
48......	52,373	35	1.22	5.00	10	......	.....	.....	....
49......	114,429	90	3.13	12.86	11	12	0.51	1.71	1
50......	41,359	51	1.77	7.29	8	21	0.89	3.00	7
51......	32,967	18	0.63	2.57	8	5	0.21	0.71	2
52......	62,751	34	1.18	4.86	8	9	0.38	1.29	2
53......	25,973	18	0.63	2.57	10	......	.....	.....	....
54......	33,425	5	0.17	0.71	2	1	0.04	0.14	.....
56......	13,566	5	0.17	0.71	5	1	0.04	0.14	1
57-58...	13,664	12	0.42	1.71	13	......	.....	.....	....
59......	43,642	66	2.30	9.43	22	14	0.60	2.00	5
60-61-66	18,104	17	0.59	2.43	13	3	0.13	0.43	2
62-63...	19,681	18	0.63	2.57	13	2	0.09	0.28	1
64-65-70	25,551	22	0.77	3.14	12	......	.....	.....	....
67......	26,557	14	0.49	2.00	8	......	.....	.....	....
68-69...	12,657	13	0.45	1.86	15	......	.....	.....	....
Total...	2,701,705	2,875	99.98	.....	......	2,348	99.99	.....	....

* Based on 70 Statistical Communities.
† Obtained from data collected by Clifford R. Shaw, Behavior Research Fund, Chicago.
‡ Based on Table 57.

effect, it is of interest to see to what extent the distribution of juvenile delinquents follows that of vice throughout Chicago. First of all, we shall consider the female Juvenile Court cases, for their greatest crime is sex delinquency and they are most affected by prostitution. The distribution of female Juvenile Court cases during 1917–23 will be compared with that for vice in the same period.

The 35 tracts of Chicago which possessed 100 per cent of the vice resorts from 1917–23 contained 84 per cent of the female delinquents, while 9 of the 35 tracts contained 92 per cent of the resorts and only 37 per cent of the delinquent girls. Thus 26 tracts which only had a

TABLE 49

TRACT DISTRIBUTION OF JUVENILE COURT BOYS' CASES
AND VICE RESORTS, CHICAGO, 1917–23

Community Area*	Population	No. of J.C. Boys 1917-23 †	Per Cent	Av. No. for 1 Year	Rate per 100,000	Vice Resorts 1917-23 ‡	Per Cent	Av. No. for 1 Year	Rate per 100,000
1-2	35,203	31	0.38	4.43	13	1	0.04	0.14	....
3	45,195	42	0.52	6.00	13	4	0.17	0.57	1
4	74,211	59	0.73	8.43	11	51	2.17	7.29	10
5	17,343	16	0.20	2.29	13	1	0.04	0.14	1
6	21,036	53	0.66	7.57	36	....	....	....	....
7	99,749	101	1.25	14.43	14	37	1.58	5.29	5
8	94,247	163	2.02	23.28	25	75	3.19	10.71	11
9	83,936	247	3.06	35.28	42	346	14.74	49.43	59
10-11-12	9,917	14	0.17	2.00	20	1	0.04	0.14	1
13	11,069	9	0.11	1.29	12	....	....	....	....
14-15	25,189	38	0.47	5.43	22	....	....	....	....
16	40,908	43	0.53	6.14	15	....	....	....	....
17	33,562	53	0.66	7.57	23	....	....	....	....
18-19	17,478	76	0.94	10.86	62	....	....	....	....
20	21,741	25	0.31	3.57	16	....	....	....	....
21	27,321	45	0.56	6.43	24	....	....	....	....
22	82,180	201	2.49	28.71	35	4	0.17	0.57	1
23	69,350	93	1.15	13.29	19	1	0.04	0.14	....
24	69,986	154	1.91	22.00	31	1	0.04	0.14	....
25	237,492	1,207	14.95	172.42	73	8	0.35	1.14	....
26	44,122	63	0.78	9.00	20	3	0.13	0.43	1
27	65,858	189	2.34	27.00	41	15	0.64	2.14	3
28	194,259	1,168	14.46	166.85	86	522	22.23	74.57	38
29	75,910	203	2.51	29.00	38	....	....	....	....
30	88,378	189	2.34	27.00	31	....	....	....	....
31	85,680	385	4.77	55.00	64	6	0.26	0.86	1
32	13,140	59	0.73	8.43	6	149	6.35	21.28	162
33	17,389	63	0.78	9.00	52	196	8.35	20.86	120
34	22,016	66	0.82	9.43	43	....	....	....	....
35	78,755	362	4.48	51.71	66	17	0.72	2.43	3
36	64,453	373	4.62	53.28	83	546	23.25	78.00	121
37-38	24,488	84	1.04	12.00	49	....	....	....	....
39	14,420	30	0.37	4.29	30	....	....	....	....
40	87,303	340	4.21	48.57	56	2	0.08	0.28	....
41	13,602	89	1.10	12.71	93	2	0.08	0.28	2
42	14,377	48	0.59	6.86	48	2	0.08	0.28	2
43	73,555	248	3.07	35.43	48	205	8.73	29.28	40

* Based on 70 Statistical Communities.
† Obtained from data collected by Clifford R. Shaw, Behavior Research Fund, Chicago.
‡ Based on Table 57.

TABLE 49—*Continued*

Community Area*	Population	No. of J.C. Boys 1917-23 †	Per Cent	Av. No. for 1 Year	Rate per 100,000	Vice Resorts 1917-23 ‡	Per Cent	Av. No. for 1 Year	Rate per 100,000
44–47–55	22,672	63	0.78	9.00	40	......	.....	.....	.....
45......	16,540	35	0.43	5.00	30	72	3.07	10.29	62
46......	30,976	34	0.42	4.86	16	13	0.55	1.86	6
48......	52,373	149	1.84	21.28	41	......	.....	.....	.....
49......	114,429	278	3.44	39.71	35	12	0.51	1.71	1
50......	41,359	93	1.15	13.29	32	21	0.89	3.00	7
51......	32,967	36	0.45	5.14	16	5	0.21	0.71	2
52......	62,751	90	1.11	12.86	20	9	0.38	1.29	2
53......	25,973	28	0.35	4.00	15	......	.....	.....	.....
54......	33,425	20	0.25	2.86	9	1	0.04	0.14	.....
56......	13,566	38	0.47	5.43	40	1	0.04	0.14	1
57–58...	13,664	54	0.67	7.71	56	......	.....	.....	.....
59......	43,642	201	2.49	28.71	66	14	0.60	2.00	5
60–61–66	18,104	29	0.36	4.14	23	3	0.13	0.43	2
62–63...	19,681	62	0.77	8.86	45	2	0.08	0.28	1
64–65–70	25,551	99	1.23	14.14	55	......	.....	.....	.....
67......	26,557	75	0.93	10.71	40	......	.....	.....	.....
68–69...	12,657	63	0.78	9.00	71	......	.....	.....	.....
Total...	2,701,705	8,076	99.99	.....	.....	2,348	99.97	.....	.....

* Based on 70 Statistical Communities.
† Obtained from data collected by Clifford R. Shaw, Behavior Research Fund, Chicago
‡ Based on Table 57.

cumulative total of 8 per cent of the vice cases, had 47 per cent of the female delinquents. The remaining 16 per cent of the delinquent girls were distributed in the non-vice tracts of the city. Female delinquency was, therefore, considerably more dispersed throughout Chicago than commercialized vice.

Eighty-two per cent of the Juvenile Court boys cases 1917–23 were distributed in the 35 tracts containing the investigated vice resorts in that period of time, although the nine tracts which quartered 92 per cent of the houses of prostitution only sheltered 31 per cent of the male juvenile offenders. The remaining 18 per cent of the

Juvenile Court boys cases were located in the non-vice tracts of the city. In their most general social geography, the boys and girls cases have practically the identical distribution in relation to the scatter and concentration of vice resorts. About two-thirds of each series of Juvenile Court cases come from those local communities which are either free or practically free of houses of prostitution.

Classifying the tracts in Chicago according to the rate of female delinquency, it was found the 61 per cent of the Juvenile Court girls and 83 per cent of the vice resorts were concentrated in these tracts with the highest rates of female delinquency. The vice rate in this quarter was about two and a half times that for Chicago as a whole, while the girl delinquency rate was 60 per cent higher in Quarter 4 than in the total city. A much higher percentage of vice resorts was associated with the concentration of Juvenile Court girls cases than the one associated with the concentration of boy delinquent cases. Compare Quarter 4 in Tables 50 and 51. In other words, there were more vice resorts in the neighborhoods which produced the majority of the officially delinquent girls than in those areas which housed the majority of officially delinquent boys. The bearing which this fact has as a background causative factor in female and male juvenile delinquents will have to be tested out in future sociological research. Our immediate concern here is that the neighborhood conditions which enable prostitution to thrive are undoubtedly the same ones which tend to produce the highest rates of juvenile delinquency in Chicago.

The coefficient of rank correlation for the tract vice rates with the tract rates of Juvenile Court girls cases

TABLE 50

QUARTER DISTRIBUTION OF VICE RESORTS ACCORDING TO TRACT RATES OF
JUVENILE COURT GIRLS' CASES, CHICAGO, 1917–23*

Quarter	Population	Per Cent	No. J. C. Girls, 1917–23	Per Cent	Rate Per 100,000, Av. 1 Year	No. Vice Resorts 1917–23	Per Cent	Rate Per 100,000, Av. 1 Year
4........	991,193	36.7	1,752	61.0	25.2	1,951	83.1	28.1
3........	632,983	23.4	561	19.5	12.7	101	4.3	2.3
2........	622,740	23.1	392	13.6	9.0	74	3.1	1.7
1........	454,789	16.8	170	5.9	5.3	222	9.5	7.0
Total..	2,701,705	100.0	2,875	100.0	15.2	2,348	100.0	12.4

* Based on Table 48.

TABLE 51

QUARTER DISTRIBUTION OF VICE RESORTS ACCORDING TO TRACT RATES OF
JUVENILE COURT BOYS' CASES, CHICAGO, 1917–23*

Quarter	Population	Per Cent	No. J. C. Boys, 1917–23	Per Cent	Rate Per 100,000 Av. 1 Year	No. Vice Resorts 1917–23	Per Cent	Rate Per 100,000, Av. 1 Year
4........	916,413	33.9	4,564	56.5	71.1	1,313	55.9	20.5
3........	688,146	25.5	1,920	23.8	39.8	587	25.0	12.2
2........	615,246	22.8	1,089	13.5	25.4	186	7.9	4.4
1........	481,900	17.8	503	6.2	14.9	262	11.2	7.7
Total..	2,701,705	100.0	8,076	100.0	42.7	2,348	100.0	12.4

* Based on Table 49.

was .49; for tract vice rates with the tract rates of Juvenile Court boys cases .17.[7] The tract vice rates show some indication of varying in magnitude with the size of the tract rates of Juvenile Court girls cases but they show very little direct connection with the variations in the tract rates of Juvenile Court boys cases. The interpreta-

[7] Thirty-five tracts with vice rates were used in the correlation with the Juvenile Court series.

tions of the results of the quarter distributions of these series seem to apply here equally as well to explain why vice rates should show more of a tendency to vary with female juvenile delinquency rates than with male juvenile delinquency rates.

POVERTY

Poverty has been one of the causes most generally held responsible for bad social conditions—especially for crime, delinquency, prostitution, desertion, and child abandonment. The popular mind has come to expect the worst to issue from or be found in the neighborhoods of the poor of the city. But it has been held by many students of social pathology that poverty is more frequently an indirect than a direct cause of social problems and still more frequently a condition associated with other problems than a cause of them.

Eighty-five per cent of the charity cases were distributed in the 28 tracts of Chicago which contained 100 per cent of the houses of prostitution (according to the investigated places on file at the Committee of Fifteen). However, in the 9 tracts which housed 90 per cent of the vice resorts only 36 per cent of the United Charity cases were distributed. The non-vice tracts and those practically free of houses of prostitution contained almost two-thirds of the families receiving aid from the charities. Poverty as a social problem was, therefore, considerably more widespread throughout Chicago than was commercialized vice, which was definitely more localized than the problem of family dependency.

In order to see whether vice concentrated in areas having the highest poverty rates, the tracts were sorted according to poverty rate by quarters. In the upper quarter

TABLE 52

Tract Distribution of United Charity Cases and Vice Resorts,
Chicago, 1920–21

Community Area*	Population	Per Cent Population	Poverty Cases Oct. 1920– Oct. 1921†	Per Cent	Rate Per 100,000	Vice Resorts 1920–21 ‡	Av. No. for 1 Year	Per Cent	Rate Per 100,000
1–2.....	32,288	1.19	5	0.09	16	......	......	......	.....
3.......	90,806	3.36	13	0.25	14	16	8.0	2.41	9
4.......	28,588	1.06	5	0.09	17	1	0.5	0.15	2
5.......	44,698	1.65	37	0.70	79	......	......	......	.....
6.......	96,357	3.57	102	1.94	106	13	6.5	1.95	7
7.......	94,247	3.49	306	5.81	325	20	10.0	3.01	11
8.......	83,936	3.11	560	10.63	667	102	51.0	15.34	61
9–10–11– 12....	9,917	0.37	6	0.11	60	......	......	......	.....
13–14...	28,006	1.04	5	0.09	18	......	......	......	.....
15–17...	29,003	1.07	14	0.27	48	......	......	......	.....
16......	43,616	1.61	11	0.21	25	......	......	......	.....
18–19...	17,997	0.67	21	0.40	117	......	......	......	.....
20......	15,618	0.58	10	0.19	64	......	......	......	.....
21......	38,093	0.41	21	0.40	55	......	......	......	.....
22......	108,733	4.02	150	2.85	138	1	0.5	0.15	.....
23......	65,575	2.43	31	0.59	47	......	......	......	.....
24......	218,130	8.07	826	15.68	379	3	1.5	0.45	1
25......	71,505	2.65	13	0.25	18	......	......	......	.....
26......	39,452	1.46	9	0.17	23	1	0.5	0.15	1
27......	58,553	2.17	31	0.59	53	5	2.5	0.75	4
28......	191,827	7.10	605	11.48	315	156	78.0	23.46	41
29......	102,482	3.79	26	0.49	25	......	......	......	.....
30......	76,213	2.82	76	1.44	100	......	......	......	.....
31......	85,680	3.17	270	5.12	315	1	0.5	0.15	1
32......	13,140	0.49	10	0.19	76	26	13.0	3.91	99
33......	17,896	0.66	77	1.46	430	55	27.5	8.27	154
34......	22,063	0.82	77	1.46	349	5	2.5	0.75	11
35......	60,178	2.23	199	3.78	331	151	75.5	22.71	125
36......	16,540	0.61	28	0.53	169	18	9.0	2.71	54
37......	17,501	0.65	82	1.56	469	......	......	......	.....
38......	76,953	2.85	120	2.28	156	54	27.0	8.12	35
39......	20,594	0.76	3	0.06	15	6	3.0	0.90	15
40......	37,568	1.39	51	0.97	136	7	3.5	1.05	9
41......	37,676	1.39	19	0.36	50	2	1.0	0.30	3
42......	60,827	2.25	45	0.85	74	3	1.5	0.45	2

* Based on 75 Census Tracts of Chicago.
† Based on a count by tracts from a spot map prepared by Erle Fisk Young and Fay B. Karpf.
‡ Based on Table 57.

TABLE 52—*Continued*

Community Area*	Population	Per Cent Population	Poverty Cases Oct. 1920-Oct. 1921†	Per Cent	Rate Per 100,000	Vice Resorts 1920-21‡	Av. No. for 1 Year	Per Cent	Rate Per 100,000
43......	32,100	1.19	32	0.61	100	......	......	......	......
44-45...	9,860	0.36	22	0.42	223	......	......	......	......
46......	40,468	1.50	161	3.06	398	9	4.5	1.35	11
47-48...	6,351	0.23	40	0.76	629	1	0.5	0.15	8
49......	28,972	1.07	36	0.68	124	1	0.5	0.15	2
50-51...	12,439	0.46	52	0.99	418	......	......	......	......
52-55...	19,859	0.73	34	0.61	171	......	......	......	......
53-54...	24,307	0.90	64	1.21	263	......	......	......	......
56-57-58	38,844	1.44	45	0.85	116	......	......	......	......
59......	22,702	0.84	40	0.76	176	......	......	......	......
60......	60,460	2.24	195	3.70	323	3	1.5	0.45	2
61......	93,425	3.46	397	7.53	425	3	1.5	0.45	2
62-63...	14,193	0.53	19	0.36	134	......	......	......	......
64-65-66	18,218	0.67	18	0.34	99	......	......	......	......
67......	55,159	2.04	53	1.01	96	......	......	......	......
68......	86,623	3.21	133	2.52	154	1	0.5	0.15	1
69......	44,104	1.63	32	0.61	73	......	......	......	......
70-71...	22,860	0.85	13	0.25	57	......	......	......	......
72-73-75§.	18,505	0.68	19	0.36	103	1	0.5	0.15	3
Total.	2,701,705	99.99	5,269	99.97	......	665	332.5	99.99	.....

* Based on 75 Census Tracts of Chicago.
† Based on a count by tracts from a spot map prepared by Erle Fisk Young and Fay B. Karpf.
‡ Based on Table 57.
§ Tract 74 not included in city limits in 1920.

containing those tracts with the highest 25 per cent of the tract rates for poverty, 76 per cent of the vice resorts were lodged. The vice rate in this quarter—Quarter 4— is almost two and a half times as high as that for entire Chicago. The quarter percentages and rates for vice and poverty decline sharply in Quarter 3, as compared with Quarter 4 and continue to descend until Quarter 1 is reached. In general, it appears that vice resorts and poverty cases tend to concentrate and to scatter themselves in the same quarter-section of the city. The quarters which

TABLE 53

QUARTER DISTRIBUTION OF VICE RESORTS ACCORDING TO TRACT RATES OF
UNITED CHARITIES CASES, CHICAGO, 1920-21*

Quarter	Population	Per Cent	Poverty Cases Oct.1920– Oct.1921	Per Cent	Rate Per 100,000	No. Vice Resorts 1920–21 Av. 1 Year	Per Cent.	Rate Per 100,000
4........	918,921	34.0	3,577	67.9	389.3	254.0	76.4	27.6
3........	588,831	21.8	1,033	19.6	175.4	41.5	12.5	7.0
2........	545,809	20.2	474	9.0	86.8	21.5	6.4	3.9
1........	648,144	24.2	185	3.5	28.5	15.5	4.7	2.4
Total..	2,701,705	100.0	5,269	100.0	195.0	332.5	100.0	12.3

* Based on Table 52.

are highest in poverty are highest in vice concentration:
those lowest in poverty lowest in vice. This must mean
that the neighborhood conditions which are conducive to
the existence of commercialized vice in its highest concentration are conducive to the acute concentration of
family dependency cases; while those community situations which give vice little quarter are the same which make
for the absence of or lowest concentration of poverty
cases.

While the incidences of vice resorts and family dependency cases vary directly by the quarter segments
of the city, the rates for vice and poverty compared tract
by tract show very little tendency to vary in magnitude
together. The coefficient of rank correlation for tract vice
and poverty rates was only .23.[8] One can understand that
since most of the vice resorts in 1920 were located in the
near central slum regions, the quarter distribution of the
vice would be expected to follow the quarter distribution

[8] Twenty-eight tracts with vice rates were used in correlation with
tract poverty rates.

of poverty cases in spite of the fact that vice and poverty rates by individual tracts did not move sympathetically together. But in 1930 by which time the vice resorts have ceased to concentrate in the poor man's land around the center of the city, one should expect that even the relationship of poverty and vice by quarter segments of the city has become much less marked.

DIVORCE

Divorce is indicative of those conditions of modern urban existence which have made for family instability and discord as well as changes in the pattern of family and neighborhood life. In a modern American city like Chicago one might expect to find the non-brothel type of prostitution flourishing in areas which show a high incidence of divorce, because family and community life therein has become unstable and changing due to the very type of population and living conditions. In 1930 50.1 per cent of the divorces granted in Chicago fell in the areas containing the vice resorts investigated by the Committee of Fifteen. The tracts which quartered 92 per cent of the vice resorts possessed 35.5 per cent of the divorce cases for 1930. Almost two-thirds of the divorce cases were scattered in the non-vice areas or in those neighborhoods practically free of prostitution. The reason why a larger proportion of the cases of family dissolution was not concentrated in the vice areas is undoubtedly due to the fact that a considerable segment of the commercialized vice still lingers in the homeless man areas of the near downtown sections which possess a non-family type of community life, and to the fact that a large part of the business of prostitution falls in the Black Belts of Chicago

TABLE 54

Tract Distribution of Divorce Cases and Vice Reports, Chicago, 1930

Community Area*	Population	1930 Divorce Cases†	Per Cent	Rate Per 100,000	1930 Vice Resorts‡	Per Cent	Rate Per 100,000
1	57,094	154	2.0	270	......	......	......
2	39,759	70	0.9	176	......	......	......
3	121,637	427	5.6	351	64	14.5	53
4	46,419	94	1.2	203	1	0.2	2
5	47,651	138	1.8	290	1	0.2	2
6	114,872	453	5.9	394	120	27.2	104
7	97,873	307	4.0	314	24	5.4	25
8	79,554	349	4.6	439	24	5.4	30
9–10	19,778	29	0.4	147	......	......	......
11–12	24,597	55	0.7	224	......	......	......
13	11,052	15	0.2	136	......	......	......
14	55,577	111	1.5	200	......	......	......
15	64,203	100	1.3	156	......	......	......
16	66,783	143	1.9	214	......	......	......
17	19,659	29	0.4	148	......	......	......
18–19	68,721	95	1.2	138	......	......	......
20	23,518	46	0.6	196	......	......	......
21	48,433	86	1.1	178	......	......	......
22	114,174	209	2.7	183	......	......	......
23	80,835	170	2.2	210	......	......	......
24	187,292	334	4.4	178	2	0.5	1
25	131,114	279	3.7	213	......	......	......
26	50,014	98	1.3	196	......	......	......
27	63,353	169	2.2	283	2	0.5	3
28	152,457	314	4.1	206	21	4.8	14
29	112,261	223	2.9	199	......	......	......
30	76,749	110	1.4	143	......	......	......
31	66,198	125	1.6	189	......	......	......
32–33	18,267	78	1.0	43	17	3.8	93
34	21,450	46	0.6	214	1	0.2	5
35	50,285	125	1.6	249	31	7.0	62
36	14,962	35	0.5	234	12	2.7	80
37	14,437	40	0.5	277	......	......	......
38	87,005	296	3.9	340	73	16.6	84
39	26,942	115	1.5	427	16	3.6	59
40	44,016	205	2.7	466	28	6.3	64
41	48,017	155	2.0	323	2	0.5	4
42	66,052	274	3.6	415	......	......	......
43	78,755	206	2.7	262	......	......	......

* Based on 75 Census Tracts of Chicago.
† Obtained from data collected by Johannes Stuart.
‡ Based on Table 57.

TABLE 54—*Continued*

Community Area*	Population	1930 Divorce Cases†	Per Cent	Rate Per 100,000	1930 Vice Resorts‡	Per Cent	Rate Per 100,000
44	36,228	67	0.9	185			
45	10,023	30	0.4	299			
46	56,683	76	1.0	134			
47–48	10,826	20	0.3	185			
49	43,206	65	0.9	150			
50–51	14,603	29	0.4	199			
52–55	24,729	34	0.4	137			
53–54	29,960	35	0.5	117			
56–57	14,170	14	0.2	99			
58	46,552	83	1.1	178			
59	22,032	23	0.3	104			
60	53,553	47	0.6	88			
61	87,103	122	1.6	140			
62–63	34,396	31	0.4	90			
64–65	14,353	32	0.4	223			
66	47,462	69	0.9	145			
67	63,845	112	1.5	175			
68	89,063	180	2.4	202	1	0.2	1
69	60,007	97	1.3	162			
70–71	58,114	78	1.0	134			
72–74	17,103	23	0.3	134			
73	17,865	30	0.4	168			
75	12,747	14	0.2	110			
Outside					1	0.2	
Total	3,376,438	7,618			441		13

* Based on 75 Census Tracts of Chicago.
† Obtained from data collected by Johannes Stuart.
‡ Based on Table 57.

where family dissolution does not usually take the legal form of divorce.

Nevertheless the great bulk of prostitution (almost 81 per cent) was found in those areas of Chicago which possessed the highest 25 per cent of the tract rates for divorce (see Quarter 4 of Table 55). The vice rate for this quarter was almost three times as high as that for Chicago as a whole. Practically 96 per cent of the vice resorts were found in the tracts which contained the highest 50 per cent of the tract divorce rates and 70 per cent of the divorce cases (combine Quarter 4 and Quarter 3 in Table 55). Only 4 per cent of the investigated resorts for prostitution occurred in the tracts with the lowest 50 per cent of the tract divorce rates and with 30 per cent of the divorce cases.

TABLE 55

QUARTER DISTRIBUTION OF VICE RESORTS ACCORDING TO TRACT
RATES OF DIVORCE CASES, CHICAGO, 1930*

Quarter	Popu- lation	Per Cent	No. Divorce Cases	Per Cent	Rate Per 100,000	No. Vice Resorts	Per Cent	Rate Per 100,000
4........	957,281	28.4	3,318	43.6	346.6	354	80.5	37.0
3........	748,291	28.1	1,980	26.0	208.8	67	15.2	7.1
2........	885,487	26.2	1,525	20.0	172.2	2	0.4	0.2
1........	585,379	17.3	795	10.4	135.8	17	3.9	2.9
Total..	3,376,438	100.0	7,618	100.0	225.6	440	100.0	13.0

* Based on Table 54.

The vice and divorce rates by tracts show some tendency to vary in magnitude together, as may be seen for a co-efficient of .42 (by rank correlation).[9] But this tendency is not marked enough to say that divorce areas are at the same vice areas. If vice resorts persist in taking up a decentralized location outside the slum regions where the poor man's family break is desertion instead of legal divorce, a greater relationship in the future might be expected to prevail between divorce and vice rates.

SUMMARY

Practically no duplications in street address (legally substantiated) were found in three years cases of places

[9] Eighteen tracts with vice rates were used in the correlation with tract divorce rates.

violating the Eighteenth Amendment and places housing prostitution. This situation contrasts markedly with the close association of liquor and vice in the pre-suppression era.

Commercialized vice in its most scattered period was found to have a much more confined location in Chicago than other social problems. Only 51 per cent of the 1926 padlock cases fell in the areas containing 100 per cent of the vice resorts; while only 47 per cent of the 1929 padlock cases fell in the areas quartering 100 per cent of the vice resorts for that year. Eighty-two per cent of the venereal disease cases (1928) 72 per cent of the males in the county jail (192ι), 84 per cent of the Juvenile Court girls cases (1917–23), 82 per cent of the Juvenile boys cases (1917–23), 85 per cent of the United Charity Cases (1920–21), and 50 per cent of the divorces (1930) were located in the areas of Chicago which contained 100 per cent of the vice resorts. Some of these series of cases, on closer inspection, are even less confined to vice areas. Only 37 per cent of the Juvenile Court girls cases, 31 per cent of the Juvenile Court boys cases, 36 per cent of the United Charity cases, and 36 per cent of the divorces were located in the tracts possessing 90 per cent of the vice emporia. In other words, almost two-thirds of the chief social problems of Chicago fell outside the important vice areas of the city.

Vice resorts concentrated in those tracts of the city which showed the highest rate of community disorganization as judged by the upper 25 per cent of the tract rates for padlock cases, venereal disease cases, adult male criminals, juvenile delinquency, poverty, and divorce. In other words, the majority of the vice resorts were situated in the tracts showing the most acute incidence of social problems.

The vice rate in the tracts with the acute incidence of social problems, i.e., in the quarter with the highest 25 per cent of the tract rates of social problems, was over twice as high as the vice rate for Chicago as a whole.

While the quarter distribution of vice resorts showed them to be concentrated in the highest quarter of the tract rates for social problems, the correlation of rates for vice and social problems by separate tracts was not as noticeable. There was a tendency for the tract vice rates to vary directly with the magnitude of the tract rates for adult male criminals and venereal disease cases; still less of a tendency for them to vary positively with tract rates for female juvenile delinquents and divorces; and practically no tendency for them to be related to the tract variations in rates for padlock cases, charity cases and male juvenile delinquents.

CHAPTER IX

THE AGENCIES OF SUPPRESSION AND CONTROL

The active suppression of commercialized vice is carried on in the Chicago field principally by the police department, the Morals Court, the States Attorney's office, the Committee of Fifteen, the Juvenile Protective Association, the Illinois Vigilance Association, the Chicago Law and Order League, and others. There are a number of other organizations whose work is significant but who fight vice at a distance, that is through arousing public opinion and exerting pressure on public officials. We shall confine ourselves to the main organizations whose full or part-time job is to proceed against the business of prostitution in the vice areas themselves. Although we may think that the suppression of vice is a police and a court responsibility solely, the fact is that the work of these public agencies has been supplemented by the resources of private ones.

THE POLICE DEPARTMENT

The Chicago police, as well as the police of other large American cities, have been of all agencies the most intimately associated with the business of vice. But this very intimacy has been a handicap to efficient control. In the days of "segregated" vice districts, the relationship between the vice interests and the local precinct police was one that might be described as benevolent and paternal. In the absence of a public policy of suppression, the vice resorts were subject to rules made by police headquarters and the whims of police captains and precinct policemen assigned to "vice duty." The police at that time were stationed in the vice areas to keep order and not for suppression. The habitués and vice lords of the districts were often subject to petty grafting on the part of the local patrol. More wholesale forms of grafting from vice resorts have been mentioned already in chapter iii. Because of this intimate association with vice resorts, either through graft or personal acquaintance, the police, when public suppression finally came, were not equipped to enforce heretofore unobserved laws in a district which had treated them so well. When Chicago's red light district was first closed it was but a short time before the resorts were running again as usual. Police efforts to close the houses of ill-fame relaxed as soon as public attention was diverted to other matters. Government by public opinion in large cities seems to fail because all the people cannot keep their minds on everything at once. American police, called upon to enforce laws made by one part of the community for the benefit of another have been, like windmills, only active when the wind was blowing.

Chicago's police were handicapped also in battling commercialized vice when law enforcement was first inaugurated, because of the lack of specialization in the department. The Chicago Vice Commission saw this and in its report, made just prior to the first closing of the district, recommended the addition of a second deputy and a morals squad to the police department, whose sole attention was to be given to the problem of vice. The new office and squad were established two years after the report of the Commission. The officers assigned to the morals squad were harassed, threatened, and one even murdered by levee hoodlums as a protest against the whole idea of a vice squad and of vice snooping. The office of Second Deputy and the Morals Squad was eventually discarded. But the plan of a raiding squad was maintained. Such a squad finally was put under the control of headquarters and sent out from there. At the beginning of the period of law enforcement against commercialized vice, police raids on open houses of prostitution were occasional and infrequent. The original morals squad introduced the program of frequent raids. The succeeding vice squad developed the nightly raids. This squad with a car had a city-wide assignment. Later on this squad, together with squads of plain clothes men from the precinct station, instituted afternoon as well as night raids. Police raiding was thus becoming continuous. The question of immunity, of previous notification of raids, of raiding for purposes of advertising, cannot be unravelled in this study.

The increase in police activity against commercialized vice has been described in Table 2 of chapter i. The frequent spurts and lags during a twenty-year period indicate already that police policy toward vice was what the administration and the public made it. In short, police activity, as far as concerns vice in Chicago, has reflected public pressure and administrative attitude to a situation in which the police department has a consistently strict legal attitude toward law enforcement apart from political and social cross-currents.

Recently the Chicago Police Department has adopted another procedure against commercialized vice. About May, 1928, the police began turning in reports to the State's Attorney's office on places against which two court convictions had been obtained. These reports come from the police captains to headquarters and from there they are sent to the Assistant State's Attorney, who notifies the property owners in a "formal notice" that they are liable to be proceeded against under the Injunction and Abatement Law unless they remove the offending tenants or activity. During 1929, the first full year of the operation of this co-operative procedure, 224 places were acted against by the police in this way. During 1931 the police filed information on 306 vice resorts at the State's Attorney's office, 87 per cent of which were found to be cheap Negro resorts in low-class neighborhoods. If this co-operative procedure between the police department and the Assistant State's Attorney's office is continued, it will certainly tend to bring these two arms of the law closer together for concerted action—a thing well nigh impossible years ago when one office blamed the other office for responsibility for lid tiltings and open vice resorts. It has still another significance. Procedure under the Injunction and Abatement Law of the state has been the main attack of the Committee of Fifteen against vice resorts. This private organization collected its evidence, sent out its notices to owners of the property on which vice activity was discovered, and if no action was obtained by notices, the Committee took the stubborn case to court. It may be that the police may be able to take over much of the responsibility for collecting evidence for the Assistant State's Attorney to use against resorts in the shadow of the Injunction and Abatement Law.

Since June, 1932, a co-operative plan for the investigation of citizens' complaints against vice resorts was worked out by the Committee of Fifteen and the Commissioner of Police. On the theory that police action (particularly raids and the press notices of them) at certain places, especially in better class neighborhoods, tends to affect property values adversely, Mr. Charles E. Miner, director of the Committee of Fifteen, asked Commissioner Allman for the opportunity to investigate citizens' complaints against suspected resorts for prostitution prior to any action by the police. This was agreed upon, and the Committee, according to the working arrangements of the plan, makes its investigations and reports its findings to the Commissioner's office within 48 hours. If evidence of prostitution is procured, the Committee can undertake the action against the case or can refer it to the police for action. Usually the Committee continues with the case, when evidence is secured. In the event of procuring no evidence, this finding is also reported to police headquarters.

This arrangement with the Committee of Fifteen only holds for complaints, originating outside the police department, which get to the Commissioner's office. Cases against houses of prostitution which are developed from the activity of the vice squad or the uniformed police, are not referred to the Committee. At any rate the plan relieves the police of the investigation of citizens' complaints against vice resorts and in turn accords the Committee the opportunity of prior investigation, which investigation avoids possible damage to property values by dramatic police action. The undramatic and undercover action of the Committee enables the owner of the property to take steps to oust the offensive tenant without publicity.

THE MORALS COURT

The arrests for commercialized vice activity in Chicago are brought mainly to the Morals Court—a specialized

branch of the Municipal Court of Chicago. The majority
of the dispositions in the total Municipal Court of the
principal cases involving commercialized vice is handled
in the Morals Court as Tables 59 to 78 in Appendix II
will show.

From 1914 to 1928 (1914 being the first full year of
operation for the Morals Court) 56 per cent of all pandering cases in the total Municipal Court (all criminal
branches) was disposed of in the Morals Court; 86.8 per
cent of total Kate Adams Law cases, 85.4 per cent of
the cases of Keeping House of Ill-Fame, 30.2 per cent of
Keeping Disorderly House cases and 85.5 per cent of
Night Walkers cases (soliciting on streets). For all these
vice cases combined 73.4 per cent of the total disposed of
in the Municipal Court were dealt with in the Morals
Court (see Tables 60–65, Appendix II).

While the Morals Court handles the major load of the
principal types of cases involving commercialized vice, it
is of interest to note that on an average throughout the
years 1914–28 this specialized branch has dealt with only
4.5 per cent of the total number of cases disposed of in the
total Municipal Court (see Table 66, Appendix II).

The Morals Court, established in 1913 was a direct out-
growth of a recommendation made in the Chicago Vice
Commission's report. Chief Justice Harry Olson of the
Municipal Court of Chicago maintained that the "Morals
Court was established at the request of the famous Chicago Vice Commission, which recommended such a court
in order to put pressure on the city authorities and the
State's Attorney to compel them to enforce the law and
wipe out the segregated district in Chicago. By bringing all such cases into one court, it was possible for the

general public without much difficulty to observe in what manner the authorities enforced the law. With all these cases in one court the activities of such persons can be controlled."[1]

Judge Harry M. Fisher in the early years of the court's operation described its functions in the following terms:

Chicago may now boast of the fact that, instead of that segregated place where vice was cultivated and encouraged, and girls and women degraded and despoiled, it has a place for the gathering up of the unfortunate offenders; where those who desire to do better find friendly aid and encouragement; where the sick are ministered to, the vicious prosecuted and punished and where all the vile influences of the underworld are exposed to view. By maintaining this separate branch, the defendants can be more or less protected from the operations of imposters; and, above all, we are given the opportunity of taking a glimpse at the social aspect of this morbid business and of ascertaining the physical, mental, and social condition of the individuals involved. A trained judge becomes expert in determining what disposition should be made of each case in the light of all the bigger facts of which he becomes cognizant, which are necessary to a proper understanding of the problem, but are not presented to him from the witness stand. He is also put in a position to call upon the many splendid social agencies for personal service whenever their aid is required.[2]

THE PERSONNEL

This description more nearly fits the work accomplished by the Juvenile Court. The present Morals Court of Chi-

[1] Taken from "The Municipal Court of Chicago," an address delivered before the Ontario Bar Association, March 4, 1920, pp. 8–9, quoted in George E. Worthington and Ruth Topping, *Specialized Courts Dealing with Sex Delinquency* (New York, 1925), p. 4.

[2] Statement by Judge Harry M. Fisher in the *Tenth and Eleventh Annual Report, Municipal Court of Chicago, 1915–1917*, pp. 85–86.

cago is little more than a specialized magistrate's court. In spite of the fact that only cases are heard there in which the right of trial by jury has been waived, it is not as ideally intended a socialized court. The personnel of the Morals Court consists of:

Judge, assigned temporarily to Morals Court duty by the Chief Justice of the Municipal Court. Municipal court judges are elected for a term of six years and qualify for any assignment.

An Assistant State's Attorney, appointed by the State's Attorney.

An Assistant City Prosecutor, appointed by the City Prosecutor.

A Public Defender (a woman), assigned by the Chief Justice of the Municipal Court, acting without salary.

Two Clerks (men) performing regular court clerk duties.

A Bailiff for men and two bailiffs for women, taking care of detention.

A personal bailiff to the Judge.

A police woman, assigned to the Health Department but detailed to the Morals Court as a contact worker between the Lawndale Hospital, where infectious venereal women's cases are sent, and the Court.

Two Social Workers, one white and one colored woman, on the payroll of the Clerk of the Municipal Court but according to campaign promises not required to do party duty or contribute to campaign funds.

An Adult Probation Officer.

A volunteer worker (a woman) from the Illinois Vigilance Society, interested in rescue work among deserving girls who are brought into court.

(All this as of September, 1932.)

HIGH TURN-OVER OF JUDGES

Although it might be highly desirable, as Judge Fisher pointed out in his statement about the Morals Court, to have one judge assigned to the court, actually there have been frequent changes of judges. In checking over assignment records of the Municipal Court from December 2, 1918, to June 23, 1930, it was found that 56 judges had been assigned at various successive intervals.[3] According to this the successive assignments of judges to the Morals Court approximated two and one half months duration ($132 \div 56$).

One is unable to say whether the established practice of temporary and rotating assignments of judges in the Municipal Court of Chicago is due to the understood but unadmitted undesirability of the Morals Court assignment or the fear that a continuous assignment might be taken advantage of by the underworld. Even if a judge had a long assignment, say for his complete term of office (six years), there are certain factors in the situation which affect the efficiency of the court. Defendants can file affidavits for a change of venue. Many defendants, especially the recidivists with counsel, demand a jury trial and consequently must be turned over to the criminal jury branch of the Municipal Court. In these ways experienced or well-counselled defendants are able to escape trial before a judge objectionable to them. Frequently, it is the counsel which is interested in the delay occasioned by "taking jury" for purposes of getting a retainer's fee. Repeaters in the Morals Court usually demand a jury trial. It is said that the majority of those who demand jury waive the jury when they get before the trial

[3] This is not a complete count of assignments to the Morals Court; for some of the old assignment sheets from which the data were taken may have been lost. The 56 assignments include some judges who repeated at the Morals Court, but repetitions if broken into by one or more different assignments were counted as different assignments. However, if the same judge was assigned two or more times in continuous succession, these unbroken assignments were counted as one assignment.

judge.[4] Moreover, the delayed hearing or trial increases the chances of being dismissed for want of prosecution. The raiding officers, who are the complaining witnesses, are able to appear the first time the case is called in the Morals Court but usually are not able to appear at a later date. Consequently, many cases which are not tried the first time when called at the Morals Court must be dismissed because of the failure of the complaining witnesses to be present.

THE PROCESS

Cases are brought to the Morals Court chiefly through police raids and arrests. The women are usually held over night for court appearance next morning. Male defendants are released if they are able to fix bail. Complaints are filed with the clerk of the Morals Court by the police. Many times these complaints, drawn up by untrained sergeants, contain defects which are taken advantage of by counsel for experienced defendants. Prior to 1931 when a case was called (and there is a tendency in the Morals Court not to split cases but to dispose of all individuals taken in a given raid or arrest at the same hearing), the judge obtained the reports on the women defendants who had been examined by the health department for infectious venereal disease. If they were found to be in an infectious state, they were sent to Lawndale Hospital and their cases continued until their discharge. Many of the judges who sat in the Morals Court, it was said, looked upon this hospitalization as a sort of sentence. At any rate

[4] Mr. George E. Worthington reports that "during six months 1920, 94.7 per cent did not take a jury trial after getting into the jury branch." *Op. cit.*, p. 21 n.

most of the Lawndale cases who were returned to court as non-infectious, were discharged or given "good behavior." Very rarely was a fine or sentence given a girl after her stay in the Lawndale Hospital. The men were not sent for examination to the Health Department unless it was shown that they had had contact with one of the female defendants who had been found to be venereally infected, although the state law of 1919 empowers judges to act equally in case of men as well as women.

The judges of the Morals Court, prior to change in the Municipal Court's administration in 1931, relied heavily on the social service department of the court to tell whether any particular girl was a repeater. The method of identification was mainly a reliance on Mrs. Julia L. McGuire's memory for names and faces. If the name was identified, the case was cleared through card records kept by Mrs. McGuire. Identification would have been more certain, because faces change almost as readily as names, if a finger print record had been kept as recommended by several critics of the Morals Court.[5]

Before 1931 there had been a tendency to dispose of women's cases in the Morals Court on the basis of the number of known appearances in court. Common observation as well as inquiry of those persons in authority at the court, led to the conclusion that a prostitute's first appearance in court seldom resulted in any disposition other than a discharge or suspended sentence during "good behavior" which is merely a warning. The second appearance usually put the offender on a sentence or

[5] See Worthington and Topping, op. cit., p. 58. See also the Nineteenth, Twentieth, Twenty-first, and Twenty-second Annual Reports of the Municipal Court of Chicago, 1924–1928, p. 116.

probation, which was hardly ever given the first offender in this court. The third appearance was commonly given a fine. The fourth appearance sometimes incurred a prison sentence although other times it drew another fine. In her 1929 report Mrs. Julia L. McGuire stated that 902 (11 per cent) of the 8,100 women's cases filed during the year were sent to the Lawndale Hospital. Her report stated further that 76.2 per cent of 7,695 women's cases disposed of in 1929 were discharged; 10.9 per cent fined; 8.1 per cent given probation; 4 per cent sentenced to houses of correction.

With the new city administration and a newly elected Chief Justice and Clerk of the Municipal Court, following the elections of 1931, certain changes in Morals Court policy were instituted. All persons booked by the police for the Morals Court are now allowed to give bail, which for the most part had only been accorded the men and the professional white prostitutes. Examinations for venereal infection are now made at the request of the sitting judge; whereas previously most, if not all, Morals Court women were given routine examination at the Health Department. When examination is requested, it is now possible to have it made in the same building which houses the court. Formerly, the cases had to be sent to the Health Department offices in the City Hall. While the men, where evidence proved they had had contact with an actively infectious prostitute, were sent to the Health Department, they are now conscripted even less frequently for medical examination and treatment. A recent report covering the dispositions of women in the Morals Court from July to December, 1931, showed that only 7 per cent of the women had been sent to Lawndale Hospital, indicating that now a lower percentage of Morals Court women is sent there than previously.

The social service workers under the new administration are not required to do identification work. Consequently, the cases are not likely to be adjudicated on the number of known or suspected appearances in court. The type of disposition is therefore left more or less entirely to the sitting judge. According to a report on the dispositions of Morals Court women's cases for the last six months of 1931, 41 per cent were given discharges and 35 per cent, fines. Thus fines and discharges combined comprise the big majority of dispositions of women's cases in the Morals Court during the first reportable six months of the new administration.

With the growing inclination on the part of the police to book cases, where the evidence of commercialized vice is clear, under the state laws, which now carry a sentence, fine, or both rather than under the city ordinances which merely carry a fine, it was felt that prison sentences could be substituted in certain cases for fines. The effect of fines in women's cases has been noted. A fine, especially a heavy one in previous years, resulted in a pimp paying the girl out and in turn indenturing her—so it was claimed. It was hoped a few years ago that the indeterminate sentence would be used in cases of female repeaters in the Morals Court, brought in under the state law, and that these recidivists would be sent to the new Women's Reformatory (Dwight), which began operating on the cottage plan. But the judges of the Morals Court for the most part have not seen fit to incarcerate sexually delinquent women in an institution which houses more serious offenders as well. Recently the new women's reformatory has added a cell block to house the women inmates who will be transferred from the penitentiary at Joliet. The cell addition will undoubtedly curb any disposition on the part of Morals Court judges to sentence sex offenders to a budding penitentiary. With no adequate facilities for commitments, where correction and rehabilitation might in some measure be assured, and with the reluctance on the part of judges to commit female offenders from the Morals Court, it is almost inevitable that fines and discharges will continue to be the principal dispositions in the Morals Court as they have been in years past.

An average of 57 per cent of the total cases disposed of in the Morals Court from 1914–28 was discharged (over half discharged) (see Table 67, Appendix II). This average percentage for discharged cases is higher when misdemeanors are singled out (62 per cent), is lower for quasi-criminal cases or the violations of city ordinances (55 per cent), and still lower for felonies (45 per cent). Isolating the principal vice cases from other kinds in the Morals Court and then combining them, we notice that for the 1914–28 span they drew an average of 56.9 per cent discharged (see Table 68, Appendix II). Of this cluster of cases, the average percentage discharged was highest for Kate Adams Law cases (66.1 per cent) and lowest for night walkers—the street walkers (40.9 per cent).

Of the misdemeanors and quasi-criminal cases disposed of by the Morals Court from 1914–28, an average of 30.2 per cent was fined. Separately considered the average for misdemeanors is less than half the average for quasi-criminal cases in regard to disposition by fines or 15.2 per cent vs. 34.8 per cent (see Table 69). Night Walkers averaged 42.7 per cent fined; Keeping Disorderly House,

36.6 per cent; Keeping House of Ill-Fame, 35.6 per cent; Kate Adams Law (House of Ill-Fame), 17.5 per cent. The average for this cluster of cases fined is 32.3 per cent or about one third (see Table 70).

If we inspect the average yearly percentages for discharges in Table 67, we notice an upward trend during the period 1914–28. Inspection of the average yearly percentages for fines shows an opposite trend—really a very remarkable decrease in fines as indicated in Table 70.

Sentences to the House of Correction for misdemeanors and quasi-criminal cases going through the Morals Court from 1914–28, averaged 5.8 per cent (see Table 71). The principal vice cases combined averaged 5.4 per cent sentenced to House of Correction, while taken separately pandering averaged 24 per cent; Night Walkers, 10.5 per cent; Kate Adams Law (House of Ill-Fame), 7.9 per cent; Keeping Disorderly House, 4.4 per cent; Keeping House of Ill-Fame, 2.9 per cent (see Table 72).

The average for non-suits in the total quasi-criminal cases disposed of in the Morals Court during 1914–28 is 2.2 per cent and for the combined principal vice cases 2.3 per cent (see Tables 73 and 74). The general average for cases dismissed for want of prosecution is also very low (1.7 per cent as Table 75 will indicate) but this average is highest for felonies (15.6 per cent) and lowest for quasi-criminal cases (1.3 per cent). The average for the principal vice cases in regard to dismissal for want of prosecution is even lower than the general average for all cases drawing this disposition in the Morals Court (1.2 per cent). Here again pandering has the highest separate average—namely 10.5 per cent (see Table 76). This relatively high average percentage for dismissals for want of prosecution should probably be connected up with the failure on part of girls to testify against pimps and keepers after the charge has been made.

The general average percentage of dispositions by probation is very small in the Morals Court (2.7 per cent) and is still smaller for the vice cases (2.2 per cent) (see Tables 77 and 78). The separate averages for pandering and Kate Adams Law (House of Ill-Fame)—both state misdemeanors—are 5.1 per cent and 5.8 respectively.

Where discharges and fines have been and are destined to remain the main dispositions, the prospect for the Morals Court as a constructive legal force is indeed in considerable doubt. It is even doubtful whether the Morals Court, assuming for the moment that sentences to correctional institutions had been the paramount disposition, would have been or could be a legal deterrent for prostitution. The greatest possibility for constructive work by the Morals Court lies in its social function—its social service work with the individual cases of girls. But the social service department of the court has never been allowed to grow.

THE SOCIAL SERVICE DIVISION

This department in the Morals Court was established in 1919, about six years after the court's first birthday. One woman worker, on the clerks of the Municipal Court payroll, was put in charge of the department. Later on when the number of Negro women increased, a colored woman worker was added—also on the clerks' payroll. While the primary intention of this department was social service for the help and care of the girls who appear in court, it had become through process of time a sort of identification and statistical bureau for the court. Its main function prior to 1931 was to keep records on the various appearances of girls in court. Its secondary function was to find temporary relief—in form of railroad fare, clothes, a place to stay, employment, etc.—for needy girls, if it can find time to do this relief work.

The cards on which the girls' records were kept were by no means adequate for socio-legal court work. But even what information was contained on the card forms was not filled out, not merely because of lack of time and help in the social service division but primarily because very early in the history of the department (perhaps the second or third year) the social worker was not allowed to question girls for purposes of putting down information on records. These card records contained only meager information such as the name and aliases, date and address at which arrested, offense and disposition of case in court. Even age and color were often left out, not to mention previous occupation, schooling, place and date of birth, marital status, etc.

If there was time for social service work, it was done mainly by calling on other agencies and institutions. The following list, supplied by Mrs. Julia L. McGuire, although not complete, will give some idea of the types of organizations called on for help.

> Big Sisters
> Bureau of Public Welfare
> Catholic Charities
> Chicago Woman's Club
> Chicago Woman's Shelter
> Chicago Urban League
> Chicago Northern District Federation
>   of Colored Women's Clubs

House of Good Shepherd
Illinois Free Employment
Immigration Bureau
Illinois Vigilance Association
Jewish Charities
Juvenile Protective Association
Juvenile Court
Polish Welfare Society
Mother's and Children's Relief Station
Salvation Army
St. Joseph's Home for the Friendless
St. Margaret's Maternity Home
St. Vincent's Orphanage
Traveler's Aid
United Charities
Woman's Church Federation
Woman's City Club.

Most of the social work done by reference to these
agencies was purely temporary relief, a matter of food,
clothing, shelter, carfare, care of child dependents. No
thoroughgoing intensive case work, pointing to the reorganization of the girl's entire personality, was done on
Morals Court girls unless they might happen to be referred
to the Juvenile Court, the Juvenile Protective Association
or one of the charity organizations (for these are primarily
case work agencies).

Following the administrative change in 1931, the social
service department was relieved of political duties and
identification work. The card system, which had formerly
recorded the number of appearances of girls in court, was
abolished. The social service workers are not called upon
to identify women before the court. The workers are still
not allowed to interview women in detention or awaiting
trial. This is a tacitly understood rule rather than an

order. Cases are received by the social service department when the judges refer them, when another agency refers them, or when the girls appeal voluntarily for help. In appealing of their own accord they frequently have in mind a possible buffer against a heavy fine or a sentence by the judge.

With such limitation imposed upon the reception of cases, the intake is necessarily small. During eleven months (from October, 1931, to September, 1932) the social service department handled 350 cases. This load would probably comprise only 6 to 8 per cent of the total number of women's cases disposed of in the Morals Court for the same period.

The newly appointed social workers appear to have the training to qualify them to do good case work. The records now kept are really social case work records. But much difficulty is experienced in doing case work with the Morals Court girls. The necessary social background information is hard to obtain from women who are so thoroughly on the defensive, while investigations in the field are often hampered by false leads and addresses. Even after the full co-operation of the girl is secured and the necessary background data are obtained, the facilities for reconstruction of the lives of these girls are so extremely limited. For one thing the great majority of the cases handled by the social service department is composed of Negro girls. And there are practically no social agencies among the Negroes themselves which can assist in a readjustment program for such cases. This is for the most part true even of the whites but for another reason. As soon as they learn that a girl is a sex offender, many white organizations, which could be of some assist-

ance, are not in position to help. The present social
workers of the Morals Court have referred cases mainly
to the Service Bureau for Women (a part of the state un-
employment relief which includes emergency care for un-
attached women); family welfare agencies, when a girl
is a part of a family unit; the Church Mission of Help
(Episcopal); venereal disease and medical clinics;
psychiatric clinics, especially the Psychiatric Division of
the University of Illinois Research Hospital.

PROBATION

The report of the secretary of the social service department of the Morals Court stated that of 7,695 girls' cases
disposed of in 1929, 8.1 per cent were put on probation.
For the last half of 1931, only 3 per cent of the girls disposed of in the Morals Court were placed on probation
(165 out of 4977). The number and per cent of probations in the Morals Court for men as well as women from
1914 to 1928 are given in Tables 77 and 78.

One probation officer is assigned to the Morals Court.
This office is usually held by a woman—an appointee of
the judge and an untrained person at that. When a girl
is placed on probation (or a man for that matter, although
this is rare in the Morals Court), she is sent to the probation officer who makes out a record of the case and sends
it to the downtown adult probation office. In the Morals
Court there is never any preliminary investigation of the
case at the request of the Judge in order to determine
whether the defendant's living conditions and past history
warrant a probation. There is no way to check on the
girl's address. The probation officer asks the girls a required set of questions and takes down the unsubstantiated

information which is often made up to "string the authorities along." Follow-up work in the field from the downtown adult probation office is practically impossible because of false names and addresses. The girls are rarely heard from until the terms of probation have been violated by subsequent arrests. While it is impossible to pick the Morals Court cases exclusively from the adult probation department's annual reports or even the ledger records, in order to check outcome and make comparisons, the probation authorities agree that the Morals Court girls as a rule are the most unsatisfactory types they have to deal with. Of 1,158 women put on probation by the Municipal Court (all criminal branches) and discharged from probation during the year ending September 30, 1927, 696 (60 per cent) were reported as being satisfactory; 384 (33 per cent), unsatisfactory. The percentage unsatisfactory is higher for those offenses involving prostitution (inmates, keepers, solicitors) than for the total Municipal Court female probation load (all offenses) for the year ending September 30, 1927, and still higher than larceny which is the single offense for which most women were probated from the city courts in that year.

THE COMMITTEE OF FIFTEEN

Chief among the private agencies dealing with commercialized vice in Chicago is the Committee of Fifteen. The Committee of Fifteen was founded in 1908 during the movement against the exploitation of white slaves, and in the early year of its existence directed its efforts toward the investigation and conviction of procurers and panders. When it was incorporated in 1911, its stated purpose was "to aid the public authorities in the enforcement of all

TABLE 56

NUMBER AND PER CENT OF SATISFACTORY AND UNSATISFACTORY OUTCOMES
BY SPECIAL OFFENSES IN WOMEN'S CASES SENT TO ADULT PROBATION
DEPARTMENT FROM THE MUNICIPAL COURT OF CHICAGO, FOR YEAR
ENDING SEPTEMBER 30, 1927.

Offenses	Satis-factory	Per Cent	Unsatis-factory	Per Cent	Total (All Out-comes)
Disorderly conduct*.........	102	63.0	45	26.6	162
Inmates disorderly house.....	54	42.5	63	49.6	127
Keepers disorderly house.....	28	44.4	29	46.0	63
Soliciting...................	22	27.5	42	52.5	80
Total for above special offenses	206	47.7	177	41.0	432
Larceny....................	326	69.2	131	28.0	471
Total for all offenses.........	696	60.1	384	33.2	1,158

* Disorderly conduct is included because it may involve prostitution.

laws against pandering and to take measures calculated to
suppress the white slave traffic." During the last half of
1912 and the first part of 1913 a somewhat new emphasis
and new procedure characterized its work. "The work of
the Committee of Fifteen had always been confined primarily to the prosecution of the men and women who procured young girls to enter an immoral life, and no direct
effort had been made to prosecute the keepers of houses in
the segregated district. Early in the month of June it became evident from the reports of our investigators that
many of the keepers were harboring girls under age and
that the officers who had charge of the 'Booking System'
failed to discriminate between hardened prostitutes and
the girls under age who were being sold into the houses."

THE DRIVE AGAINST KEEPERS

"The active campaign against the keepers began the
first week in August, when, within a period of a few days,

five girls, all under the age of eighteen, were found in houses of prostitution on the South Side. Warrants were sworn out for the arrest of seven keepers and all of them became fugitives from justice, but the houses continued open and the police captain of the district said that he was powerless to close them, and declined even to report the situation to the chief or to the mayor."[6]

This attack on the keepers of the resorts in question did not stop here but continued. The Committee wrote the mayor about the situation on August 23, 1912, and Mayor Harrison on August 24, 1912, issued an order to the Chief of Police to close five of the houses in question and revoked the saloon license of a notorious red light café also in question.

The following week the fugitives began to return to the city and surrendered themselves to the officers. "Dago" Frank Lewis and Harry Cusick were the first to be brought into court, and while their preliminary hearings were still pending, all evidence in the seven cases was presented to the September Grand Jury by witnesses produced by the Committee of Fifteen. The indictments were promptly returned and the Grand Jury announced that it was prepared to make a general investigation of vice conditions in Cook County. For three days evidence was presented involving the different sections of the City of Chicago and West Hammond. As a result of the revelations thus made, John E. W. Wayman, State's Attorney, announced that he would exercise the power vested in him by law, and close every house of prostitution in Cook County and have warrants issued for the keepers, inmates and owners of the property. This plan was carried out as to the red light district. Many of the owners and proprietors were either fined in court or given written notice that such violation of the Statutes would no longer be tolerated.[7]

[6]*Annual Report of the Committee of Fifteen for the Year Ending April 30, 1913*, pp. 1–2.

[7]*Ibid.*, pp. 3–4.

It was not intended to rehearse the steps leading up to the Wayman raids on the Twenty-second Street red light district; for the versions of this bit of history are varied and conflicting, one even going so far as to claim that an important railroad system wanted the property occupied by the vice area. The point I intended to bring out is that in 1912 and 1913 the Committee of Fifteen's attack flanked to include a drive against the keepers of houses as well as procurers and panders. This is important to note because in succeeding years the Committee's action against white slave traffickers decreases while its direct action against the houses (i.e., vice resorts) increases.

EJECTION OF TENANTS

In its 1914 report (for the year ending April 30, 1914) the Committee of Fifteen stated that it "has directed its efforts chiefly to the work of destroying market places for traffic in women (i.e., closing up vice resorts). We have much evidence to prove that many owners have directly, or through the police, ejected many tenants. The chief weapon used in this warfare has been publicity, the publishing of the names of the owners of real estate, in connection with the keepers of immoral resorts."

Action against pandering is continued. "Our records show," so states the 1914 report, "that 94 persons have been arrested for pandering and related crimes. 49 persons have been convicted and punished, by fine or by both fine and imprisonment."

The 1915 report of the Committee mentions a continuation of the drive to close resorts by police methods and by use of publicity in newspapers. On a superficial check up by investigators, the Committee claimed that 1,178 vacant

places were found in the area east of Clark Street and between Sixteenth and Twenty-sixth Streets—the area formerly infested with vice resorts. Only 18 persons were
reported as arrested for pandering, 16 of whom were convicted.

PROCEDURE UNDER INJUNCTION AND
ABATEMENT LAW

During 1915 the outstanding innovation in method of
attack on vice resorts was inaugurated and that was the
use of the newly passed Injunction and Abatement Law.
This law was passed July 1, 1915. According to its pro-
visions any citizen who can show by competent evidence
that certain property in the state is being used for purposes
of prostitution, the premises can be closed and their use
for any purpose abated for a period of one year. The Committee discovered that in most instances it was only necessary to inform the owners of such property that action
would be brought against them if the offending tenants
were not removed and the premises kept "clean." This
constituted the informal notice. If owners showed indifference or stubbornness another informal notice might be
sent; if they still remained untouched, a formal notice was
sent indicating that the Committee would take legal action
under the Injunction and Abatement Law of the State.
"During the year (ending April 30, 1917) we have procured evidence against 170 places and have sent the owners
of each property the informal notice. It is gratifying to
report that 119 of these owners have taken such action as
to make it unnecessary to serve the formal notice. Fifty-
one formal notices have been served on that number of
owners. This has been so effective as to make it necessary

to apply for only 6 injunctions which have been granted and are now in force."[8]

The Injunction and Abatement Law was therefore used in substitution for newspaper exposure of owners of offending property, and the major load of the Committee's work was directed toward the suppression of resorts; for only 22 persons were reported as convicted for pandering (in the 1917 report) through the efforts of a special vigilance officer maintained by the Committee. The rest of the staff besides the superintendent and his clerical assistants was composed of investigators who collected evidence against the operation of resorts by field investigation and visits to houses of ill-fame.

SUMMARY OF WORK 1918–32

The major emphasis now rests squarely on the Injunction and Abatement Law. There is a decreasing emphasis on pandering. This may be due to the fact that following the agitation against the white slave traffic it became increasingly difficult to make a bona fide case of procuring and pandering, because male exploiters were more cautious and their female victims refused, either through inclination or intimidation, to prefer charges. The growing cooperation with the State's Attorney's office, the police department and federal government is noteworthy, especially in the last six years. The Committee branched out from time to time on closely related problems, like cabarets and roadhouses. But by 1927 it had confined itself largely to the investigation and dislodging of vice resorts in Chicago.

While the dislodgment of vice resorts has become the

[8]*Annual Report of the Committee of Fifteen for the Year Ending April 30, 1917*, pp. 5–6.

major emphasis of the Committee's program rather than prosecution of pandering cases, cabarets, roadhouses, or the dissemination of vigilance or social hygiene propaganda, there has been an effort to gain more insight and control over the work at hand by statistical studies. When Mr. Charles E. Miner as general director took charge of the active direction of the Committee's field work, he tied in with the scientific and statistical study of community problems in Chicago as conducted by the Department of Sociology of the University of Chicago and by the research sociologists of the Institute for Juvenile Research and the Behavior Research Fund. Mr. Miner has kept tabs on the distribution of vice resorts by local community areas for which there have been worked out rates on crime, delinquency, divorce, desertion, suicide, poverty, etc., in fact on all the social pathological phenomena in all the various sections of Chicago.[9]

In the 1929 report Mr. Miner listed the distribution of the 342 vice resorts closed, by the local areas adopted for statistical study. In this report also he classified the 342 resorts by type of building in which they were found to be lodged. "Of the 342 resorts closed by the action of the Committee in 1929, there were 171 in apartment buildings (with more than six individual apartments), 115 in flat buildings (with six or less individual apartments), 12 in apartment hotels and 21 detached houses." Mr. Miner's thoroughgoing restudy at the end of 1929 of the 942 resorts closed in 1927, 1928, and 1929 represents an attempt to discover in an objective, scientific way just what the results of the Committee's action have been. In 1928

[9] See the following studies: C. R. Shaw, *Delinquency Areas;* Ruth S. Cavan, *Suicide;* E. R. Mowrer, *Family Disorganization.*

a similar large-scale rechecking study was reported on.

To have the facts at hand, the entire staff of investigators was assigned during June to re-investigate every address then in the active records. There were 1,307 of these addresses. One hundred and forty-one of this number were listed as operating when the check-up began. Out of the 1,166 listed as closed, 12 were found to have reopened and were operating at the time of the investigation. Still other studies were conducted in 1928 to discover "what changes had taken place in the general location of the resorts" in order to see "whether a repressive program results in scattering resorts into sections not previously invaded."

The first of these was of the locations of resorts as published in the Chicago newspapers. From 1905 to 1925 the Chicago newspapers published the addresses of 262 resorts. All of these were found to be located within 12 of the 80 districts in which the city is divided for statistical purposes. All of them were located in the areas in which are the resorts now being acted against by the Committee.

The second of these studies of possible changes in locations of resorts was of various lists of addresses, the first published in 1894; the records of the Committee for several years past; reports for several years from the Morals Court; a series of confidential reports made by agents of the federal government from 1917 to 1923; and the current list of addresses in the records of the Committee. The study seems to show that all of the different addresses of resorts, approximately 8,400, from 1894 to date, have been found within less than 23 per cent of the total area of the City.

Such studies represent research and the bringing to bear of science on the practical problems of administration and control.

THE JUVENILE PROTECTIVE ASSOCIATION

Indirectly through its interest in child welfare and protection, the Juvenile Protective Association has made from time to time investigations of vice conditions with the idea of cleaning up the city environment children have to live in. Although the Juvenile Protective Association now is partly a case work organization, it reserves part of its program for the making of surveys of bad urban environmental conditions affecting child life. Consequently, it has investigated dance halls, cabarets, roadhouses, commercialized vice; has tried to bring pressure on lax officials to enforce laws; has prosecuted violators when necessary; and has lobbied for modern social legislation to fit certain new situations.

THE BEGINNINGS

Originally the Juvenile Protective Association emerged out of the Juvenile Court Committee. This precursor of the present organization was founded in the early days of the Juvenile Court in Chicago, to take care of juvenile detention and probation. When the Juvenile Court Committee was able to get the county (Cook County of Illinois) to take over these phases of the court's work, it turned to a program of protective work and became the Juvenile Protective Association (June 4, 1909). "The purpose of this work as its name indicates is to take another preventive step on behalf of the children of the city and to remove as far as possible the temptations and dangers, which carelessness and greed place about too many children." The tabulated report of the Juvenile Protective Association for the year ending October 23, 1909, reproduced only in part below, gives some idea of the lines of effort and activity in the first year of preventive-protective work.

Total Complaints Received..............5047
(reproduced in part only)
Complaints of selling liquor to minors
investigated 295

Complaints of selling tobacco to minors
investigated 52
Complaints of selling obscene postcards to
minors investigated 49
Complaints of pool rooms investigated...... 203
Complaints of dance halls investigated...... 92
Five and Ten Cent Theatres visited........1013
Penny Arcades visited 61
Saloons visited 735
Visits to ice cream parlors................ 356
Visits to candy stores.................... 805

Total Prosecutions in Court.............. 738
(reproduced in part only)
Abandonment 99
Contributing to delinquency and dependency
of children 232
Disorderly conduct 141
Immoral dancing 4
Prostitution cases 6
Pandering .... 1[10]

"CONDITION" WORK

In the succeeding years the work on "conditions" as
well as with cases of children is continued. In the 1916
annual report the following statement occurs. "Fully as
significant as the work with individuals just described,
though less in volume, is the investigation of demoralizing
conditions which are reported to this organization or which
the officers discover in their routine work. During the
last year 590 complaints concerning adverse conditions in
saloons, cabarets, places of amusement, stores, poolrooms,
etc., have been investigated."[11]

[10] From *Annual Report of Juvenile Protective Association, Chicago,
1909*, pp. 13–14.

[11] P. 19.

In the 1918 annual report of the Juvenile Protective Association's activity it appears that in initiating these surveys "there has been kept in mind the two-fold function of the Society. First, that of a 'checking-up' agency designed to assist the Public Departments in the enforcement of laws relating to the protection of children; second, that of an Association engaged in the practical social research from which can spring more adequate legislation and new forms of constructive effort."[12] Chief among investigations listed were: Saturday Half Holiday Investigation, 300 Comfort Stations on Chicago Elevated Lines, Junk Investigation (relative to selling of junk and juvenile delinquency), a Survey of 100 Uncertified Child Placing Agencies, Dance Halls Selling Liquor (445 investigated), Excursion Boats, and Nine Picnics (evidently at picnic groves).[13]

THE 1922 EXPOSURE OF VICE

The piece of "condition work," which received the greatest amount of publicity in newspapers as well as the greatest emphasis in time, money and effort, was the Association's 1922 investigation of vice conditions in Chicago leading to a Grand Jury investigation. Critics have said that the Juvenile Protective Association went out of its way in this investigation to expose the police department, the city administration, and even the Committee of Fifteen, for in those days co-operation between agencies, both private and public, was not as good as it is today. The Juvenile Protective Association's Vice Investigation developed as follows:

[12] Pp. 12–15.
[13] *Op. cit.*, 1918, pp. 15–18.

"We gradually realized that our Police Department had no policy for suppression of vice or perhaps I had better say that it was a policy of practically ignoring all vice conditions." And so a trained investigator of vice was brought on from the American Social Hygiene Association (headquarters in New York City). In three weeks this investigator investigated 18 cabarets; 12 saloons; 14 furnished rooms; 44 go-betweens including cab drivers, "light houses," bell boys, bartenders and bootblacks; 33 hotels, and 70 "regulation" (whatever that might be) houses of prostitution. After this the Juvenile Protective Association's own officers and workers checked this paid investigator's survey and discovered many other openly violating places besides. "We knew that it was futile to take this report to the Mayor, to the Chief of Police, or any organization and we presented a petition to Judge Michael McKinley asking for a special grand jury investigation." The Grand Jury met in January-February 1922, the field investigation having taken place the last part of 1921.[14]

CONDITION WORK IN LATER YEARS

Two years later, we learn that from the Juvenile Protective Association's report for the year ending November 30, 1924, the largest class of complaints acted on and cared for was that belonging to "questionable conditions" (513 out of a total of 2,485). Included within the complaints and special investigations were cabarets which were said to keep late hours and to sell liquor; the "closed dance halls," large ballrooms (public dance halls at which 125,-000 young people were estimated to attend 12 of the large halls alone), prostitution(the report takes credit for closing the famous Cort Hotel and mentioning better police action on vice under Mayor Dever's administration), roadhouses (the report states that the Juvenile Protective Association brought pressure on Sheriff Hoffman to close

[14]*Annual Report, Juvenile Protective Association, Chicago, 1921–1922*, pp. 15–17.

places like the Speedway Inn and the Blue Goose on threat of impeachment proceedings), carnivals, movies and theaters, literature, and obscene postcards.

A condition, heretofore unreported by the Juvenile Protective Association, was subject to special inquiry in the summer of 1925. This was the homosexual association and practices of men and young boys—mostly hobos and vagrant males—headquartering in the Grant Park fresh air camp. Besides this condition, other conditions like Closed Dance Halls, Taxi Cab Stands, Lady Barber Shops, and Greek Restaurants were reported on in the 1925 report. "Questionable Places or Conditions" comprised the largest class of complaints again in this annual statement. Gambling, vice, cabarets were claimed to be improved, while roadhouses still presented a challenging problem.

The yearly tabulations of the Juvenile Protective Association's activity have not been emphasized in order to stress the condition work. The tabulated statement of the 1928 report is, however, included for comparison with the tabulations given for 1909.

Total Number of Complaints Received..... 3,035
Cases and Conditions Cared for
 (reproduced in part)................ 2,303
Adult Conditions That Contribute to the
 Dependency and Delinquency of Chil-
 dren 1,069
Offenses against Children.............. 88
Delinquent Boys and Girls............. 409
Child Labor 206
Community Conditions 378
Special Investigations 153
Referred to Other Agencies............ 590
Complaints Not Confirmed............ 142

During 1928 the Juvenile Protective Association found that the roadhouses, cabarets, taxi-dance halls among other community conditions needed public attention.

THE ILLINOIS VIGILANCE ASSOCIATION

Founded in 1908 at the time the public was organizing against white slavery, the Illinois Vigilance Society has continued from that time with an interest in all the various phases of commercialized vice. A small pamphlet recently issued lists the objects of the Association as follows:

A. *Repression* of white slavery by oath bound, tax paid officials.
B. *Prevention* of social diseases by warning and instruction.
C. *Education* in sex morality by lectures and literature.
D. *Elimination* of unclean conditions in commercialized amusements.
E. *Suppression* of indecent pictures, magazines, and books.
F. *Protection* of girls who are victims of vicious conditions.

The part of the work covered by items B and C is carried on chiefly through talks, pamphleteering, and posters. Items A, D, and E are accomplished by making special investigations from time to time, notifying public officials of laxities in law enforcement, newspaper publicity of particular findings, prosecution in court of sellers of obscene literature. Item F is covered by a full-time paid worker who devotes her time to rescue work among girls in the Morals Court. Mr. Philip Yarrow, superintendent of the Illinois Vigilance Association, claimed that Mrs. Aldrich—the worker assigned to the Morals Court—assisted in a material way, during 1929, 225 girls brought into the court. Most of the help consisted in sending girls home, or providing food, shelter, clothes, or a job. Many girls used the good auspices of the rescue worker, it has been said, to get a free ride to a destination they temporarily claimed as home.

The Association's work has been described facetiously as "purity racketeering," since the state law provides that, in cases of prosecution of sellers of obscene literature one half of the fine is to be turned over to the law enforcement organization acting as plaintiff. Mr. Yarrow states that $50 was collected in 1929 from fines which resulted from prosecution of this sort. More constructive critics might urge that the Association is spreading its resources over too many fields.

SUMMARY COMMENT: SUPPRESSION VERSUS PREVENTION

In summary, one may say that most of the work of public or private agencies, dealing with the problem of prostitution, is suppressive. Very few persons, nowadays, actively engaged in the suppression of vice as a business believe that what the Vice Commission recommended and hoped for, namely, complete destruction of the traffic, is possible. The Committee of Fifteen today does not believe that vice can be harried out of Chicago and kept out. It conceives its own task well done if it can keep the business of vice at a minimum or keep it from growing.

Suppressive agencies are in somewhat the same position as public health work was when its aim was simply to combat the spread of contagious disease, that is, before public health work took the form of preventive medicine.

It may be assumed that the work of combating the spread of commercialized vice will become more and more efficient—certainly if increased efficiency in, and co-operation between the police department, the State's Attorney's office, and private agencies continues. If preventive work were possible in this field, it would have to take into account the forces and conditions in social life which foster prostitution. Correctional work—sending violators to an institution—was originally conceived as a means of preventing delinquency. As a matter of fact it is doubtful whether very many persons discharged from penal and reform institutions are really improved. Some follow-up studies of juvenile delinquents and male prisoners discharged from institutions of Illinois, have been made, but none have been made of Morals Court women. The few that have received prison sentences have been corrected, if at all, by the House of Correction and the County Jail.

Besides correctional work, there have been attempts to do rescue work—to induce girls to reform and go straight. In 1925 the Juvenile Protective Association undertook to do intensive case work on Morals Court girls 18 years and over. These cases were referred by the public health nurse whom the Health Department employed at that time to follow up Lawndale cases. The Juvenile Protective Association claims that these were very exasperating cases to deal with. A review of these records indicates that most of the effort was made to establish residence in other towns and to verify contacts for the purpose of sending the girls home. Sending a case back to its place of origin is held to be good case work practice. Any attempt to deal with chronic runaway boys by trying to send them back to their places of origin would also be beset with difficulty and for the same reason, since the home town may be the very place these vagrants want to escape.

If there is to be an extensive and continuous case work with Morals Court girls—work which attempts to readjust them and prevent recidivism—the prevailing opinion of social workers of Chicago seems to be that this work should be done by a trained staff attached to the court itself rather than divided up among the private agencies.

CHAPTER X

REMEDIAL POSSIBILITIES

The enthusiastic hope, which early crusaders had, of exterminating commercialized vice has now been tempered with the practical difficulties of law enforcement. The recommendations in this chapter, therefore, are based on the assumption that law enforcement in its most effective form can only reduce to a minimum the evils of commercialized vice.

THE LIMITS TO LAW ENFORCEMENT

When the Vice Commission of 1910 undertook the suppression of vice and when in 1912 the policy was inaugurated, certain future developments which have hampered the workings of law enforcement were not foreseen. I refer particularly to:

a) The social changes incident to modern urban life—changes, like increased mobility and leisure time, growth in urban population, changing neighborhood life, greater freedom for women in social and public activities, the breakdown of the caste of the prostitute.

b) The tendency for commercialized vice to seek those areas of the city in which it could hide from or survive the hammer blows of suppression—areas like disorganized neighborhoods which lack the morale to resist the inroads of vice both morally and politically, areas like apartment districts where life is nondescript and resorts can bask undetected under the protective coloring of respectability and areas like those on the outskirts of the city where political and social control are difficult to maintain.

c) The inability of our urban political order to combat social evils—an inability born mainly of political heritages which lag behind modern exigencies. [These exigencies have been created by the developments of city life and are the unprecedented social changes referred to in *a*) above].

URBAN TRENDS VS. SUPPRESSION

While public suppression, in so far as it was effective, has wrought certain definite changes in the form and distribution of prostitution in Chicago, the greatest changes it seems to me, have come about through changes in the conditions of life—the rapid growth of Chicago; the decline of the old form of local community life; the decay of neighborhoods; the problems of adjustment of incoming peoples without families; Negroes and immigrants from abroad; the development of transportation facilities including the automobile; the changes in the status of women; the development of mechanized living conditions in apartments; the growth of leisure and the declining influences of the home and neighborhood. It so happened that the effect of these urban changes was registered on commercialized vice during the era of public suppression. We can see where such changes have undermined at certain points the workings of law enforcement and where they have brought about results which on the surface appear to have been brought about by suppression. At no time while these undercurrents in city life have been operating on the problem of vice have measures of suppression been effective.

POLICE POLICY

Organized vice has controlled the police during the suppression era even more than the police have controlled vice. Affiliation, almost inevitable in American city politics, between vice and politics, was a heritage from an earlier period, when the policy of the police was to keep up a decent appearance, while tolerating vice. This had assumed the character of a system. In the first place the police were opposed to the idea of vice suppression. After many years experience with a customarily tolerated vice, they naturally clung to the notion that "segregation" was the *only* policy and were not easily converted to a program of suppression. In the second place the police were not equipped to do a thoroughgoing piece of law enforcement. For political reasons it has never been possible for them to plunge "scot free" into the vice-cleansing business. In making raids they have not always been legal-minded; they frequently erred in "booking" cases and in the presentation of evidence in court. They have not been able to follow the many continuances of cases in court. Until recently they have been in conflict with the courts, the State's Attorney's office and private investigating bodies—all of which have made them group conscious, sometimes stubborn, and many times unco-operative.

In this connection the recent working relationship between the police, the Committee of Fifteen, and the State's Attorney's office should be commended and furthered. Out of this the police have discovered how to proceed in the collection of evidence against resorts for prosecution under the Injunction and Abatement Law. Out of it also they have found that well-kept records of raids against places can be used as effective legal weapons. If a permanent set of vice records, containing accurate details of raids and investigations made by raiding squads and by the precinct stations, could be accumulated and kept on file at headquarters, it would guide police drives as well as constitute the basis for legal action. If some better method could be devised by which the police could avoid errors in booking arrests and drawing up complaints in vice cases, and more care was exercised in following the process of the cases in the municipal courts, especially the Morals Court, the efficiency of the police department in vice suppression could be enormously increased.

MORALS COURT POLICY

The Morals Court has not been as effective as it could and should be. It has been charged that the vice cases are permitted to lapse or are too frequently dismissed. A few years back the police were saying: "We catch them and they [the court] let them go; what's the use." On the other hand the court's reply was: "Why don't they [the police] raid the 'big places'? They only send us in the small fry, often with faulty complaints and then half the time they do not appear when the case is called." Both of these contentions have been partially true and both conditions could be corrected.

The tables in the Appendix indicate a surprisingly low percentage of the cases sentenced, fined, or placed on probation. The large number of dismissals indicates an all too lenient policy. Prior to 1931 the judges too frequently seemed to interpret a girl's isolation in the Lawndale Hospital for venereal infection as an adequate punishment. The small number of sentences shows how far from stern court reprimands are. The small number of cases of probation is due to the fact that the judges do not use it because they feel it cannot work. The high percentage of fines in the Morals Court has been criticized on the ground that fines encourage women to stay in the business to "break even" or to indenture themselves to cadets who will pay their fines.

Effective suppression is likewise minimized by the over use of continuances which give the openings for eventual dismissals. The lack of proper detention facilities means that the state can seldom induce a woman to testify against a keeper or exploiter who is able directly or indirectly to prevent the witness from testifying against him. Even cursory study of the records indicates that the rate of recidivism is high, that the present organization of the Morals Court is not effective either for suppression or correction.

Here again certain changes could be profitably made without drastic steps in public or political house cleaning. A committee made up of a judge who has sat on the Morals Court bench, a civic-minded lawyer, a representative of the staff of the American Institute of Criminal Law and Criminology; a representative each from the Committee of Fifteen, Crime Commission, and the Juvenile Protective Association, with the Chief Justice of the Municipal Court of Chicago as chairman, could certainly work out a constructive program to increase the effectiveness of the Morals Court. It might even be possible to devise a practical plan for handling the Morals Court cases—one based on more effective use of sentences, including the indeterminate sentence, more efficient probation, and more certain identification of both men as well as women (fingerprints if necessary) and founded at the same time on the first, second or third appearance of the individual in court. If such a standardized policy or program for disposing of cases in the Morals Court could be adopted by the Municipal Court it would be possible to check the percentages of various types of dispositions made in the Morals Court at the end of each year to see if the sitting judges were carrying out the accepted policies and to see how the scheme is working.

REHABILITATION WORK AT COURT

Suppression by itself is not sufficient. It must be supplemented by rehabilitation work. Well-intentioned rescue work has never met the problems of delinquent women. Thoroughgoing case work holds greater promise of reconstructing lives of disordered individuals. Prior to the assignment of two trained workers to the social service department of the Morals Court in 1931, very little adequate and constructive case work was done in the court. Even with the present staff of two workers, thoroughgoing case work with sexually delinquent women is restricted to a very small percentage of the cases (estimated to be between 6 and 8 per cent) and is hampered considerably by the lack of welfare agencies which can assist in the adjustment of adult female delinquents.

Since it seems to be the prevailing opinion among social workers in Chicago that the case work rehabilitation of delinquent women should be done by workers attached to the Morals Court itself rather than by an outside agency, the possibilities for such a program could be taken up by the same Committee constituted to study the possibilities for more effective legal handling of Morals Court cases. A subcommittee of technical advisors could be assigned the task of devising and presenting a program to supplement the legal disposition of cases with a social disposition. They should be able to develop a plan, not calling for any elaborate increase in the court's budget, by which the Morals Court could be patterned after the Juvenile Court or the Court of Domestic Relations in so far as they are socialized courts with both the legal (i.e., the suppressive) and the rehabilitation (i.e., the constructive and preventive) programs combined. With a well-organized rehabilitation program of case work for the Morals Court, it would be possible to use adequate detention and probation facilities, follow-up supervision, and the services of the Health Department, the Psychopathic Laboratory, and other medical and psychiatric clinics to great advantage.

The same problems would have to be met if and when a Woman's Court,[1] which would largely assume in its total load the functions of the present Morals Court, was established. Although this new court might, on paper at least, appear to be set up as a socialized court, such as the Court of Domestic Relations, the Boys' Court, the Juvenile Court, etc., care would have to be exercised at the very beginning to insure provision for adequate case work facilities. Technical advisors, particularly trained students of social welfare (e.g., social workers and sociologists) could be called upon to work out an effective social rehabilitation program for the delinquent women who would come under the court's jurisdiction.

COMMUNITY REHABILITATION

While we have touched on suggestions for bolstering up the law enforcement and rehabilitation programs as focused on the police department and Morals Court, there still remains another attack on the problem of commercialized vice—a still more difficult one which can be projected on the areas in which resorts find a location. This attack, therefore, is directed at the disorganized neighborhoods and conditions in which and with which commercialized vice is sheltered and associated. Social workers

[1] Since this book was written, the Morals Court has been superseded by a new Woman's Court, which was established October 3, 1932.

and reformers made the start in this direction years ago when they instituted neighborhood rehabilitation, community center and social settlement programs. The strategy of attack has been on two supporting flanks: first, the direction of the lives of people needing help and guidance, and second, the building up of a local neighborhood morale capable of combating and handling social problems. Since these early efforts, community rehabilitation and reorganization work has gone far. But before it is practical to proceed with the application of this program to one which is intended to check the invasion and survival of vice resorts, studies should be made of the existing local community rehabilitation agencies both within and without the areas possessing the vice distribution in Chicago. We should know the extent and character of community organization work being done in vice areas as compared with areas free of commercialized vice. We should discover whether the existing efforts to rehabilitate neighborhoods falling within the vice distribution are of the kind peculiarly adapted to combat vice and the disorganization associated with it or whether these efforts are merely well-intentioned but actually ill-directed ones. By this means it would be possible to work out a program of community reorganization suited to the particular area. The programs of many agencies working toward neighborhood betterment in the vice areas of Chicago are not adapted to make much of a dent on the local conditions. Perhaps instead of making their programs fit the area, they are trying to make the area fit their programs.

APPENDIX I

DISTRIBUTION OF COMMITTEE OF FIFTEEN CASES (1910–30)

APPENDIX I

TABLE 57

COMMITTEE OF FIFTEEN CASES: DISTRIBUTION OF SEPARATE ADDRESSES BY LOCAL COMMUNITY AREAS AT WHICH EVIDENCE OF COMMERCIALIZED VICE WAS SECURED, CHICAGO, 1910–30

NAME OF LOCAL COMMUNITIES†	1910 No.	1910 Per Cent	1911 No.	1911 Per Cent	1912 No.	1912 Per Cent	1913 No.	1913 Per Cent	1914 No.	1914 No. Cent
Rogers Park	0	0.0	0	0.0	0	0.0	0	0.0	0	0.0
Uptown	0	0.0	0	0.0	0	0.0	0	0.0	0	0.0
Ravenswood	0	0.0	0	0.0	0	0.0	0	0.0	0	0.0
North Center	0	0.0	0	0.0	0	0.0	0	0.0	0	0.0
Lake View	0	0.0	0	0.0	0	0.0	1	0.8	5	1.8
Lincoln	0	0.0	0	0.0	0	0.0	0	0.0	4	1.5
Lower North	6	17.6	4	6.1	2	2.9	14	10.5	53	19.5
Jefferson Park	0	0.0	0	0.0	0	0.0	0	0.0	0	0.0
Belmont-Cragin	0	0.0	0	0.0	0	0.0	0	0.0	0	0.0
Logan Square	0	0.0	0	0.0	0	0.0	0	0.0	2	0.7
West Humboldt	0	0.0	2	0.0	0	0.0	0	0.0	0	0.0
Lower Northwest	0	0.0	2	3.0	1	1.4	2	1.5	3	1.1
Near West	8	23.5	15	22.7	12	17.4	11	8.3	16	5.9
East Garfield	0	0.0	0	0.0	0	0.0	1	0.8	1	0.4
West Garfield	0	0.0	0	0.0	0	0.0	0	0.0	0	0.0
Austin	0	0.0	0	0.0	0	0.0	0	0.0	0	0.0
North Lawndale	0	0.0	0	0.0	0	0.0	0	0.0	0	0.0
Lower West	0	0.0	0	0.0	0	0.0	0	0.0	0	0.0
Loop	3	8.8	5	7.6	6	8.7	9	6.8	29	10.7
Armour Square	0	0.0	0	0.0	1	1.4	1	0.8	0	0.0
Bridgeport	0	0.0	0	0.0	0	0.0	0	0.0	0	0.0
Canaryville	0	0.0	0	0.0	0	0.0	0	0.0	0	0.0
Fuller Park	0	0.0	0	0.0	0	0.0	0	0.0	0	0.0
New City	0	0.0	0	0.0	0	0.0	0	0.0	0	0.0
Englewood	0	0.0	0	0.0	0	0.0	0	0.0	1	0.4
Auburn-Gresham	0	0.0	0	0.0	0	0.0	0	0.0	0	0.0
Morgan Park	0	0.0	0	0.0	0	0.0	0	0.0	0	0.0
Near South	14	41.2	23	34.8	42	60.9	69	51.9	94	34.6
Douglas	0	0.0	8	12.1	1	1.4	14	10.5	47	17.3
Oakland	0	0.0	1	1.5	0	0.0	1	0.8	5	1.8
Grand Boulevard	0	0.0	0	0.0	0	0.0	6	4.5	9	3.3
Kenwood	0	0.0	0	0.0	0	0.0	0	0.0	1	0.4
Hyde Park	0	0.0	0	0.0	0	0.0	0	0.0	0	0.0
Woodlawn	0	0.0	1	1.5	0	0.0	0	0.0	0	0.0
Washington Park	0	0.0	0	0.0	0	0.0	0	0.0	1	0.4
South Shore	0	0.0	0	0.0	0	0.0	0	0.0	0	0.0
South Chicago	2	5.9	4	6.1	4	5.8	2	1.5	1	0.4
Calumet Heights	0	0.0	0	0.0	0	0.0	0	0.0	0	0.0
Roseland	0	0.0	0	0.0	0	0.0	0	0.0	0	0.0
Riverdale	0	0.0	0	0.0	0	0.0	0	0.0	0	0.0
Outside city limits	1	2.9	3	4.5	0	0.0	2	1.5	0	0.0
Unclassified	0	0.0	0	0.0	0	0.0	0	0.0	0	0.0
Total	34	100.0	66	100.0	69	100.0	133	100.0	272	100.0

† By combination these areas can be made to fit the corresponding ones in the scheme of 70 statistical communities or the plan of 75 tracts.

TABLE 57—*Continued*

NAME OF LOCAL COMMUNITIES†	1915 No.	1915 Per Cent	1916 No.	1916 Per Cent	1917 No.	1917 Per Cent	1918 No.	1918 Per Cent	1919 No.	1919 Per Cent
Rogers Park	0	0.0	0	0.0	0	0.0	0	0.0	0	0.0
Uptown	1	0.4	0	0.0	1	0.3	6	1.8	11	3.6
Ravenswood	0	0.0	0	0.0	0	0.0	0	0.0	1	0.3
North Center	0	0.0	0	0.0	0	0.0	0	0.0	1	0.3
Lake View	1	0.4	0	0.0	1	0.3	9	2.7	6	2.0
Lincoln	1	0.4	2	0.7	7	1.8	18	5.4	15	5.3
Lower North	37	14.3	76	26.4	97	25.5	43	13.0	45	14.9
Jefferson Park	0	0.0	0	0.0	0	0.0	0	0.0	1	0.3
Belmont-Cragin	0	0.0	0	0.0	0	0.0	0	0.0	0	0.0
Logan Square	0	0.0	2	0.7	1	0.3	2	0.6	0	0.0
West Humboldt	0	0.0	0	0.0	0	0.0	1	0.3	0	0.0
Lower Northwest	1	0.4	2	0.7	1	0.3	2	0.6	1	0.3
Near West	39	15.1	50	17.4	78	20.5	79	23.8	73	24.1
East Garfield	0	0.0	1	0.3	1	0.3	3	0.9	5	1.7
West Garfield	0	0.0	0	0.0	1	0.3	1	0.3	0	0.0
Austin	0	0.0	0	0.0	0	0.0	1	0.3	0	0.0
North Lawndale	1	0.4	0	0.0	0	0.0	0	0.0	0	0.0
Lower West	0	0.0	0	0.0	0	0.0	0	0.0	0	0.0
Loop	24	9.3	10	3.5	32	8.4	22	6.6	29	9.6
Armour Square	0	0.0	2	0.7	0	0.0	2	0.6	1	0.3
Bridgeport	0	0.0	0	0.0	0	0.0	1	0.3	0	0.0
Canaryville	0	0.0	0	0.0	0	0.0	0	0.0	0	0.0
Fuller Park	0	0.0	0	0.0	0	0.0	0	0.0	1	0.3
New City	0	0.0	0	0.0	0	0.0	0	0.0	0	0.0
Englewood	0	0.0	0	0.0	4	1.1	6	1.8	1	0.3
Auburn-Gresham	0	0.0	0	0.0	1	0.3	0	0.0	0	0.0
Morgan Park	0	0.0	1	0.3	1	0.3	0	0.0	1	0.3
Near South	49	18.9	58	20.1	34	8.9	32	9.6	29	9.6
Douglas	83	32.0	59	20.5	77	20.3	52	15.7	28	9.2
Oakland	8	3.1	7	2.4	13	3.4	18	5.4	14	4.6
Grand Boulevard	6	2.3	9	3.1	23	6.1	17	5.1	18	5.9
Kenwood	0	0.0	2	0.7	1	0.3	3	0.9	3	1.0
Hyde Park	0	0.0	0	0.0	1	0.3	0	0.0	2	0.7
Woodlawn	0	0.0	0	0.0	0	0.0	0	0.0	2	0.7
Washington Park	0	0.0	0	0.0	1	0.3	3	0.9	6	2.0
South Shore	0	0.0	0	0.0	0	0.0	0	0.0	0	0.0
South Chicago	2	0.8	0	0.0	0	0.0	0	0.0	4	1.3
Calumet Heights	0	0.0	0	0.0	0	0.0	0	0.0	0	0.0
Roseland	0	0.0	0	0.0	0	0.0	0	0.0	0	0.0
Riverdale	0	0.0	1	0.3	0	0.0	0	0.0	0	0.0
Outside city limits	6	2.3	6	2.1	4	1.1	11	3.3	4	1.3
Unclassified	0	0.0	0	0.0	0	0.0	0	0.0	0	0.0
Total	259	100.0	288	100.0	380	100.0	332	100.0	303	100.0

† By combination these areas can be made to fit the corresponding ones in the scheme of 70 statistical communities or the plan of 75 tracts.

TABLE 57—*Continued*

NAME OF LOCAL COMMUNITIES†	1920		1921		1922		1923		1924	
	No.	Per Cent	No.	Per Cent	No.	Per Cent	No.	Per Cent	No.	Per Cent
Rogers Park	0	0.0	0	0.0	1	0.3	0	0.0	0	0.0
Uptown	9	3.1	7	1.9	5	1.3	12	3.9	19	8.0
Ravenswood	1	0.3	0	0.0	1	0.3	1	0.3	0	0.0
North Center	0	0.0	0	0.0	0	0.0	0	0.0	0	0.0
Lake View	6	2.1	7	1.9	4	1.0	4	1.3	4	1.7
Lincoln	6	2.1	14	3.7	5	1.3	9	3.0	1	0.4
Lower North	57	19.6	45	12.0	29	7.5	30	9.8	15	6.3
Jefferson Park	0	0.0	0	0.0	0	0.0	0	0.0	0	0.0
Belmont-Cragin	0	0.0	0	0.0	0	0.0	0	0.0	0	0.0
Logan Square	1	0.3	0	0.0	0	0.0	0	0.0	0	0.0
West Humboldt	0	0.0	0	0.0	0	0.0	0	0.0	0	0.0
Lower Northwest	1	0.3	2	0.5	0	0.0	1	0.3	4	1.7
Near West	70	24.1	86	23.0	71	13.3	65	21.3	29	12.2
East Garfield	2	0.7	3	0.8	0	0.0	1	0.3	2	0.8
West Garfield	1	0.3	0	0.0	0	0.0	0	0.0	0	0.0
Austin	0	0.0	0	0.0	0	0.0	0	0.0	0	0.0
North Lawndale	0	0.0	0	0.0	0	0.0	0	0.0	0	0.0
Lower West	0	0.0	1	0.3	1	0.3	4	1.3	1	0.4
Loop	12	4.1	14	3.7	19	4.9	21	6.9	14	5.9
Armour Square	0	0.0	5	1.3	1	0.3	2	0.7	1	0.4
Bridgeport	0	0.0	3	0.8	1	0.3	1	0.3	0	0.0
Canaryville	0	0.0	1	0.3	1	0.3	0	0.0	0	0.0
Fuller Park	0	0.0	0	0.0	0	0.0	1	0.3	0	0.0
New City	0	0.0	2	0.5	0	0.0	0	0.0	0	0.0
Englewood	0	0.0	1	0.3	0	0.0	0	0.0	0	0.0
Auburn-Gresham	0	0.0	0	0.0	0	0.0	0	0.0	0	0.0
Morgan Park	1	0.3	0	0.0	0	0.0	0	0.0	0	0.0
Near South	28	9.6	27	7.2	30	7.8	16	5.2	17	7.1
Douglas	43	14.8	108	28.9	163	42.1	75	24.6	65	27.3
Oakland	12	4.1	6	1.6	8	2.1	1	0.3	5	2.1
Grand Boulevard	21	7.2	33	8.8	43	11.1	50	16.4	58	24.4
Kenwood	5	1.7	1	0.3	0	0.0	0	0.0	0	0.0
Hyde Park	2	0.7	0	0.0	0	0.0	0	0.0	0	0.0
Woodlawn	2	0.7	1	0.3	2	0.5	2	0.7	0	0.0
Washington Park	4	1.4	3	0.8	2	0.5	2	0.7	1	0.4
South Shore	0	0.0	0	0.0	0	0.0	1	0.3	0	0.0
South Chicago	7	2.4	2	0.5	0	0.0	0	0.0	0	0.0
Calumet Heights	0	0.0	1	0.3	0	0.0	0	0.0	0	0.0
Roseland	0	0.0	1	0.3	0	0.0	1	0.3	0	0.0
Riverdale	0	0.0	0	0.0	0	0.0	0	0.0	0	0.0
Outside city limits	0	0.0	0	0.0	0	0.0	5	1.6	2	0.8
Unclassified	0	0.0	0	0.0	0	0.0	0	0.0	0	0.0
Total	291	100.0	374	100.0	387	100.0	305	100.0	238	100.0

† By combination these areas can be made to fit the corresponding ones in the scheme of 70 statistical communities or the plan of 75 tracts.

TABLE 57—*Continued*

NAME OF LOCAL COMMUNITIES†	1925 No.	1925 Per Cent	1926 No.	1926 Per Cent	1927 No.	1927 Per Cent	1928 No.	1928 Per Cent
Rogers Park	1	0.3	0	0.0	0	0.0	1	0.2
Uptown	39	10.0	47	10.5	45	10.2	60	12.5
Ravenswood	0	0.0	0	0.0	1	0.2	2	0.4
North Center	0	0.0	0	0.0	0	0.0	0	0.0
Lake View	15	3.9	13	2.9	37	8.4	52	10.8
Lincoln	6	1.5	9	2.0	12	2.7	21	4.4
Lower North	27	6.9	32	7.2	68	15.4	64	13.3
Jefferson Park	0	0.0	0	0.0	0	0.0	0	0.0
Belmont-Cragin	0	0.0	0	0.0	0	0.0	1	0.2
Logan Square	0	0.0	0	0.0	1	0.2	0	0.0
West Humboldt	1	0.3	0	0.0	0	0.0	1	0.2
Lower Northwest	3	0.8	0	0.0	0	0.0	1	0.2
Near West	39	10.0	35	7.8	32	7.3	34	7.1
East Garfield	6	1.5	8	1.8	6	1.4	1	0.2
West Garfield	1	0.3	0	0.0	0	0.0	0	0.0
Austin	0	0.0	0	0.0	0	0.0	0	0.0
North Lawndale	1	0.3	1	0.2	0	0.0	0	0.0
Lower West	0	0.0	0	0.0	0	0.0	0	0.0
Loop	10	2.6	12	2.7	4	0.9	7	1.5
Armour Square	0	0.0	0	0.0	0	0.0	1	0.2
Bridgeport	0	0.0	0	0.0	0	0.0	0	0.0
Canaryville	0	0.0	0	0.0	0	0.0	0	0.0
Fuller Park	0	0.0	0	0.0	0	0.0	0	0.0
New City	0	0.0	0	0.0	0	0.0	0	0.0
Englewood	0	0.0	1	0.2	1	0.2	0	0.0
Auburn-Gresham	0	0.0	0	0.0	0	0.0	0	0.0
Morgan Park	0	0.0	0	0.0	0	0.0	0	0.0
Near South	21	5.4	16	3.6	11	2.5	13	2.7
Douglas	127	32.6	132	29.6	68	15.4	67	14.0
Oakland	9	2.3	6	1.3	10	2.3	5	1.0
Grand Boulevard	66	17.0	113	25.3	124	28.1	103	21.5
Kenwood	6	1.5	8	1.8	4	0.9	20	4.2
Hyde Park	2	0.5	0	0.0	0	0.0	3	0.6
Woodlawn	1	0.3	4	0.9	1	0.2	0	0.0
Washington Park	2	0.5	9	2.0	15	3.4	23	4.8
South Side	0	0.0	0	0.0	1	0.2	0	0.0
South Chicago	0	0.0	0	0.0	0	0.0	0	0.0
Calumet Heights	0	0.0	0	0.0	0	0.0	0	0.0
Roseland	0	0.0	0	0.0	0	0.0	0	0.0
Riverdale	0	0.0	0	0.0	0	0.0	0	0.0
Outside city limits	4	1.0	0	0.0	0	0.0	0	0.0
Unclassified	2	0.5	0	0.0	0	0.0	0	0.0
Total	389	100.0	446	100.0	441	100.0	480	100.0

† By combination these areas can be made to fit the corresponding ones in the scheme of 70 statistical communities or the plan of 75 tracts.

TABLE 57—*Continued*

NAME OF LOCAL COMMUNITIES†	1929 No.	1929 Per Cent	1910–29 No.	1910–29 Per Cent	1930 No.	1930 Per Cent
Rogers Park	1	0.2	4	*	0	0.0
Uptown	96	20.9	358	6.0	64	14.5
Ravenswood	0	0.0	7	0.1	1	0.2
North Center	0	0.0	1	*	1	0.2
Lake View	58	12.6	223	3.8	120	27.2
Lincoln	6	1.3	136	2.3	24	5.4
Lower North	33	7.2	778	13.1	24	5.4
Jefferson Park	0	0.0	1	*	0	0.0
Belmont-Cragin	0	0.0	1	*	0	0.0
Logan Square	0	0.0	8	0.1	0	0.0
West Humboldt	0	0.0	3	*	0	0.0
Lower Northwest	0	0.0	27	0.5	2	0.5
Near West	31	6.8	873	14.7	21	4.8
East Garfield	0	0.0	41	0.7	2	0.5
West Garfield	0	0.0	4	*	0	0.0
Austin	0	0.0	1	*	0	0.0
North Lawndale	0	0.0	3	*	0	0.0
Lower West	0	0.0	7	0.1	0	0.0
Loop	5	1.1	287	4.8	5	1.1
Armour Square	0	0.0	17	0.3	1	0.2
Bridgeport	0	0.0	6	0.1	0	0.0
Canaryville	0	0.0	2	*	0	0.0
Fuller Park	0	0.0	2	*	0	0.0
New City	0	0.0	2	*	0	0.0
Englewood	0	0.0	15	0.3	1	0.2
Auburn-Gresham	0	0.0	1	*	0	0.0
Morgan Park	0	0.0	4	*	0	0.0
Near South	9	2.0	632	10.6	12	2.7
Douglas	50	10.9	1267	21.3	31	7.0
Oakland	6	1.3	135	2.3	12	2.7
Grand Boulevard	125	27.2	824	13.9	73	16.6
Kenwood	11	2.4	65	1.1	16	3.6
Hyde Park	2	0.4	12	0.2	2	0.5
Woodlawn	0	0.0	16	0.3	0	0.0
Washington Park	26	5.7	98	1.6	28	6.3
South Side	0	0.0	2	*	0	0.0
South Chicago	0	0.0	28	0.5	0	0.0
Calumet Heights	0	0.0	1	*	0	0.0
Roseland	0	0.0	2	*	0	0.0
Riverdale	0	0.0	1	*	0	0.0
Outside city limits	0	0.0	48	0.8	1	0.2
Unclassified	0	0.0	2	*	0	0.0
Total	459	100.0	5945	100.0	441	100.0

* Less than one-tenth of 1 per cent.
† By combination these areas can be made to fit the corresponding ones in the scheme of 70 statistical communities or the plan of 75 tracts.

APPENDIX II

POLICE, MUNICIPAL, AND MORALS COURT STATISTICS

TABLE 58

POLICE ARRESTS FOR PRINCIPAL OFFENSES INVOLVING COMMERCIALIZED VICE, CHICAGO, 1908–28

(Based on Annual Reports of Police Department)

Year	Pan.	I.K.D.H	I.H.I.F.	K.H.I.F.	K.A.L.	S.F.P.	Combined	Total Arrests incl. Summons	No. Police	Population*
1908		530	236	68		1,731	2,565	68,220	4,293	2,096,977
1909	73	782	580	222		1,778	3,435	70,575	4,288	2,146,264
1910	92	996	347	149		1,619	3,203	81,269	4,260	2,196,238
1911	60	660	617	264		1,730	3,331	84,838	4,437	2,249,363
1912	68	1,405	1,663	396		1,516	5,048	86,950	4,436	2,301,946
1913	36	1,654	3,195	486		1,645	7,016	109,764	4,443	2,354,529
1914	50	5,548	2,178	324		2,006	10,106	116,895	4,420	2,410,806
1915	62	7,875	155	68		2,079	10,239	121,714	5,331	2,464,189
1916	40	4,401	61	16	644	742	5,904	111,527	5,277	2,517,172
1917	74	6,593	1,113	198	1,216	537	9,731	137,910	5,199	2,509,755
1918	40	3,884	445	119	441	476	5,405	110,819	4,706	2,622,338
1919	44	2,930	164	19	365	202	3,724	96,676	5,120	2,674,921
1920	49	3,353	392	64	270	167	4,295	94,453	5,152	2,728,022
1921	45	4,090	1,055	210	523	597	6,520	125,843	5,140	2,780,655
1922	52	3,092	1,868	170	802	549	6,533	143,185	6,184	2,833,288
1923	37	7,735	3,055	502	737	387	12,453	192,278	5,965	2,886,971
1924	51	13,890	3,249	582	1,696	498	19,966	256,345	6,010	2,939,605
1925	39	17,728	1,701	135	2,945	97	22,645	282,260	5,862	2,995,239
1926	53	20,827	2,372	147	3,012	115	26,526	281,268	6,080	3,048,000
1927	46	9,424	4,801	984	3,351	794	19,400	223,848	6,078	3,102,800
1928	64	13,414	7,925	2,124	126	745	24,398	209,878	6,098	3,157,400
Total							212,443	3,006,515		

Pan.—Pandering.
I.K.D.H.—Inmate or Keeper of Disorderly House.
I.H.I.F.—Inmate of House of Ill-Fame.
K.H.I.F.—Keeper of House of Ill-Fame.

K.A.L.—Kate Adams Law.
S.F.P.—Soliciting for Prostitution.
*Population estimates obtained from Health Dept., City of Chicago and based on United States estimates.

TABLE 59

PRINCIPAL CASES OF COMMERCIALIZED VICE DISPOSED OF IN MUNICIPAL COURT, CHICAGO, 1908–28

Year	Enticing Female*	Pandering	Kate Adams Law	Keeper House of Ill-Fame	Keeper Disorderly House	Night Walker	Combined	Total Dispositions	Per Cent
1908	...	...	...	70	447	1,664	2,181	74,930	2.9
1909	1	92	...	182	697	1,665	2,545	78,371	3.2
1910	3	62	...	134	934	1,619	2,782	87,922	3.2
1911	2	72	...	205	598	1,633	2,500	92,730	3.0
1912	8	54	...	1,863	1,075	1,569	4,587	106,369	4.3
1913	5	42	...	3,345	1,608	1,846	6,858	121,333	5.7
1914	6	67	...	3,120	5,191	2,093	10,452	134,048	7.7
1915	1	35	...	241	7,691	2,254	10,254	130,971	7.8
1916	...	64	...	63	4,518	834	5,450	123,873	4.4
1917	2	40	...	1,135	5,641	502	7,344	149,268	4.9
1918	...	35	...	727	4,258	613	5,638	124,397	4.5
1919	2	48	...	190	3,013	210	3,450	111,276	3.1
1920	1	57	...	403	3,272	195	3,919	103,150	3.8
1921	10	57	613†	1,137	4,249	571	6,637	162,190	4.1
1922	6	54	712	1,748	3,121	536	6,177	184,362	3.4
1923	3	58	1,214	3,294	7,271	429	12,269	219,705	5.6
1924	1	50	1,942	3,620	13,318	575	19,506	279,960	7.0
1925	8	63	4,246	1,997	18,378	29	24,721	317,352	7.8
1926	2	68	4,537	2,520	21,685	52	28,864	324,444	8.9
1927	4	60	5,926	6,130	12,220	677	25,017	296,082	8.4
1928	...	84	7,201	5,764	11,812	713	25,574	251,370	10.2
Total	...	...	...	...	...	...	216,725	3,474,103	6.2

* Enticing female into house of prostitution.
† The Municipal Court did not classify cases under the Kate Adams Law until 1921 when the law was approved in its present form, although a less comprehensive form of the same statute bearing the same name was approved in 1916.

TABLE 60

NUMBER AND PER CENT PANDERING CASES DISPOSED OF IN MORALS
COURT OF TOTAL SUCH CASES DISPOSED OF IN MUNICIPAL
COURT (ALL BRANCHES), CHICAGO, 1914–28

Date	Total Mun. Ct.	Total Morals Ct.	Per Cent
1914.............	42	36*	85.7
1915.............	67	48	71.6
1916.............	35	25	71.4
1917.............	64	35	54.7
1918.............	40	19	47.5
1919.............	35	24	68.6
1920.............	48	31	64.6
1921†............	....	....	....
1922.............	54	25	46.3
1923.............	58	28	48.3
1924.............	50	30	60.0
1925.............	63	20	31.7
1926.............	68	40	58.8
1927.............	60	22	36.7
1928.............	84	47	56.0
Total........	768	430	56.0

* 1914 is the first full year of operation of the Morals Court.
† 1921 must be left blank due to misplacement of the proper tabulations for this year.
Those given in the Municipal Court reports for the Morals Court as of 1921 are wrong.

TABLE 61

NUMBER AND PER CENT KATE ADAMS LAW CASES DISPOSED OF IN MORALS
COURT OF TOTAL SUCH CASES DISPOSED OF IN MUNICIPAL
COURT (ALL BRANCHES), CHICAGO, 1922–28

Date	Total Mun. Ct.	Total Morals Ct.	Per Cent
1922...............	712	573	80.5*
1923...............	1,214	740	61.0
1924...............	1,942	1,826	94.0
1925...............	4,246	3,304	77.8
1926...............	4,537	4,229	93.2
1927...............	5,926	5,259	88.7
1928...............	7,201	6,438	89.4
Total..........	25,778	22,369	86.8

* 1921 was the first year that the police booked under the Kate Adams Law.

TABLE 62

NUMBER AND PERCENT

KEEPING HOUSE OF ILL-FAME CASES (QUASI-CRIMINAL) DISPOSED OF IN THE
MORALS COURT OF TOTAL SUCH CASES DISPOSED OF IN THE
MUNICIPAL COURT, CHICAGO, 1914–28

Date	Total Mun. Ct.	Total Morals Ct.	Per Cent
1914...............	3,120	3,006	96.3
1915...............	241	213	88.4
1916...............	63	46	73.0
1917...............	1,135	605	53.3
1918...............	727	383	52.7
1919...............	190	146	76.8
1920...............	403	357	88.6
1921...............	....	....	....
1922...............	1,748	1,587	90.8
1923...............	3,294	2,509	76.2
1924...............	3,620	3,375	93.2
1925...............	1,997	1,410	70.6
1926...............	2,520	2,271	90.1
1927...............	6,130	5,490	89.6
1928...............	5,764	5,027	87.2
Total..........	30,952	26,425	85.4

TABLE 63

NUMBER AND PER CENT KEEPING DISORDERLY HOUSE CASES IN MORALS
COURT OF TOTAL SUCH CASES DISPOSED OF IN MUNICIPAL
COURT, CHICAGO, 1914–28

Date	Total Mun. Ct.	Total Morals Ct.	Per Cent
1914	5,191	4,728	91.1
1915	7,691	6,536	85.0
1916	4,518	2,585	57.2
1917	5,641	2,655	47.1
1918	4,258	2,389	56.1
1919	3,013	2,069	68.7
1920	3,272	2,408	73.6
1921	....	....	....
1922	3,121	2,024	64.9
1923	7,271	1,356	18.6
1924	13,318	3,150	23.7
1925	18,378	2,251	12.2
1926	21,685	1,914	8.8
1927	12,220	1,334	10.9
1928	11,812	1,242	10.5
Total	121,389	36,641	30.2

TABLE 64

Number and Per Cent Night Walking Cases in Morals Court of
Total Such Cases Disposed of in Municipal Court,
Chicago, 1914–28

Date	Total Mun. Ct.	Total Morals Ct.	Per Cent
1914...............	2,093	2,085	99.6
1915...............	2,254	2,016	89.4
1916...............	834	579	69.2
1917...............	502	308	61.4
1918...............	613	395	64.4
1919...............	210	203	96.7
1920...............	195	182	93.3
1921...............	....	....	....
1922...............	536	525	97.9
1923...............	429	392	91.4
1924...............	575	547	95.1
1925...............	61	55	90.2
1926...............	52	40	76.9
1927...............	677	408	60.3
1928...............	713	595	83.5
Total.........	9,744	8,330	85.5

TABLE 65

NUMBER AND PER CENT PRINCIPAL CASES* OF COMMERCIALIZED VICE OR TOTAL CASES DISPOSED OF IN MORALS COURT, CHICAGO, 1914–28

Date	Vice Cases	Total Morals Ct.	Per Cent
1914	9,855	12,645	77.9
1915	8,813	12,361	71.3
1916	3,135	6,581	47.6
1917	3,603	7,271	49.6
1918	3,186	5,822	54.7
1919	2,442	4,510	54.1
1920	2,978	4,678	63.7
1921	....	....	....
1922	4,734	7,280	65.0
1923	5,025	7,291	68.9
1924	8,928	11,106	80.4
1925	7,040	8,464	83.2
1926	8,494	10,127	83.9
1927	12,513	14,549	86.0
1928	13,349	15,438	86.5
Total	94,095†	128,123†	73.4

* Consisting of pandering, House of Ill-Fame—misdemeanor; and Houses of Ill-Fame, Disorderly Houses and Night Walker—quasi-criminal.
† Exclusive of 1921 figures.

TABLE 66

TOTAL CASES DISPOSED OF IN MORALS COURT OF TOTAL DISPOSED
OF IN MUNICIPAL COURT, CHICAGO, 1914–28

Date	Total Mun. Ct.	Total Morals Ct.	Per Cent
1914.............	134,048	12,645	9.4
1915.............	130,971	12,361	9.4
1916.............	123,873	6,581	5.3
1917.............	149,268	7,271	4.9
1918.............	124,397	5,822	4.7
1919.............	111,276	4,510	4.1
1920.............	193,150	4,678	2.4
1921.............	162,190	6,471	4.0
1922.............	184,362	7,280	3.9
1923.............	219,705	7,291	3.3
1924.............	279,960	11,106	4.0
1925.............	317,352	8,464	2.7
1926.............	324,444	10,127	3.1
1927.............	296,082	14,549	4.9
1928.............	251,370	15,438	6.1
Total..........	3,002,448	134,594	4.5

TABLE 67

Number and Per Cent of Discharges for Felonies, Misdemeanors and Quasi-Criminal Cases Disposed of in Morals Court, Chicago, 1914–28

Date	Felonies			Misdemeanors			Quasi-Criminal			Combined		
	Total	No. Dis.	Per Cent	Total	No. Dis.	Per Cent	Total	No. Dis.	Per Cent	Total	No. Dis.	Per Cent
1914	49	18	36.7	589	211	35.8	12,007	3,809	31.7	12,645	4,038	31.9
1915	36	19	52.8	497	180	36.2	11,828	4,231	35.8	12,361	4,430	35.8
1916	53	31	58.5	763	353	46.3	5,765	3,018	52.4	6,581	3,402	51.7
1917	41	24	58.5	1,290	660	51.2	5,940	3,065	51.6	7,271	3,749	51.6
1918	33	20	60.6	745	365	49.0	5,044	3,201	63.5	5,822	3,586	61.6
1919	38	17	44.7	718	404	56.3	3,754	2,556	68.1	4,510	2,977	66.0
1920	26	6	23.1	553	318	57.5	4,099	2,831	69.1	4,678	3,155	67.4
1922	22	3	13.6	936	367	39.2	6,322	3,045	48.2	7,280	3,415	46.9
1923	22	10	45.5	1,134	441	38.9	6,135	3,235	52.7	7,291	3,686	50.6
1924	20	11	55.0	2,173	1,252	57.6	8,913	5,649	63.4	11,106	6,912	62.2
1925	42	17	40.5	3,630	2,112	58.2	4,792	2,761	57.6	8,464	4,890	57.8
1926	19	6	31.6	4,555	2,803	61.5	5,553	3,310	59.6	10,127	6,119	60.4
1927	25	9	36.0	5,522	3,847	69.7	9,002	6,103	67.8	14,549	9,959	68.5
1928	10	4	40.0	6,820	5,201	76.3	8,608	6,988	81.2	15,438	12,193	79.0
Total*	436	195	44.7	29,925	18,514	61.9	97,762	53,802	55.0	128,123	72,511	56.6

* Exclusive of figures for 1921.

TABLE 68

NUMBER AND PER CENT DISCHARGES PANDERING, KEEPING HOUSE OF ILL-FAME, KEEPING DISORDERLY HOUSE, NIGHT WALKING, KATE ADAMS LAW CASES DISPOSED OF IN MORALS COURT, CHICAGO, 1914-28

DATE	PANDERING			KEEPING HOUSE OF ILL-FAME			KEEPING DISORDERLY HOUSE			NIGHT WALKERS			KATE ADAMS LAW			COMBINED		
	Total	No. Dis.	Per Cent	Total	No. Dis.	Per Cent	Total	No. Dis.	Per Cent	Total	No. Dis.	Per Cent	Total	No. Dis.	Per Cent	Total	No. Dis.	Per Cent
1914	36	13	36.1	3,006	641	21.3	4,728	1,688	35.7	2,085	443	21.2				9,855	2,785	28.3
1915	48	20	41.7	213	93	43.7	6,536	2,265	34.7	2,016	571	28.3				8,813	2,949	33.5
1916	25	7	28.0	46	29	63.0	2,585	1,365	52.8	579	310	53.5				3,235	1,711	52.9
1917	35	17	48.6	605	290	47.9	2,655	1,453	54.7	308	139	45.1				3,603	1,899	52.7
1918	19	8	42.1	383	220	57.4	2,389	1,503	62.9	395	165	41.8				3,186	1,896	59.5
1919	24	8	33.3	146	112	76.7	2,069	1,474	71.2	203	124	61.1				2,442	1,718	70.4
1920	31	19	61.3	357	227	63.6	2,408	1,744	72.4	182	94	51.6				2,978	2,084	70.0
1922	25	6	24.0	1,587	729	45.9	2,024	1,201	59.3	525	192	36.6	573	200	34.9	4,734	2,328	49.2
1923	28	12	42.9	2,509	1,296	51.7	1,356	787	58.0	392	199	50.8	740	293	39.6	5,025	2,587	51.5
1924	30	18	60.0	3,375	1,702	50.4	3,150	2,225	70.6	547	296	54.1	1,826	1,018	55.8	8,928	5,259	58.9
1925	20	11	55.0	1,410	774	54.9	2,251	1,324	58.8	55	37	67.3	3,304	1,942	58.8	7,040	4,088	58.1
1926	40	21	52.5	2,271	1,332	58.7	1,914	1,081	56.5	40	22	55.0	4,229	2,639	62.4	8,494	5,095	60.0
1927	22	14	63.6	5,490	3,639	66.3	1,334	922	69.1	408	319	78.2	5,259	3,727	70.9	12,513	8,621	68.9
1928	47	20	42.6	5,027	4,060	80.8	1,242	1,028	82.8	595	499	83.9	6,438	4,965	77.1	13,349	10,572	79.2
Total	430	194	45.1	26,425	15,144	57.3	36,641	20,060	54.7	8,330	3,410	40.9	22,369	14,784	66.1	94,195	53,592	56.9

TABLE 69

NUMBER AND PER CENT FINED IN MISDEMEANORS AND QUASI-CRIMINAL
CASES DISPOSED OF IN MORALS COURT, CHICAGO, 1914–28

DATE	MISDEMEANORS			QUASI-CRIMINAL			COMBINED		
	Total	No. Fined	Per Cent	Total	No. Fined	Per Cent	Total	No. Fined	Per Cent
1914..	589	30	5.1	12,007	6,924	57.7	12,596	6,954	55.2
1915..	497	33	6.6	11,828	5,892	49.8	12,325	5,925	48.1
1916..	763	59	7.7	5,765	1,712	29.7	6,528	1,771	27.1
1917..	1,290	135	10.5	5,940	2,089	35.2	7,230	2,224	30.8
1918..	745	66	8.9	5,044	1,112	22.0	5,789	1,178	20.3
1919..	718	93	13.0	3,754	820	21.8	4,472	913	20.4
1920..	553	69	12.5	4,099	927	22.6	4,652	996	21.4
1922..	936	364	38.9	6,322	2,837	44.9	7,258	3,201	44.1
1923..	1,134	412	36.3	6,135	2,373	38.7	7,269	2,785	38.3
1924..	2,173	696	32.0	8,913	2,881	32.3	11,086	3,577	32.3
1925..	3,630	581	16.0	4,792	1,655	34.5	8,422	2,236	26.5
1926..	4,555	1,142	25.1	5,553	1,946	35.0	10,108	3,088	30.6
1927..	5,522	387	7.0	9,002	1,705	18.9	14,524	2,092	14.4
1928..	6,820	492	7.2	8,608	1,175	13.7	15,428	1,667	10.8
Total.	29,925	4,559	15.2	97,762	34,048	34.8	127,687	38,607	30.2

TABLE 70

NUMBER AND PER CENT OF FINED IN PRINCIPAL CASES OF COMMERCIALIZED VICE DISPOSED OF IN MORALS COURT, CHICAGO, 1914–28

DATE	KEEPING HOUSE OF ILL-FAME			KEEPING DISORDERLY HOUSE			NIGHT WALKER			KATE ADAMS LAW			COMBINED		
	Total	No. Fined	Per Cent	Total	No. Fined	Per Cent	Total	No. Fined	Per Cent	Total	No. Fined	Per Cent	Total	No. Fined	Per Cent
1914	3,006	2,176	72.4	4,728	2,590	54.8	2,085	1,291	61.9	....	....	....	9,819	6,057	61.7
1915	213	70	32.9	6,536	3,451	52.8	2,016	1,085	53.8	....	....	....	8,765	4,606	52.5
1916	46	7	15.2	2,585	843	32.6	579	125	21.6	....	....	....	3,210	975	30.4
1917	605	274	45.3	2,655	927	34.9	308	90	29.2	....	....	....	3,568	1,291	36.2
1918	383	115	30.0	2,389	597	25.0	395	105	26.6	....	....	....	3,167	817	25.8
1919	146	24	16.4	2,069	441	21.3	203	42	20.7	....	....	....	2,418	507	21.0
1920	357	95	26.6	2,408	540	22.4	182	64	35.2	....	....	....	2,947	699	23.7
1922	1,587	792	49.9	2,024	697	34.4	525	287	54.7	573	336	58.6	4,709	2,112	44.9
1923	2,509	1,082	43.1	1,356	459	33.8	392	153	39.0	740	382	51.6	4,997	2,076	41.5
1924	3,375	1,514	44.9	3,150	853	27.1	547	199	36.4	1,826	682	37.3	8,898	3,248	36.5
1925	1,410	560	39.7	2,251	786	34.9	55	13	23.6	3,304	567	17.2	7,020	1,926	27.4
1926	2,271	848	37.3	1,914	755	39.4	40	12	30.0	4,229	1,128	26.7	8,454	2,743	32.4
1927	5,490	1,099	20.0	1,334	313	23.5	408	37	9.1	5,259	360	6.8	12,491	1,809	14.5
1928	5,027	752	15.0	1,242	144	11.6	595	57	9.6	6,438	463	7.2	13,302	1,416	10.6
Total	26,425	9,408	35.6	36,641	13,396	36.6	8,330	3,560	42.7	22,369	3,918	17.5	93,765	30,282	32.3

TABLE 71

NUMBER AND PER CENT OF SENTENCES TO HOUSE OF CORRECTION IN MIS-
DEMEANORS AND QUASI-CRIMINAL CASES DISPOSED OF BY
MORALS COURT, CHICAGO, 1914–28

DATE	MISDEMEANORS			QUASI-CRIMINAL			COMBINED		
	Total	No. H.C.	Per Cent	Total	No. H.C	Per Cent	Total	No. H.C.	Per Cent
1914..	589	65	11.0	12,007	639	5.3	12,596	704	5.6
1915..	497	82	16.5	11,828	909	7.7	12,325	991	8.0
1916..	763	169	22.1	5,765	669	11.6	6,528	838	12.8
1917..	1,290	200	15.5	5,940	591	9.9	7,230	791	10.9
1918..	745	141	18.9	5,044	482	9.6	5,789	623	10.8
1919..	718	66	9.2	3,754	106	2.8	4,472	172	3.8
1920..	553	27	4.9	4,099	39	1.0	4,652	66	1.4
1922..	936	60	6.4	6,322	191	3.0	7,258	251	3.5
1923..	1,134	67	5.9	6,135	266	4.3	7,269	333	4.6
1924..	2,173	97	4.5	8,913	284	3.2	11,086	381	3.4
1925..	3,630	497	13.7	4,792	154	3.2	8,422	651	7.7
1926..	4,555	325	7.1	5,553	133	2.4	10,108	458	4.5
1927..	5,522	403	7.3	9,002	208	2.3	14,524	611	4.2
1928..	6,820	552	8.1	8,608	216	2.5	15,428	768	5.0
Total.	29,925	2,751	9.2	97,762	4,887	5.0	127,687	7,368	5.8

TABLE 72

NUMBER AND PER CENT SENTENCES TO HOUSE OF CORRECTION IN PRINCIPAL CASES OF COMMERCIALIZED VICE DISPOSED OF BY MORALS COURT, CHICAGO, 1914–28

DATE	KEEPING HOUSE OF ILL-FAME			KEEPING DISORDERLY HOUSE			NIGHT WALKER			PANDERING			KATE ADAMS LAW			COMBINED		
	Total	No. H.C.	Per Cent	Total	No. H.C.	Per Cent	Total	No. H.C.	Per Cent	Total	No. H.C.	Per Cent	Total	No. H.C.	Per Cent	Total	No. H.C.	Per Cent
1914	3,006	72	2.4	4,728	205	4.3	2,085	229	11.0	36	15	41.7	.....	.....	.....	9,855	521	5.3
1915	213	22	10.3	6,536	414	6.3	2,016	243	12.1	48	15	31.3	.....	.....	.....	8,813	694	7.9
1916	46	8	17.4	2,583	242	9.4	579	104	18.0	25	0	0.0	.....	.....	.....	3,235	354	10.9
1917	605	37	6.1	2,655	194	7.3	308	68	22.1	35	11	31.4	.....	.....	.....	3,603	310	8.6
1918	383	28	7.3	2,389	182	7.6	395	100	25.3	19	8	42.1	.....	.....	.....	3,186	318	10.0
1919	146	1	0.7	2,069	47	2.3	203	12	5.9	24	5	20.8	.....	.....	.....	2,442	65	2.7
1920	357	1	0.3	2,408	15	0.6	182	3	1.6	31	4	12.9	.....	.....	.....	2,978	23	0.8
1922	1,587	45	2.8	2,024	49	2.4	525	23	4.4	25	7	28.0	573	16	2.3	4,734	140	3.0
1923	2,509	86	3.4	1,356	60	4.4	392	27	6.9	28	6	21.4	740	27	3.6	5,025	206	4.1
1924	3,375	137	4.1	3,150	50	1.6	547	45	8.2	30	3	10.0	1,826	80	4.4	8,928	315	3.5
1925	1,410	51	3.6	2,251	45	2.0	55	2	3.6	20	5	25.0	3,304	456	13.8	7,040	559	7.9
1926	2,271	54	2.4	1,914	29	1.5	40	2	5.0	40	9	22.5	4,229	295	7.0	8,494	389	4.6
1927	5,490	90	1.6	1,334	33	2.5	408	4	1.0	22	5	22.7	5,259	372	7.1	12,513	504	4.0
1928	5,027	125	2.5	1,242	39	3.1	595	14	2.4	47	10	21.3	6,438	510	7.9	13,349	698	5.2
Total	26,425	757	2.9	36,641	1,604	4.4	8,330	876	10.5	430	103	24.0	22,369	1,756	7.9	94,195	5,096	5.4

TABLE 73

NUMBER AND PER CENT NON-SUITS* IN QUASI-CRIMINAL CASES
DISPOSED OF IN MORALS COURT, CHICAGO, 1914–28

Date	Total	No. N.S.	Per Cent
1914..............	12,007	430	3.6
1915..............	11,828	621	5.3
1916..............	5,765	68	1.2
1917..............	5,940	17	0.3
1918..............	5,044	44	0.9
1919..............	3,754	10	0.3
1920..............	4,099	24	0.6
1921..............	....	....	....
1922..............	6,322	52	0.8
1923..............	6,135	56	0.9
1924..............	8,913	10	0.1
1925..............	4,792	38	0.8
1926..............	5,553	13	0.2
1927..............	9,002	754	8.4
1928..............	8,608	46	0.5
Total†.........	97,762	2,183	2.2

* No non-suits for other types of cases.
† Exclusive of figures for 1921.

TABLE 74

NUMBER AND PER CENT OF NON-SUITS IN PRINCIPAL CASES OF
COMMERCIALIZED VICE DISPOSED OF IN MORALS
COURT, CHICAGO, 1914–28

DATE	KEEPING HOUSE OF ILL-FAME			KEEPING DISORDERLY HOUSE			NIGHT WALKERS			COMBINED		
	Total	No. N.S.	Per Cent	Total	No. N.S.	Per Cent	Total	No. N.S.	Per Cent	Total	No. N.S.	Per Cent
1914.	3,006	87	2.9	4,728	219	4.6	2,085	23	1.1	9,819	329	3.4
1915.	213	26	12.2	6,536	338	5.2	2,016	71	3.5	8,765	435	5.0
1916.	46	...	....	2,585	21	0.8	579	5	0.9	3,210	26	0.8
1917.	605	...	....	2,655	10	0.4	308	...	...	3,568	10	0.3
1918.	383	10	2.6	2,389	27	1.1	395	2	0.5	3,167	39	1.2
1919.	146	...	....	2,069	6	0.3	203	...	...	2,418	6	0.2
1920.	357	8	2.2	2,408	14	0.6	182	...	...	2,947	22	0.7
1922.	1,587	11	0.7	2,024	20	1.0	525	4	0.8	4,136	35	0.8
1923.	2,509	9	0.4	1,356	14	1.0	392	1	0.3	4,257	24	0.6
1924.	3,375	...	....	3,150	5	0.2	547	...	...	7,072	5	0.1
1925.	1,410	1	0.1	2,251	9	0.4	55	...	...	3,716	10	0.3
1926.	2,271	3	0.1	1,914	5	0.3	40	...	...	4,225	8	0.2
1927.	5,490	563	10.3	1,334	25	1.9	408	38	9.3	7,232	626	8.7
1928.	5,027	26	0.5	1,242	2	0.2	595	8	1.3	6,864	36	0.5
Total	26,425	744	2.8	36,641	715	2.0	8,330	152	1.8	71,396	1,611	2.3

TABLE 75

Number and Per Cent Dismissed for Want of Prosecution
in Cases Disposed of in Morals Court,
Chicago, 1914–28

Date	Felonies			Misdemeanors			Quasi-Criminal			Combined		
	Total	No. D.W.P.	Per Cent	Total	No. D.W.P.	Per Cent	Total	No. D.W.P.	Per Cent	Total	No. D.W.P.	Per Cent
1914.	49	11	22.4	589	89	15.1	12,007	42	0.3	12,645	142	1.1
1915.	36	4	11.1	497	47	9.5	11,828	90	0.8	12,361	141	1.1
1916.	53	5	9.4	763	66	8.7	5,765	232	4.0	6,581	303	4.6
1917.	41	9	22.0	1,290	82	6.4	5,940	90	1.5	7,271	181	2.5
1918.	33	5	15.2	745	79	10.6	5,044	110	2.2	5,822	194	3.3
1919.	38	8	21.1	718	91	12.7	3,754	197	5.2	4,510	296	6.6
1920.	26	3	11.5	553	63	11.4	4,099	174	4.2	4,678	240	5.1
1922.	22	3	13.6	936	36	3.8	6,322	85	1.3	7,280	124	1.7
1923.	22	4	18.2	1,134	103	9.1	6,135	38	0.6	7,291	145	2.0
1924.	20	1	5.0	2,173	33	1.5	8,913	40	0.4	11,106	74	0.7
1925.	42	9	21.4	3,630	53	1.5	4,792	55	1.1	8,464	117	1.4
1926.	19	6	31.6	4,555	155	3.4	5,553	91	1.6	10,127	252	2.5
1927.	25	....	....	5,522	...	....	9,002	....	...	14,549	....	...
1928.	10	....	....	6,820	...	....	8,608	....	...	15,438	....	...
Total	436	68	15.6	29,925	897	3.0	97,762	1,244	1.3	128,123	2,209	1.7

TABLE 76

Number and Per Cent Dismissed for Want of Prosecution in the Principal Cases of Commercialized Vice Disposed of by Morals Court, Chicago, 1914–28

Date	Pandering			Keeping House of Ill-Fame			Keeping Disorderly House			Night Walker			House of Ill-Fame			Combined		
	Total	No. D.W.P.	Per Cent	Total	No. D.W.P.	Per Cent	Total	No. D.W.P.	Per Cent	Total	No. D.W.P.	Per Cent	Total	No. D.W.P.	Per Cent	Total	No. D.W.P.	Per Cent
1914	36	4	11.1	3,006	9	0.3	4,728	11	0.2	2,085	5	0.2				9,855	29	0.3
1915	48	…	…	213	1	0.5	6,536	30	0.5	2,016	18	0.9				8,813	49	0.6
1916	25	5	20.0	46	2	4.3	2,585	102	3.9	579	14	2.4				3,235	123	3.8
1917	35	2	5.7	605	2	0.3	2,655	33	1.2	308	2	0.6				3,603	39	1.1
1918	19	2	10.5	383	2	0.5	2,389	41	1.7	395	17	4.3				3,186	62	1.9
1919	24	4	16.7	146	7	4.8	2,069	77	3.7	203	8	3.9				2,442	96	3.9
1920	31	3	9.7	357	22	6.2	2,408	59	2.5	182	16	8.8				2,978	100	3.4
1922	25	1	4.0	1,587	5	0.3	2,024	23	1.1	525	8	1.5	573	1	0.2	4,734	38	0.8
1923	28	4	14.3	2,509	2	0.1	1,356	1	0.1	392	1	0.3	740	11	1.5	5,025	19	0.4
1924	30	7	23.3	3,375	9	0.3	3,150	9	0.3	547	3	0.5	1,826	5	0.3	8,928	33	0.4
1925	20	…	…	1,410	4	0.3	2,251	29	1.3	55	1	1.8	3,304	16	0.5	7,040	50	0.7
1926	40	9	22.5	2,271	28	1.2	1,914	16	0.8	40	4	10.0	4,229	73	1.7	8,494	130	1.5
1927	22	1	4.5	5,490	55	1.0	1,334	5	0.4	408	2	0.5	5,259	60	1.1	12,513	123	1.0
1928	47	3	6.4	5,027	29	0.6	1,242	17	1.4	595	7	1.2	6,438	147	2.3	13,349	203	1.5
Total	430	45	10.5	26,425	177	0.7	36,641	453	1.2	8,330	106	1.3	22,369	313	1.4	94,195	1,094	1.2

TABLE 77

NUMBER AND PER CENT PROBATIONS IN CASES DISPOSED OF IN
MORALS COURT, CHICAGO, 1914–28

Rate	FELONIES			MISDEMEANORS			QUASI-CRIMINAL			COMBINED		
	Total	No. Prob.	Per Cent	Total	No. Prob.	Per Cent	Total	No. Prob.	Per Cent	Total	No. Prob.	Per Cent
1914.	49	.....	.....	589	.....	.....	12,007	.....	.....	12,596	.....	.....
1915.	36	.....	.....	497	54	10.9	11,828	85	0.7	12,325	139	1.1
1916.	53	.....	.....	763	93	12.2	5,765	66	1.1	6,528	159	2.4
1917.	41	.....	.....	1,290	201	15.6	5,940	88	1.5	7,230	289	4.0
1918.	33	.....	.....	745	82	11.0	5,044	94	1.9	5,789	176	3.0
1919.	38	.....	.....	718	54	7.5	3,754	65	1.7	4,472	119	2.7
1920.	26	.....	.....	553	56	10.1	4,099	104	2.5	4,652	160	3.4
1922.	22	.....	.....	936	65	6.9	6,322	112	1.8	7,258	177	2.4
1923.	22	.....	.....	1,134	85	7.5	6,135	167	2.7	7,269	252	3.5
1924.	20	.....	.....	2,173	68	3.1	8,913	49	0.5	11,086	117	1.1
1925.	42	.....	.....	3,630	356	9.8	4,792	129	2.7	8,422	485	5.8
1926.	19	.....	.....	4,555	123	2.7	5,553	60	1.1	10,108	183	1.8
1927.	25	.....	.....	5,522	572	10.4	9,002	146	1.6	14,524	718	4.9
1928.	10	.....	.....	6,820	323	4.7	8,608	89	1.0	15,428	412	2.7
Total	436	.....	.....	29,925	2,132	7.1	97,762	1,254	1.3	127,687	3,386	2.7

TABLE 78

NUMBER AND PER CENT PROBATIONS IN PRINCIPAL CASES OF COMMERCIALIZED VICE
DISPOSED OF IN MORALS COURT, CHICAGO, 1914–28

Date	Pandering			Keeping House of Ill-Fame			Keeping Disorderly House			Night Walker			Kate Adams Law			Combined		
	Total	No. Prob.	Per Cent	Total	No. Prob.	Per Cent	Total	No. Prob.	Per Cent	Total	No. Prob.	Per Cent	Total	No. Prob.	Per Cent	Total	No. Prob.	Per Cent
1914	36	0	0.0	3,006	0	0.0	4,728	0	0.0	2,085	0	0.0	....	....	....	9,855	0	0.0
1915	48	2	4.2	213	1	0.5	6,536	38	0.6	2,016	28	1.4	....	....	....	8,813	69	0.8
1916	25	2	8.0	46	0	0.0	2,585	12	0.5	579	21	3.6	....	....	....	3,235	35	1.1
1917	35	1	2.9	605	2	0.3	2,655	38	1.4	308	9	2.9	....	....	....	3,603	50	1.4
1918	19	1	5.3	383	8	2.1	2,389	39	1.6	395	17	4.3	....	....	....	3,186	65	2.0
1919	24	5	20.8	146	2	1.4	2,069	24	1.2	203	8	3.9	....	....	....	2,442	39	1.6
1920	31	1	3.2	357	4	1.1	2,408	36	1.5	182	5	2.7	....	....	....	2,978	46	1.6
1922	25	1	4.0	1,587	5	0.3	2,024	34	1.7	525	14	2.7	573	13	2.3	4,734	67	1.4
1923	28	1	3.6	2,509	36	1.4	1,356	35	2.6	392	11	2.8	740	26	3.5	5,025	109	2.2
1924	30	0	0.0	3,375	13	0.4	3,150	8	0.3	547	4	0.7	1,826	37	2.0	8,928	62	0.7
1925	20	0	0.0	1,410	20	1.4	2,251	58	2.6	55	2	3.6	3,304	303	9.2	7,040	383	5.4
1926	40	1	2.5	2,271	6	0.3	1,914	28	1.5	40	0	0.0	4,229	90	0.2	8,494	125	1.5
1927	22	1	4.5	5,490	44	0.8	1,334	36	2.7	408	8	2.0	5,259	539	10.2	12,513	628	5.0
1928	47	6	12.8	5,027	35	0.7	1,242	12	1.0	595	10	1.7	6,438	289	4.5	13,349	352	2.6
Total.	430	22	5.1	26,425	176	0.7	36,641	398	1.1	8,330	137	1.6	22,369	1,297	5.8	94,195	2,030	2.2

INDEX

INDEX

311

83; and divorce, 228–31; foreign-born whites, 189–92; home
ownership in, 187–89; and juvenile delinquency, 217–24;
location of, 165–67; as natural
areas, 164–67; Negro population, 192–95; and padlock cases,
198–208; population count in,
167–69; and poverty, 224–28;
and residences of male criminals, 213–17; shortage of children in, 185–87; and venereal
diseases, 208–13
Vice Commission of Chicago, 4
Vice suppression, 1–10, 234–69;
limited by urban trends, 271
Vice trusts, 69–71
Vote trading, 88–89

Wayman, State's Attorney, 4, 7–8
Wegg, Jervis, 122
White slavery, 32 ff.; brutality, 45–
48; cases of, 36–38, 38–39, 43–
50; 56–57; rumor of, 46–47;
traffickers in, 40–43
Wickersham Commission, 88
Woman's Court, 277n.
Working girl, and prostitution, 52–
54
Worthington, George E., and Ruth
Topping, 240, 243, 244

Yarrow, Philip, 267
Young People's Civic League, 6

Zuta, Jack, 94, 103–104; murder
of, 80